Deregulation and the New Airline Entrepreneurs

MIT Press Series on the Regulation of Economic Activity

General Editor
Richard Schmalensee, MIT Sloan School of Management

Deregulation and the New Airline Entrepreneurs

John R. Meyer and Clinton V. Oster, Jr.

with
Marni Clippinger, Andrew McKey,
Don H. Pickrell, John Strong,
and C. Kurt Zorn

The MIT Press
Cambridge, Massachusetts
London, England

This book was set in Times Roman
by The MIT Press Computergraphics Department
and printed and bound by The Murray Printing Co.   Halliday Lithograph
in the United States of America

Library of Congress Cataloging in Publication Data

Main entry under title:

Deregulation and the new airline entrepreneurs

  (MIT Press series on the regulation of economic activity; 9)
  Bibliography: p.
  Includes index.
  1. Aeronautics, Commercial—United States.
2. Airlines—United States. 3. Aeronautics and state—United States.
I. Meyer, John Robert. II. Oster, Clinton V. III. Series.
HE9803.A35A57   1984   387.7'12   84–7935
ISBN 0–262–13198–6

Contents

List of Contributors

Marni Clippinger, Center for Business and Government, Harvard University

Andrew McKey, New York Air

John R. Meyer, Center for Business and Government, Harvard University

Clinton V. Oster, Jr., School of Public and Environmental Affairs, Indiana University

Don H. Pickrell, Kennedy School of Government, Harvard University

John Strong, Center for Business and Government, Harvard University

C. Kurt Zorn, School of Public and Environmental Affairs, Indiana University

List of Tables and Figures

Tables

Figures

Series Foreword

Government regulation of economic activity in the United States has grown dramatically in this century, radically transforming government-business relations. Economic regulation of prices and conditions of service was first applied to transportation and public utilities and was later extended to energy, health care, and other sectors. In the early 1970s explosive growth occurred in social regulation, focusing on workplace safety, environmental preservation, consumer protection, and related goals. Though regulatory reform has occupied a prominent place on the agendas of recent administrations, and some important reforms have occurred, the aims, methods, and results of many regulatory programs remain controversial.

The purpose of the MIT Press series, Regulation of Economic Activity, is to inform the ongoing debate on regulatory policy by making significant and relevant research available to both scholars and decision makers. Books in this series present new insights into individual agencies, programs, and regulated sectors, as well as the important economic, political, and administrative aspects of the regulatory process that cut across these boundaries.

Although most economists applaud airline deregulation as a significant, positive reform, it remains controversial, in part because the industry still seems far from equilibrium. Debates about deregulation focus on its effects on the established carriers and are marked by a low ratio of analysis to rhetoric. This study by John Meyer, Clinton Oster, and their colleagues should serve both to shift that focus somewhat and to increase the analytical base available for future debates. They concentrate not on the established carriers but on the new entrepreneurs, commuters and new entrant jet carriers active in short- and medium-haul markets, that have grown rapidly at the expense of the established carriers. Their important and well-supported findings should be of interest to economists and others concerned with the rapid evolution of this fascinating industry and to those interested in entrepreneurship in general, as well as to specialists in transportation.

Preface

The Airline Deregulation Act of 1978 (enacted in October of that year) formalized and hastened a process of regulatory reform that had begun with administrative actions of the Civil Aeronautics Board as early as 1976. In the spring of 1979 the Harvard Faculty Project on Regulation began a study of the effects of that deregulation. Recognizing that the full effects of this major shift in public policy would not be observable for some time, the Harvard Study was designed to monitor developments in the airline industry over several years. The first report of this effort, *Airline Deregulation: The Early Experience* published in 1981, examined the industry's initial adaptations to deregulation. This book is the project's second report and examines one of the major post-deregulation trends, the rapid growth of entrepreneurial low-cost jet carriers and commuter airlines.

This study owes a considerable debt to several institutions and many individuals. The Harvard Business School's Division of Research and the United Parcel Service Foundation provided both the seed money that launched the effort in 1979 and subsequent support as well. The John A. Olin Foundation provided funds needed to undertake a major expansion of the scope of the study. The John F. Kennedy School of Government at Harvard has provided from the very beginning a physical home for the study team and has provided administrative and logistical support which has been essential to our efforts. In addition the U.S. Department of Transportation and Indiana University provided funding for a detailed study of commuter airline safety that served as the basis for chapter 5.

Research assistance for this study has been provided by Benjamin Berman, Rene Riecke, Andy Schneck, Rosemary Booth, and Elise Junn. Ben and Elise prepared the data and did much of the initial analysis of the demand for commuter service in chapter 3. Rene's efforts provided much of the background for chapter 2, and she also assisted in the analyses presented in chapter 5. Andy was responsible for the difficult job of data collection and much of the analysis of chapter 10. Rosemary did much of the groundwork for the analysis of new entrant jet carrier route strategies in chapter 7. The authors are very grateful for the splendid help and support rendered by all these individuals—and particularly the contributions of Berman and Schneck whose participation in the initial design and writing of this study was interrupted by their departure to other responsibilities.

Many people in the commuter airline industry also provided early and invaluable help. We would especially like to thank Bryce Appleton of Midstate Airlines, John Sullivan of Air North, Dean Sparkman of Mississippi Valley Airlines, John Van Arsdale, Sr., of Provincetown-Boston Airlines, and Watson Whitesides of Air Wisconsin.

The Civil Aeronautics Board and staff also gave freely of their time and provided much useful data. In particular, Dan Kaplan of the CAB staff helped us at several stages in the research and was most generous in sharing with us not only data but preliminary results of his own research.

Finally, our special thanks are given to Eleanor Lintner, who has served as production coordinator for the entire project. She has dealt admirably with a sizable group of authors and many draft chapters and has made innumerable other contributions to keep the project running smoothly.

In any project undertaken by a group the question of authorship arises. The entire Harvard Airline Deregulation Study has been marked by considerable interaction among all involved. All of the chapters in this book have benefited from inputs of the group. Where possible, we have identified the authorship contributions of those other than the editors. The remaining chapters have been authored by the editors with help from others on the project.

Finally, of course, the conclusions and opinions are those of the authors and do not necessarily represent those of the individuals or institutions that have provided us with support or assistance.

Part I

INTRODUCTION AND HISTORICAL PERSPECTIVE

Chapter 1

Opportunities in a Deregulated Industry

The U.S. Airline Deregulation Act of 1978 marked a major step toward deregulation of a once highly regulated industry. Most of the public debate prior to passage, and most subsequent analyses of the major impacts of deregulation, focused on what would and would not be done by the established carriers—those trunk and local service airlines that were operating prior to deregulation. Largely overlooked was the possibility that new opportunities would not only be created for the established carriers but for entirely new carriers as well.

Regulation, to understate the case, was not conducive to entrepreneurship, at least of the classic Schumpeterian type concerned with capitalistic innovations that expand general economic well-being.[1] The regulatory authorities often—indeed almost invariably—thwarted any attempt to introduce new or different market concepts. To the extent there was rivalry, let alone competition, under regulation, it was largely restricted to currying advantage from the highly legalistic and politicized regulatory process (e.g., keeping competition out of one's own markets and trying to gain access to theirs). These efforts could absorb considerable energy and imagination but seldom represented entrepreneurship of the classic capitalistic form—providing a better product at a lower price so as to enhance total economic satisfaction. To the extent there was any tendency toward entrepreneurship under regulation, it was usually a pale imitation stressing "service" or "quality" differences that at best may have appealed to a limited clientele (e.g., piano bars, larger canapes, younger and more vigorous cabin crews, more and dryer champagne, first-run movies, rerunning of last week's football highlights). Only occasionally did the rivalry spill over into lower fares, and then the regulator's acquiescence was often grudging. Experimentation with new *combinations* of services and fares was particularly rare. With deregulation, however, airline managers have had far greater freedom, and the result has been a rebirth of true economic or Schumpeterian entrepreneurship in the industry. This rebirth has been manifested in two major forms.

First, deregulation unleashed a surge of activity by commuter airlines offering scheduled short-haul service in low-density markets using small propeller-driven aircraft. Specifically, deregulation has greatly enhanced the number of market opportunities for the commuter airlines, as established trunk and local service carriers have used their new freedoms to withdraw from short-haul routes (which have usually been unprofitable for large, jet-equipped airlines).

A second surge of post-deregulation entrepreneurship has involved the introduction of simple, no-frills service and low fares in short to medium hauls (200 to 1,000 miles). In these markets most of the new competition has come from entirely new jet-equipped carriers or from expansion of what were previously intrastate carriers confined by regulation to operations within one state (e.g., California, Texas, and Florida).

Somewhat surprisingly, the entrepreneurship unleashed by deregulation has been largely confined to short-haul markets. Fundamentally, opportunities for almost all of the new entrepreneurs arose because air transportation in short-haul markets was not highly profitable under CAB regulation, and most established airlines served these markets reluctantly—primarily as a means of feeding passengers to their longer and more profitable flights. Competition to the established trunks on longer hauls has been provided since deregulation by what once were known as "supplemental carriers" (or charter operators), but these unleashed supplementals have not had a major impact. Many of their airplanes have proved ill-adapted to high fuel costs, and they have been swamped by the unexpectedly intense post-deregulation competition among the established trunks on the longer-haul routes. Just as short-haul routes were usually not profitable under regulation, long-haul routes were often especially lucrative. Prior to deregulation the trunk carriers therefore ordered what proved to be a surfeit of wide-bodied planes suitable for long-haul service. That surfeit manifested itself under deregulation in intense rate and service competition in many long-haul markets, with the supplementals adding, but only marginally, to the melee![2]

Of course any surfeit of long-haul aircraft need not last forever. New equipment cycles may eventually result in just the opposite occurring— too many small planes leading to intense competition on short-haul routes. But because of the long lead times involved, it is obvious that to understand the airline industry after deregulation, and the possibility of new and different competitive cycles, something must also be known about the point of departure: how the industry operated under regulation.

The Impact of Regulation

Regulation of airline passenger service formally began in the United States with the creation of the Civil Aeronautics Authority (CAA) in 1938, which was reorganized into the Civil Aeronautics Board (CAB) in 1940. The major elements of airline economic regulation remained essentially unchanged from then until 1976, when the move toward less regulation began.

Under CAB regulation an airline was required to have a Certificate of Public Convenience and Necessity, before offering scheduled airline service on any route.[3] When economic regulation began in 1938, 16 carriers were granted grandfather certificates to continue their existing operations. Through mergers these 16 carriers had evolved into 10 domestic trunk airlines by the mid-1970s (just before deregulation began). Although many applications and attempts were made over the years, no new trunk carriers (with the limited exception of the now-defunct Northeast Airlines) were allowed to enter the industry under CAB regulation.[4]

Authority to issue certificates also allowed the CAB to control the route structure of every major scheduled airline. The certificates specified both the pair of cities that were the end points of a route and the intermediate stops. The specification of intermediate stops was quite detailed and often included stops that had to be made, stops that could be made, and stops that could not be made. In some cases there were also limitations on carrying passengers between intermediate stops.

The CAB was only slightly more permissive about the entry of existing carriers into new city-pair markets than of new carriers into the industry. When a route was already served by an incumbent carrier, the CAB was usually reluctant to allow new entry if the incumbent objected on the grounds that such entry would divert existing traffic and cause financial hardship. As a further restriction, route awards necessitated an application procedure and hearings that were very lengthy and often quite expensive. In these proceedings legal and political skills were often important, and executive recruitment and promotion at the airlines came to reflect these considerations.

The CAB used route awards to pursue diverse policy objectives. Monopoly routes were sometimes given to carriers in a weak financial position in an attempt to maintain stability in the industry. Through route awards attempts were also made to reduce the subsidies needed by so-called local service airlines for service to small communities. Small community service was further protected by using certificates to control exit, since a carrier could not stop serving a route without CAB approval.

Another critical aspect of CAB regulation was its authority over fares. The CAB controlled fares in two different ways: (1) by approving, modifying, or rejecting requests for fare changes filed by individual carriers and (2) by directly setting either the exact fares or a narrow range of permissible fares. Both approaches were used extensively. Fare offerings generally were limited to coach and first-class fares based on the mileage traveled, although the CAB allowed limited experimentation with discount or promotional fares at various times.

CAB approval was also necessary for airline companies to merge. In general, the CAB took a restrictive view of mergers, granting approval only to maintain industry stability when one of the merger candidates was in serious financial trouble.

Deregulation Changes the Rules

With the passage of the Airline Deregulation Act of 1978 the CAB no longer had complete control over such matters as entry, exit, routes, and fares. Indeed, the act even scheduled the disbanding of the CAB itself (in 1984) and the transfer of its few remaining regulatory functions to the Department of Transportation.

Two specific changes in the deregulation act were crucial to opening opportunities for entrepreneurship. The first change was a provision that an applicant for a route found "fit, willing, and able to perform air transportation properly" will not be denied route authority on the grounds that granting the certificate would divert traffic from an existing carrier. Under this provision the CAB has processed applications quickly so that entry into any domestic route has become virtually automatic, with minimal delay for any qualified carrier.

The second crucial change was to give carriers freedom to set their own fares within a wide range without CAB approval. The range just after formal deregulation extended from 5 to 10 percent above to as much as 50 percent below the Standard Industry Fare Level (SIFL) established by the CAB. The range of permissible fare increases was subsequently broadened so that the CAB effectively gave up virtually all control over fares. Most important for the unleashing of entrepreneurship in short-haul markets, the CAB abandoned all control over short-haul fares very shortly after deregulation (apparently because of a fear that service to many small communities might not otherwise be available).

These two changes—freedom to add routes and to set fares—allowed the new jet and former intrastate carriers to enter the markets they chose and to establish a presence quickly by charging much lower fares than the incumbents. Their service was also usually simpler and lower in cost with fewer on-board amenities such as meals, movies, or free drinks. Costs were often further reduced by using nonunion and lower-seniority labor, utilizing secondary airports, and not providing interlining with other carriers. Prior to deregulation the CAB effectively prevented such low-fare, no-frills combinations and provided minimal incentives to hold costs in check.

Although commuter carriers were never subject to formal CAB regulation (other than some data-reporting requirements), as long as they operated aircraft below a specified size, several features of the Airline Deregulation Act had important implications for these carriers as well. The most direct change was raising the maximum-size aircraft a commuter could operate from 30 seats to 60 seats. The ability to use these larger aircraft opened up new market opportunities for commuters. For those commuters wishing to operate still larger aircraft, deregulation made it easier to become a certificated carrier and thus operate without aircraft size restrictions.

Elimination of most rate and entry regulations (especially in the short hauls) helped the commuter airlines just as it helped the new jet and intrastate carriers—but for somewhat different reasons. Basically, subsidized competition was eliminated from many of the markets that on efficiency grounds naturally belonged to the commuters. The local service carriers that prior to deregulation received government subsidies to provide jet service on low-density short-haul routes found it attractive after deregulation to redeploy their aircraft to new higher-density and longer routes where they could realize a higher return on their investments. Furthermore, where the local service carriers stayed in low-density short-haul markets, they used their new rate freedom to set fares at levels that were fully compensatory, thus removing an artificially low rate umbrella that previously inhibited commuter entry.

Another feature of the act, easing exit restrictions on the certificated carriers, further helped the commuters. As the local service carriers withdrew from short-haul low-density markets (which they found un-profitable or only marginally profitable) in search of higher returns elsewhere, commuters were able to enter these markets as replacement carriers. With their smaller and more fuel-efficient aircraft commuters usually found these services at least compensatory, and sometimes quite profitable. In response to a widespread fear that under deregulation exit from small community service might become rampant, the act also included a provision guaranteeing essential air service for 10 years to communities receiving certificated service prior to deregulation and authorized a new subsidy program to insure that this air service would be maintained. Commuters were declared eligible to provide this service and to receive subsidy, if warranted. Prior to deregulation there had been subsidies for small community service, but commuters had been ineligible to receive them. Also for the first time the act made commuters eligible for government loan guarantees to acquire aircraft.

Ironically, the change in exit requirements, which represented a re-laxation of regulation for certificated carriers, increased the regulation of commuters. Prior to deregulation a commuter carrier could stop serving a community at will without prior notice or permission of either the CAB or the community. As part of the deregulation act, however, a commuter had to give a 30-day notice before stopping service to a community that had previously received service from a certificated carrier. Moreover, as will be discussed in chapter 10, if the commuter's departure would leave the community with too little air service, the commuter could be forced to continue serving the community indef-initely, albeit with financial compensation for any losses incurred.

Overview and Plan of Study

The first two chapters of this book (part I) provide an introduction and historical perspective. Chapter 2 discusses the limited enterpreneurial opportunities in the industry before deregulation and traces the de-velopment of the new entrepreneurs' "ancestors": the pre-deregulation commuters, the local service airlines, and the intrastate jet carriers.

Because of the fundamental importance of short-haul markets for entrepreneurial activity, the basic elements of short-haul air transpor-tation are addressed in part II, chapters 3 through 5. The particular focus in these chapters is determining to what extent different short-haul airline markets lie along a continuum so that carriers serving one market might or might not be expected to compete in other markets if opportunities presented themselves. In terms of the "traditional" economic concepts of industrial organization the essential question is to what extent airline markets are easy to enter and therefore subject to competitive limitations on market power. In more modern formulations it is the notion of "contestability," defined to include ease of exit as well as entry, that comes to the fore.[5]

Chapter 3 investigates the nature of demand for air travel with an emphasis on short- and medium-haul markets, focusing on the relative role of fares and service in stimulating demand under different circumstances. Chapter 4 examines the cost structure of short- and medium-haul air service as provided by different kinds of aircraft. It addresses both the issue of under what circumstances a particular type of aircraft has a cost advantage over another type and the magnitude and sources of any cost advantage of the new entrant jet carriers. Chapter 5 contains a systematic investigation of airline safety, with particular emphasis on evaluating the commonly held perception that commuter airlines are unacceptably less safe than certificated jet carriers, thereby possibly creating a bifurcation that prevents commuter carriers from providing an effective competitive alternative to other airlines.[6]

Part III, chapters 6 through 8, examines the various management strategies used by the new entrepreneurs. In these chapters financial strategies as well as operating strategies with regard to route networks and fare policies are examined and compared with those pursued by the older established airlines.

Chapter 6 examines how the new entrant jet and commuter carriers have financed their expanding operations. It explores the relative roles of federal loan guarantees, private capital (in the form of both equity and debt), subsidies from foreign governments, and recent changes in U.S. tax laws. Chapter 7 focuses on the operating strategies of the new entrant and former intrastate jet carriers, and chapter 8 examines the commuter airlines' strategies.

The final section of the book, part IV (chapters 9 through 11), turns to the larger issues of public policy that arise from the presence of the entrepreneurial carriers. Chapter 9 examines airport congestion and how it has changed since deregulation; it focuses especially on the extent to which congestion at major airports may have hindered access for new entrant carriers and thus impeded their development. Airport and airway facilities are of course a basic element of air transportation. Unlike the elements discussed in part II, however, decisions about the provision and use of airports and airways are much more in the domain of public policy than under the control of the airlines themselves (as the events surrounding the PATCO strike of 1981 so graphically demonstrated).

Chapter 10 examines airline service to small communities and federal subsidies for this service in light of the post-deregulation eligibility of commuter carriers to receive subsidies; in particular, the effectiveness of the old or pre-deregulation subsidy program is compared with that of the program established by the 1978 deregulation act.

Chapter 11 draws on the analyses of the preceding chapters to discuss the implications of these entrepreneurial carriers for the eventual structure of the airline industry. The new entrant jet carriers, with their lower cost structures and simplified service patterns, represent a significant break with practices of the established trunk and local service airlines. Their impact on the airline industry could far exceed what might be implied by the limited number of passengers they carried in their early or developmental years. Similarly, the new opportunities presented to commuter carriers should allow them to increase their role in the nation's air transportation system.

Indeed, a central theme in the chapters that follow will be that the most significant long-run impacts of airline deregulation may derive not from the obvious initial adaptations of the established carriers to deregulation but instead from the more fundamental and long-run changes stimulated by the rebirth of airline entrepreneurship, among the established carriers as well as the new.[7] Even though the new entrepreneurs may never account for more than a small percentage of total activity, they have irrevocably changed the fundamentals of the industry. Furthermore their presence will create new competitive pressures and checks that will influence the future structure of the industry in ways yet to be determined.

Chapter 2

Progenitors: Entrepreneurial Opportunities before Deregulation

Although opportunities for entrepreneurship in the airline industry were severely limited before deregulation, three avenues were open for firms to enter the fringes of the industry and provide limited passenger air service. These were (1) local service airlines, several of which eventually came to resemble small trunk carriers; (2) supplemental carriers that orginally offered only nonscheduled charter service but from which both commuter airlines and jet charter carriers developed; and (3) intrastate carriers that, free from CAB regulation, experimented with different combinations of fare and service and became a model for many of the post-deregulation new entrants.

Much of the entrepreneurial response to the easing of restrictions accompanying the Airline Deregulation Act of 1978 came in fact from carriers that had developed prior to deregulation via one of these avenues. Even post-deregulation new entrants looked to the experiences of these carriers as a guide. Consequently, to understand post-deregulation developments in commercial air transportation, pre deregulation experiences of at least the local service carriers, commuters and intrastate carriers must be examined.

Local Service Airlines

In the early 1940s pressure built for expansion of air transportation services to smaller communities. But the CAB, despite receiving requests by various applicants to serve over 16,000 miles of such feeder routes, was reluctant to permit entry into this type of service.[1]

The CAB feared that feeder routes (short-haul low-density segments connecting smaller communities in outlying areas with larger airports) would face stiffer competition from rail, bus, and automobile transportation than did the longer trunk routes. Furthermore the typical communities proposed as recipients of feeder air service—with populations of less than 50,000—were not expected to generate adequate daily passenger traffic to support profitable operation. The CAB also believed that the industry's primary passenger transport aircraft at the time, the DC-3, was designed for "long-haul" transportation. In short-haul low-density services these planes would thus be burdened with high operating costs. Moreover the aircraft industry did not appear ready to supplement the DC-3 with a comparable aircraft for shorter distance operations.[2]

A 1943–44 CAB Investigation of Local, Feeder, and Pick-up Air Service seemingly confirmed these fears and reservations.[3] The examiners compiled traffic data for 88 cities with populations of less than 50,000 that had received air service as of September 1940. In this group the 18 cities with populations below 10,000 had generated an average of only 4.03 arriving and departing passengers per day.[4] The 31 cities in the 10,000 to 20,000 population bracket averaged 5.7 passengers per day, while even the 39 cities with populations of 20,000 to 50,000 averaged only 13.4 per day.[5] The future success of feeder airlines was further called into question by a 1944 survey conducted by United Air Lines in which airline feeder hops of less than 100 miles were found not competitive with surface transportation.[6]

Despite these negative findings, the CAB in 1945, influenced by the eagerness of the proponents of the service, established feeder service on an experimental basis. Two safeguards, however, were incorporated into the route awards made to carriers on feeder segments: (1) such authorizations were limited in time (three years in most cases), and (2) operations were to be confined to those that did not require unacceptable levels of subsidy.[7]

The CAB also considered the question of whether feeder service should be provided by the established 16 trunk carriers or by entirely new carriers. The advantages of using the existing carriers included: "(1) the lower overhead expenses involved in extending routes of existing carriers as opposed to expenses incurred by a separate enterprise; (2) the ability of the existing carriers to absorb losses on local routes with profits from long-haul services; (3) greater utilization of existing equipment; and (4) the higher quality of service existing carriers would be able to provide."[8] By contrast, the proposals from the new carriers emphasized "economy and less luxurious standards of service" with smaller aircraft (e.g., the 9-passenger Lockheed L-10s and the 10-passenger Boeing B-247s) and the elimination of stewardesses and some ground personnel.[9] After considerable evaluation of these conflicting tendencies, the examiners eventually concluded that an entirely new class of local service carriers was needed.[10]

The CAB examiners also anticipated a potential problem with competition between new carriers and trunks. To prevent this, several witnesses proposed that a certificate issued to a feeder airline contain a provision requiring the carrier to stop at every intermediate point on every flight. The examiners, however, believed that such a limitation would prevent an operator from developing a market for the business traveler who wanted to go from a small town to a large city with a minimum of delay, so they suggested that an operator should be allowed some flexibility in accommodating this type of traffic through skip-stop or nonstop operations.[11] Despite this recommendation the CAB initially adopted a policy requiring feeder flights to originate and terminate at points on the carrier's certificate and to stop at every intermediate point. This policy was later modified to allow shuttle service between any two points named consecutively in a local service certificate.[12] However, a minimum of two round trips per day was also required over each route segment.

While the every-stop-on-every-flight requirement assured more frequent service to intermediate points than would otherwise have been provided, it also effectively insulated the trunks from new competition. That such restrictions were indeed aimed at preventing competition between feeder and trunk airlines (rather than improving service) was revealed by the CAB's deviation from the every-stop requirement when trunk airlines were involved in feeder service. For example, TWA was granted feeder routes in Indiana and Ohio in 1946, but no restrictions were placed on these routes.[13] In general, the trunks were allowed to experiment with a variety of nonstop and skip-stop operations to avoid impairing the quality of their service.

Establishing Small Community Subsidies
From the outset the CAB believed that a subsidy would be necessary if air service was to be extended to small communities unable to generate enough daily passenger traffic to support regular air service.[14] However, the CAB rejected using a fixed rate subsidy stating: "In the absence of any definite maximum limit on mail pay incorporated into the certificates that are granted, the issuance of temporary certificates will serve as a safeguard against a static or progressively increasing dependence on the Government, and will permit the subsequent issuance of permanent status only to such carriers who, based on their performance during the temporary period, have shown that they are capable of operation without undue cost to the Government."[15] Although concerned that

using a temporary rate schedule might effectively place an airline on a "cost-plus" subsidy system with reduced incentives for efficient operation, the CAB nevertheless established temporary rates based on the particular conditions of individual carriers.[16] The temporary rate system was based on Section 406(a) of the Civil Aeronautics Act of 1938, which empowered the CAB "to fix and determine from time to time, after notice and hearing, the fair and reasonable rates of compensation for the transportation of mail" and "to make such rates effective from such date as it shall determine to be proper."[17] The basis for temporary mail rates was "to insure the performance of mail service," but the CAB also stressed the importance of mail compensation which, "together with all its other revenue, would enable the carrier under honest, economical and efficient management to maintain and continue the development of air transportation to the extent and of the character and quality required for the commerce of the United States, the Postal Service, and the National defense."[18]

This decision to compensate not only for mail service but to include considerations of developing the air transportation network led to what in essence became a cost-plus subsidy system. The CAB recognized the potential problems with such a system: "Heretofore, we have refused to establish future mail rates on a tentative basis subject to later readjustments. We have held that the adoption of mail rate determination pattern upon a 'cost plus' system would tend to destroy a carrier's incentive to maintain costs at a reasonable level and to develop its nonmail business."[19] Sliding-scale rates based on load factors were thus tested with the goal of inducing carriers to increase their load factors and develop nonmail business.[20] The results were disappointing, and the subsidy remained largely cost-plus in nature.

The level of subsidy to the newly established carriers consistently exceeded expectations. In part, the indirect costs were found to be greater than anticipated in the original feeder proposals. Carriers often underestimated the cost of ticket offices, ground equipment, personnel, and hangar space at intermediate and terminal points. Higher costs also stemmed from unanticipated restrictions placed on the feeder operators by the CAB, such as the every-stop-on-every-flight requirement.

The biggest source of higher subsidies, however, was the use of larger aircraft. The cost estimates presented in the Investigation of Local, Feeder, and Pick-up Air Service assumed new carriers would use 9- to 10-seat aircraft—and indeed, that was the major reason for favoring the creation of new carriers to provide such service. Remarkably, certification of feeder carriers was *not* made contingent on the use of equipment suitable to such routes. Although several of the first feeder carriers began service with small aircraft suitable to these low-density routes, these aircraft were often later replaced by DC-3s.[21] Some feeder airlines even began operation with DC-3s, without bothering to use smaller aircraft. War surplus military versions of the DC-3 (C-47) were readily available, inexpensive, and easily converted to civilian passenger service. The Surplus Property Board, established by Congress on October 3, 1944, transferred nearly 30,000 planes to the civilian sector.[22] Furthermore the DC-3 remained an important part of the trunks' fleets. By operating aircraft similar to the trunk airlines, local service airlines improved their public image and on some routes were able to compete with the trunks. Surprisingly, the high operating cost of the DC-3s in low-density service did not prompt the board to restrict their use by the local service carriers. Subsidies were increased as the small gains in passenger loads accompanying the switch to DC-3s failed to cover the increased cost of flying the larger aircraft. By its inaction the CAB indicated to the carriers that the greater operating costs of this aircraft would not preclude its use in subsidized service, and by 1948 the DC-3 had become the principal aircraft of the local service airlines."[23] Indeed, all local service carriers that had acquired DC-3s had their certificates renewed, whereas the three airlines that had not flown DC-3s lost their certification![24]

In 1955 Congress moved to make the certificates of the local service airlines permanent, and in 1957 the Government Guaranty of Equipment Loans Act authorized the CAB to guarantee equipment loans for local service airlines to modernize their fleets. The subsidy level had continued to rise throughout the 1950s, and as the local service airlines began to reequip with ever larger planes, the subsidy shot up dramatically. From a subsidy level of $33 million in 1958, the payments more than doubled to $67 million by 1962.

Concerned by the rising level of subsidy, the CAB in 1953 attempted to reduce the subsidy by following a policy of limited route strengthening. This policy consisted of four facets: (1) liberalizing the route restrictions placed on the local service airlines; (2) transferring those weaker points served by trunks to local service airlines; (3) implementing a "use it or lose it" policy stating that each locality had to enplane at least five passengers per day or lose its service; and (4) adding new routes, often to points that had previously been without airline service.

Route strengthening, however, did not stop the rise of subsidies. The liberalized route policy largely took the form of easing the every-stop requirement and allowing some reduction of minimum daily frequencies. Even with this liberalization, local service airlines were rarely permitted to offer nonstop service in a market also served by trunks. Transferring weak points from trunks to local service airlines almost certainly helped the trunks more than it did the locals. The transferred points generated little traffic and had been a financial drain on the trunks—and proved to be almost as much a drain on the locals. The "use it or lose it" policy was not formalized until 1958 and even then was applied so loosely that many points enplaning fewer than five passengers per day remained on the certificates of the local service airlines.

Class-Rate Subsidies

To meet these and other problems, a new subsidy policy for local service airlines was adopted in 1961 (following the Local Service Class Subsidy Rate Investigation of 1958). A single set of subsidy rates was established to supersede the individual treatments formerly accorded the carriers—though the class-rate system was subsequently amended to allow also for an individual carrier's "need."

The subsidy to local service airlines nevertheless continued to grow and to be a cause for concern. In 1962 a request by President Kennedy to the CAB to reduce the subsidies did not produce immediate results. Indeed, the subsidy level rose in 1963 and continued thereafter at high levels. Thus in 1966 the CAB again embarked on an even more ambitious program aimed at strengthening the local service carriers' route structures. The CAB abandoned the long-held idea of the locals being specialized carriers concentrating on feeder markets and avoiding direct competition with the trunks. The local service airlines were provided profitable unsubsidized opportunities in higher-density medium-haul markets to cross-subsidize the losses incurred on their feeder routes. The trunks were felt to be strong enough by the late 1960s to withstand any such competition.

Concurrently, the CAB allowed the local service airlines to introduce jet aircraft (ostensibly to increase earnings and reduce subsidy) and to merge when that would strengthen their position. Both jets and mergers were avidly pursued by the locals (with three mergers taking place by 1972). While subsidies fell sharply, the fall in the locals' profits was even greater! As a result the CAB abruptly abandoned this approach in 1970 and returned to the class-rate formula—and subsidies once again began to rise.

The general character of the various class-rate formulas in effect from 1970 to the beginning of deregulation was much the same. An amount was paid for (1) the number of days each eligible point was served, (2) the number of departures from each eligible point, and (3) the number of plane miles flown in subsidy-eligible service. An offset was made for the number of revenue passengers and the number of revenue passenger miles flown on the subsidized flights. The subsidy did not vary, however, by time of day; the subsidy rate was no higher for a conveniently scheduled flight than for an inconvenient one. In fact, because of the offset for revenue passengers and revenue passenger miles, a conveniently scheduled flight was likely to earn less subsidy (although more passenger revenue) than an inconvenient one. Thus an aircraft used to fly both subsidy and nonsubsidy routes generally could earn more revenue plus subsidy by flying the nonsubsidy route during the peak period (when there were more passengers) and the subsidy route during the off-peak period (when there were fewer passengers). Furthermore, because a subsidy was paid for each aircraft departure from an eligible point (up to a limit), more subsidy could be earned by an aircraft flying a multistop route among subsidy-eligible points than by an aircraft flying nonstop or one-stop routes.

The use of jet aircraft was also encouraged by the manner in which the subsidies were paid. In addition to the subsidy paid according to the class-rate formulas, a "need adjustment" subsidy was paid to allow the carriers to earn reasonable rates of return on the investment used in subsidy operations. A carrier purchasing a jet was allowed to include part of the capital investment in the subsidy-eligible investment base, with the portion included determined by the amount the aircraft was used in subsidy-eligible (as against subsidy-ineligible) markets. A jet purchased to meet peak period demands in markets ineligible for subsidy could therefore have its return partially guaranteed through this need adjustment (by using it during off-peak periods in markets eligible for subsidy). The resulting use of jets, with the accompanying need adjustment, was thus quite parallel with the earlier use of DC-3s and the then accompanying cost-plus arrangement using temporary mail-subsidy rates.

It is therefore hardly surprising that on the eve of deregulation, the larger of the local service airlines had grown to resemble small trunk airlines. The CAB, in the pursuit of cross-subsidies, had placed the locals in competition with the trunks in many short- and medium-haul routes of moderate density. The local service carriers had also in effect been given subsidies to acquire modern jet aircraft similar or identical to those used by the trunks. The local service airlines' transition to becoming jet carriers was therefore largely complete by the time deregulation began.

Nonscheduled Services and the Development of the Commuter Carriers

The commuter airline industry grew out of so-called on-demand nonscheduled operators. In these operations a small aircraft with a pilot could be hired on a nonscheduled basis for short-distance passenger or cargo transportation. Since obtaining the service was similar to hiring a taxicab, this form of nonscheduled service became known as air taxi service.[25]

After World War II an influx of surplus transport planes, and a large number of military pilots returning to civilian life, provided the impetus for a rapid expansion of air taxi service, primarily in short-haul low-density markets where scheduled service was unavailable. Nonscheduled operators grew rapidly between 1944 and 1946, with the number estimated at 2,730 in 1946. Most of these operations proved to be short-lived, and by 1951 there were fewer than 50 in operation.[26] Although veterans' wartime flying skills and cheap planes made entry into the fledgling industry relatively easy, most operators lacked sufficient managerial skills to maintain profitable air service. The development of air taxi services was also impeded by the creation of the local service airlines. As subsidized local service airlines began extending air service to small communities, the unsubsidized air taxis found that their only opportunities were to serve still smaller communities, many of which could not support even nonscheduled service.

Nonscheduled operations had always been exempt from CAB certification requirements and economic regulation (since the CAB's inception in 1938). On July 26, 1944, the CAB authorized an investigation into nonscheduled air transportation "to determine what should be the nature and extent of permanent economic regulation, if any, of nonscheduled operations, and to inquire into the general problems concerning the desirability of revising or terminating the general exemption order, Section 292.1 of the Economic Regulations."[27]

In defining the meaning of nonscheduled or irregular service, the CAB stated, in its opinion, that "the term nonscheduled has far more restrictive meaning than the mere absence of a published timetable. The operation ceases to be a nonscheduled operation, within the meaning of the exemption order, when the point is reached at which the operator and passenger tacitly assume that trips will be operated between specific points with a fair degree of regularity, and that the only question is whether space will be obtained on such flights."[28] In 1946 the CAB issued an initial ruling that an airline would need to have fairly unpredictable service and make 10 or fewer round trips between two points in a month. Carriers failing to meet this test would have to become certificated in order to continue operating.

Reaction to this ruling was, predictably, mixed. The local service and trunk airlines of course favored the decision. They argued that nonscheduled carriers were avoiding regulation under the previous imprecise definitions and that these "nonscheds" should be forced to stop conducting regular operations without a certificate. Furthermore many of the nonscheds were using large aircraft such as the ubiquitous DC-3s and were posing unwanted and unneeded competition for the certificated carriers. The nonscheds, by contrast, considered the ruling a threat to their existence. Certification could prove extremely expensive for small operators. Since the nonscheduled carriers were not receiving government subsidy, opponents of the ruling argued that nonscheduled operations were independent enterprises and should not be subject to economic regulation.[29]

In a final decision, announced on May 17, 1946, the exemption of nonscheduled operations from the economic regulations of the Civil Aeronautics Act of 1938 was continued in effect. However, the CAB amended the regulations to require that all nonscheduled carriers register their names with the board and furnish information that would indicate the extent of their transportation services. The CAB also empowered itself to issue cease and desist orders if it found a nonscheduled carrier "engaging in unfair methods of competition."[30]

In 1947 the CAB created "irregular air carriers" as a new class of nonscheduled airlines. These carriers were defined as carriers not holding a certificate but engaged in interstate air transportation of persons or property to varying destinations in a nonscheduled manner. In 1948 a distinction was drawn between large and small irregular carriers. Small irregular carriers were originally limited to the operation of aircraft with a gross takeoff weight of not more than 10,000 pounds, or three or more planes whose aggregate takeoff weight did not exceed 25,000 pounds.[31] In 1949 the CAB raised the takeoff weight limit to 12,500 pounds (about half the gross takeoff weight of a DC-3) for small irregular carriers to bring their weight limit in line with that of the Federal Aviation Administration (FAA).

In 1969 the CAB established a subclass of small irregular carriers (or air taxis) known as commuter air carriers who were exempt from the normal economic regulations of scheduled airlines. Commuter carriers were defined by the CAB as operators that performed at least five round trips per week between two or more points and published flight schedules specifying the times, days of the week, and places between which flights were performed.[32] The commuter airlines were also required to register with the CAB, carry passenger liability insurance, and provide the board with a copy of their schedule of fares, rates, and charges. In 1972, instead of the previous operating standard of 12,500 pounds takeoff weight limit, the board relaxed the aircraft restriction to allow commuter operators to conduct operations in aircraft seating 30 or fewer passengers.[33]

This relaxation of the CAB weight limit, combined with a greater CAB tolerance of trunk and local airlines' withdrawal from small towns or low-density routes, opened up new opportunities for commuter service during the 1970s. Between 1971 and 1978 commuter enplanements grew at an average annual rate of 12.1 percent. During the same period, by contrast, the local service airlines grew at a rate of 8.5 percent, and the trunks grew at 6.7 percent. Although deregulation certainly did not hurt commuters, aggregate commuter growth during the two years following deregulation was actually no greater than during the two years immediately preceding deregulation.

Growth within the commuter industry has not, however, been uniform. In outlying regions (e.g., Alaska, Hawaii, and the Caribbean) commuters serve a much different function than in more densely developed areas; among islands or in mountainous areas commuters are often the primary or only practical means of transportation. As a consequence commuter service in these areas developed earlier and more rapidly, accounting for about 40 percent of total commuter enplanements in 1972. Since then the rate of growth in these regions has slowed to about 0.5 percent per year. By contrast, in the 48 contiguous states as a whole the average annual rate of growth was 13.6 percent between 1972 and 1980. By 1980 therefore island and mountainous regions accounted for only about 20 percent of total commuter traffic.

Commuter airlines serve an important role in the U.S. transportation system. In 1980 commuter enplanements represented 5 percent of total U.S. airline enplanements, up from 3 percent in 1972. By several measures, moreover, the role of commuters is much larger than the enplanement figures would indicate. As of June 1, 1980, 618 airports in the contiguous 48 states received scheduled passenger air service. Of these, 505 were served by commuters with 292 receiving only commuter service. Commuters serve primarily a feeder function with approximately 70 percent of commuter passengers connecting to another flight. Most commuter airlines also estimate that between 80 and 90 percent of their passengers travel for business purposes.

Intrastate Airlines

The intrastate segment of the airline industry was not large prior to deregulation and has remained small since deregulation in terms of passengers carried or passenger miles. Nevertheless, the operations of intrastate carriers have been a crucial aspect of the entire deregulation experience. In the debate prior to the passage of the deregulation act intrastate jet carriers in Texas and California were cited as examples of what was possible with less regulation.[34] These carriers had been able to offer frequent service at fares far below comparable interstate fares, and they had been generally profitable. The influence of these carriers continued after deregulation as many of the new entrant jet carriers patterned their operations, to a large degree, after these earlier intrastate operations.

Prior to deregulation three intrastate carriers were particularly prominent—two in California and one in Texas. The largest intrastate carrier was Pacific Southwest Airlines (PSA) which began operations in California in 1949; it was the first to begin low-fare, no-frills jet service which came to characterize not only intrastate carriers but subsequent new entrant jet carriers as well. A second important California intrastate carrier was Air California which began operations in 1967. In Texas, Southwest Airlines began service in 1971 following a long legal battle and patterned itself after PSA. Intrastate carriers were not subject to regulation by the Civil Aeronautics Board but operated instead under regulation administered by their respective state agencies (the California Public Utilities Commission, or CPUC, and the Texas Aeronautics Commission). Under these regulatory regimes, the carriers were able to offer fare and service combinations not permitted under CAB regulation.

The regulatory authority of the CPUC was quite similar to that of the CAB in that it could control entry, exit, fares, and set maximum and minimum limits on flight frequency.[35] Although its authority was similar, the CPUC nevertheless proceeded quite differently. For example, the CPUC was much more liberal with respect to entry than was the CAB. Between 1946 and 1975, 18 carriers were permitted to enter into California intrastate service. Entry, however, was no guarantee of success as only 3 of the 18 remained in service by 1975. The CPUC controlled exit but, unlike the CAB, was quite willing to allow carriers to exit if a route was considered unprofitable.

Using its entry and exit control, the CPUC also controlled the routes each carrier could fly. Route control was also used to promote the use of uncongested satellite airports, such as Oakland, Ontario, Burbank, and Santa Ana. After the fashion of the CAB, however, the CPUC also largely avoided having intrastate carriers competing head to head on identical routes.

A major difference between CPUC and CAB fare policies was that the CPUC based fares on the experience of the lowest-cost carrier rather than an industry average, as was the CAB's practice. Thus PSA's high load factors, high seating densities, no-frills service, and good aircraft utilization were reflected in the regulated fares. Low fares and frequent service also stimulated high market growth with accompanying high load factors and profitable operations.

In Texas, the Texas Aeronautics Commission had control over entry but had no authority to regulate fares. As a result Southwest Airlines had complete freedom to set fares and, not too surprisingly, was the first airline to make extensive use of differentiated peak and off-peak pricing. Southwest not only charged low fares during peak daytime weekday flights but applied even lower fares to evening and weekend flights. Southwest also used close-in secondary airports in Dallas and Houston rather than the major international airports that were more distant from the central business district in these cities.

The intrastate services that evolved under the somewhat different regulatory environments of Texas and California shared several important characteristics. The most obvious, given that these were intrastate markets, was that the service was confined to short-haul markets, enabling the carriers to specialize in a single type of service. Some of the passengers using the intrastate carriers were of course drawn from the older established airlines. The phenomenal growth of the intrastate markets, however, came primarily from drawing passengers away from private autos and stimulating new trips with very low fares.

This very high traffic growth suggested that both fare and service elasticities were much more substantial than conventionally believed. Although attention was largely focused on the high-density markets of Dallas–Houston and Los Angeles–San Francisco, the intrastate carriers also had good market growth and profitable operations in medium-density markets such as Dallas–San Antonio, Houston–San Antonio, San Diego–San Jose, and Los Angeles–Fresno.

The route structures and service patterns of these carriers also contributed to the low cost of their operations. In varying degrees much of their activity was confined to simple turnaround services, where aircraft are flown back and forth between two points. Turnaround service greatly simplified scheduling and maintenance, and it enabled the carriers to achieve high aircraft utilization. Few of these carriers had interlining agreements with other airlines. Reservations, ticketing, and baggage handling were thus also simplified.

The intrastate carriers used the same small jet equipment as the trunk and local service carriers used for short-haul flights. In intrastate use, however, the aircraft were configured in high-density single-class seating. Coupled with high load factors and good aircraft utilization, the result was excellent productivity. Their operations were also enhanced by extensive, although not exclusive, use of secondary airports. The carriers found more favorable terms on gate space and ground facilities at these airports and experienced fewer delays than were typical at major airports. High productivity, coupled with low overhead and operating costs, resulted in relatively high profit levels—making it obvious why the jet carrier entrepreneurs of the post-deregulation period closely followed intrastate carrier precedents when establishing their operations.

Indeed, it is essentially impossible—and irrelevant—to distinguish post-deregulation between the old intrastate carriers and the new jet entrepreneurs. Seven new entrant jet carriers are examined in some detail in the chapters that follow. Of the seven, four are totally new entrants: Midway, Muse, New York Air, and People Express. The other three—Air Florida, Pacific Southwest Airlines (PSA), and Southwest—operated as intrastate carriers before deregulation and have subsequently expanded jet service to interstate markets. Collectively, these new entrant carriers accounted for 3.9 percent of domestic certificated revenue passenger miles and 4.2 percent of passenger revenues in the second quarter of 1981. As will be seen, however, their impact on the nation's air transportation system far exceeds that implied by these figures.

Summary

The experience prior to deregulation of the local service airlines, non-scheduled carriers, commuters, and intrastate carriers largely shaped entrepreneurial developments after deregulation. The nonscheds went directly into competition with the trunks, mainly on long hauls, just as expected. The local service airlines, formed initially to provide service similar to that now provided by commuters, had slowly but surely progressed from small prop planes to jets even before deregulation; by the time deregulation occurred, the local service carriers often competed directly with the trunks, and deregulation simply hastened and heightened that tendency.

The local service carriers "found" the aircraft to compete with the trunks after deregulation by swiftly withdrawing from subsidized loss or marginally profitable operations in lower-density and smaller markets. This evolution of local service airlines into medium-haul jet carriers provided major opportunities for commuter airlines. The commuters moved quickly to serve the markets vacated by the local service airlines following deregulation, sometimes with subsidy but more often without. In doing this, the commuters were essentially extending a process that started in the late stages of regulation—but a process that was sharply accelerated under deregulation. As the commuters grew with their new market opportunities, and occasional subsidies, a few of the larger and more aggressive of them began to enter markets that continued to be served by local service airlines, extending the scope of competition in the industry one step further. Indeed, some of the commuters even acquired jets after deregulation and operated much like the new entrants, entering directly into competition with the established carriers.

Virtually all of the key elements of the new entrant jet carriers' business strategies had their origins, at least conceptually, in the pre-deregulation operations of intrastate carriers. Thus even the most distinctive of post-deregulation innovations—the new jet carriers—had a progenitor in pre-deregulation experience. Most important, however, these progenitors, the intrastate carriers, were themselves the creations of a few special pockets of "relaxed" regulation and opportunity, mainly in California and Texas.

In general, entrepreneurial activity has always been just "beneath the surface" in the airline industry, mainly manifesting itself in efforts to find a special market niche—rendering lower fares (derived from lower costs), providing a better service, or flying in a market not otherwise served. Deregulation greatly expanded the scope of that search, opening up countless new opportunities. It also significantly "ratcheted" the entire entrepreneurial activity up a notch by opening up a whole new range of opportunities for commuter operations in smaller markets. A most important question, though, is whether all these activities tend to overlap. Is it an easy step (including both entry and exit) for a carrier anywhere in the size hierarchy to contemplate competing with a bigger or smaller "brother," thus making airline markets in the terminology of modern economics highly "contestable" and therefore competitive in their market behavior? These and related questions are investigated in the next few chapters.

Part II

THE BASIC ELEMENTS OF SHORT-HAUL AIR TRANSPORTATION

Chapter 3

The Demand for Short-Haul Air Service
by Don H. Pickrell

Markets are likely to perform competitively if many potential producers can, at relatively low cost, begin and cease operations in response to variations in demand. The ease with which suppliers can enter and exit markets depends in turn on the characteristics of both the demand for a product and the cost of supplying it. Insofar as these characteristics vary continuously, movement from one market or market segment to another should be relatively easy. In contrast, the greater the degree of differentiation among the characteristics of demand or cost of supplying a product in different markets, the more difficult it will be for producers to move from one segment to another.

This chapter examines the demand for scheduled air service in short-haul markets, including lightly traveled routes served by commuters and the more heavily traveled routes that have been the main target of entry by new jet carriers. The analysis is intended to provide insights into the underlying demand characteristics of the two types of markets served by these entrepreneurial carriers and a basis for examining their fare and route development strategies in chapters 7 and 8. A second goal is to assess the extent to which differences in the nature of demand between the two types of markets represent barriers to commuter airlines entering competition with jet carriers in denser markets.

Determinants of the Demand for Air Travel

The demand for travel to and from a city is influenced by the levels of economic and social activity that occur there, as well as its cultural, recreational, and other attractions. The cost of traveling between cities, including both dollar outlays and time required, also affects the level of trip making that occurs. The demand for air travel also depends on the delay to travelers' schedules imposed by the available frequency and specific scheduling of aircraft departures. More frequent flights or a wider choice of departure times generally reduce the schedule disruption entailed in traveling by air, thereby increasing the convenience offered. On the other hand, there is also some evidence that larger, more comfortable planes will attract more patronage, thus posing a marketing trade-off between plane size and schedule frequency.[1]

Various means of ground travel, principally the private automobile, are also usually available between cities connected by commercial airline service. Travelers choose among these competing modes by comparing their prices, travel times, and other important service characteristics, such as departure frequency and schedule convenience.[2]

Unfortunately, few reliable estimates of the sensitivity of air travel demand to the level of service provided in markets commonly served by commuter air carriers appear to be available.[3] Thus the effects of flight frequency, aircraft size, and other dimensions of service quality on the demand for short-haul air service to small communities remain poorly understood even though understanding these relationships is particularly important to assessing the prospects for competition on such routes.

A Model of the Demand for Commuter Air Service

To evaluate the sensitivity of demand for air service in short-haul low-density markets, a sample of 135 routes served by commuters was analyzed. Each route connected a single small community classified by the CAB as a nonhub with the nearest medium or large hub to which regularly scheduled airline service was offered.[4] Travel volumes on this sample of routes ranged from 100 to 650 one-way passengers per month departing from the nonhub for the large hub.[5] Population, which averaged slightly under 33,000 for the nonhub cities included in the sample, was the most readily available index of the level of travel-generating activity in the communities in which trips originated. Although perhaps a less accurate index of business and other trip-producing activities than employment or income levels, population is more readily available and consistently measured than other potential indicators.

The attractiveness of destination cities in the sample was measured by the number of passenger enplanements at the large-hub airport, which reflects both the level of local economic activity and the number of available connections to onward flights. Departure frequencies, flying times, and passenger fares for commuter airline service were available directly from the *Official Airline Guide* (*OAG*). Published air fares ranged from $27 to $132 for the selected sample of routes; however, many passengers transferring to onward flights actually pay fares considerably lower than those published through joint fare agreements between commuter and certificated jet carriers. As a consequence the published fare probably consistently overstates the average fare actually paid by air travelers on most routes. City-pair distances were concentrated in the 100- to 300-mile range, with scheduled flying times averaging slightly less than one hour.

The frequency of scheduled aircraft departures was used as an index of the schedule delay air travelers encounter in using commuter airline service. Because schedule delays are likely to be especially affected by the availability of flights at particularly convenient hours, the frequency of departures during early morning and evening hours was used as an alternate index of delay. Departure frequencies averaged about 20 per week, nearly half of which were scheduled for morning or evening hours (6 to 9 A.M. and 5 to 8 P.M.). Because the seating capacity of aircraft operated by commuter carriers (7 to 56 passengers in this sample) affects the probability of actually obtaining a seat at a specific departure time, it was used as another dimension of the schedule delay air travelers can experience on routes served by infrequent departures. Aircraft seating capacity probably also reflects the level of comfort experienced by passengers, which may affect their willingness to use commuter air service.

The characteristics of travel by private auto, the principal alternative mode for most commuter airline trips, proved somewhat more difficult to measure. Driving time was estimated using assumed routes between cities and resulting distances traveled at various average speeds. Although driving costs depend partly on distance traveled, they are also influenced by charges levied for parking at the trip destination, which can range up to several dollars per day. Unfortunately information on the duration of trips and the type of parking facilities used was unavailable, so it was necessary to use estimates of the average values of per mile operating costs and parking charges.

Further it was difficult to develop indexes of schedule delay and passenger comfort for auto travel that were comparable to those for commuter air travel. This difficulty was partly because auto departures can be readily scheduled to minimize disruption or delay in a single traveler's schedule, although groups traveling together by auto may experience greater disruption. In addition the comfort level afforded by driving depends largely on specific features of the vehicle and highway used, which probably vary widely among trips but in ways that are difficult to measure accurately. As a result of these complications the characteristics of auto travel used in the model were limited to driving time and estimates of the out-of-pocket cost over each route.

Using these data, a conventional gravity-type model of air travel was estimated. Details of the actual specification of the model, the estimation procedure employed, and the results are described in the appendix to this chapter. An important problem in estimating the effect of commuter air service levels on volumes of air traffic arises because the volume itself may in turn affect the level of service carriers provide, as well as perhaps the fares at which they offer that service. Air carriers commonly vary the passenger-carrying capacity they offer on specific routes in response to fluctuations in the level of passenger traffic by changing the frequency of departures or varying aircraft seating capacities.

One consequence of ignoring this supply response can be an unreliable estimate of the magnitude of demand response to variations in the level of service offered. To minimize this potential problem, the demand functions tested in this analysis were estimated simultaneously with a short-run "supply" or capacity relationship specifically incorporating the response of flight frequency to variation in passenger volumes. In this supply function the number of flights scheduled on a particular route depends on the passenger volume actually carried as well as on the fixed seating capacity of aircraft in service on the route.[6]

Results of the Model

The results of this analysis suggest that costs and other characteristics of the two competing travel modes do influence the number of passenger trips made by commuter air service. In conjunction with the levels of travel-generating activities in the origin and destination cities, the cost and service characteristics used in the model account for approximately half of the observed variation in passenger volumes among the 135 markets sampled. The estimated effects of several of the individual variables are also illuminating. First, within reasonable limits a given percentage increase in the air fare on a route apparently reduces air travel on it by a roughly equal percentage.[7] Or, conversely, a fare reduction of 10 percent will lead to approximately a 10 percent increase in the number of airline trips.

This result is somewhat surprising since much of the travel in the type of markets sampled is apparently for business purposes, which is usually hypothesized to be relatively insensitive to price variation.[8] A

partial explanation may be that the ready availability of auto transportation as a substitute for air travel on the relatively short routes
raises the sensitivity to air fares. This price elasticity estimate must be
viewed with caution, however, because of the lack of information on
joint fares for commuter flights that connect to jet air service at major
hub airports.[9] Joint fares (discussed more fully in chapter 8) reduce the
actual fare paid by connecting travelers to levels considerably below
the published full fare, which may cause the fare elasticity to be overestimated. Although precise figures are unavailable, slightly more than
half the passengers on the sample routes probably made use of such
joint fares. Nevertheless, it does appear that demand for short-haul air
service may be more responsive to fares charged than much conventional
wisdom about business travel price sensitivity would suggest.

Second, commuter air travel demand appears to be extremely sensitive
to both flying and driving times. In fact travelers appear to respond
almost identically to variation in flying and driving time; that is, a
given increase in flying time on a particular route has the same effect
on air travel as an equal reduction in driving time. Thus travelers'
choices between air and auto travel are sensitive to the time *savings*
offered by the faster mode. As an illustration of this time sensitivity,
the mean city-pair separation in the sample was about 210 miles, requiring one and a half hours to fly or about five hours to drive. A half
hour reduction in driving time, say from the introduction of a more
direct route, would, according to the results obtained here, reduce the
number of airline trips between such a city pair by 17 to 19 percent.
On the other hand, an identical reduction in flying time, say from the
introduction of nonstop service, might increase air travel by as much
as 50 percent. Of course such changes are likely to be accompanied by
significant airfare increases as well as by a reduction in the frequency
of air service (as when frequent indirect flights are replaced by less
frequent nonstop service), and these are likely to have partly offsetting
effects on air travel demand.

After accounting for the effect of carriers' aircraft size and scheduling
decisions, air travel also appears quite sensitive to the frequency of air
service. This result seems reasonable, since average departure frequencies in the markets sampled are fewer than four per weekday, of
which two are typically scheduled for morning or evening travel hours.
As an example, adding a single daily departure on such a route would
increase the predicted number of air trips by 10 to 15 percent. This
increase would include some entirely new trips made because the in-

creased departure frequency reduces the elapsed travel time and schedule disruption entailed in intercity travel. It would also include some trips formerly made by auto that are shifted to air travel because of the improvement in service frequency and total elapsed travel time.

Air travel also appears to be moderately sensitive to average aircraft size, a measure that captures several aspects of service quality. For example, an increase in the size of aircraft used to serve the average market in the sample from 19 to 30 seats (without a corresponding reduction in the frequency of flights) seemingly increases predicted air travel by 10 to 20 passengers (or 18 to 20 percent) per day in the typical market. This response probably captures travelers' reactions to several differences in the characteristics of different aircraft, including the improved seating comfort, presence of more in-flight amenities or services, and increased smoothness of ride offered by progressively larger aircraft.

Higher seating capacity may also be associated with increased air travel simply because larger aircraft make more seats available at specific departure times that are particularly convenient. By increasing the probability that an individual traveler can obtain a seat at a specific, desirable departure time, larger aircraft may raise the fraction of all trips made by air in situations where flights are infrequent but conveniently scheduled. Nearly half of all departures serving the sample routes are scheduled for morning or evening hours, suggesting that the additional capacity at convenient departure times offered by larger aircraft may affect air travel volumes as much as their commonly hypothesized greater public acceptance.

Another result of the analysis is that air travel is slightly more sensitive to the frequency of flights than to aircraft size. Thus a fixed number of seat departures provided by more frequent flights using smaller aircraft may be preferred by travelers to service using larger aircraft departing less frequently. The results obtained here suggest that the former combination may lead to slightly more air travel because of the increased schedule flexibility it offers travelers, despite the fact that it requires them to make sacrifices in comfort or amenity levels and slightly reduces each individual traveler's chance of obtaining a seat at a specific departure time.

The analysis also indicates that the population of the small communities sampled is not a particularly good index of the scale of travel-generating activities taking place there. For example, the model indicates that a community of 40,000 (slightly above the average of those sampled) is likely to generate only about 8 to 15 percent more air trips to the nearest large-hub city than an otherwise comparable town of 20,000 receiving similar air service. Further, there is a wide range of uncertainty around these estimates since the sample of city pairs selected apparently encompasses considerable variation in the amount of air travel to and from communities of similar population.

On the other hand, the results suggest that passenger enplanements at the large-hub airport is a useful index of that city's desirability as both a final travel destination and a transfer point. Furthermore air travel from small communities to large cities appears to be fairly sensitive to this measure of the latter's attractiveness.[10] Thus a community with equivalent air service to two large hubs would exhibit more air travel to the larger because of its greater attractiveness as a destination and the larger number of onward flight connections it offers. The proportional difference in travel volumes destined for the two large hubs is estimated to be about 40 percent of their proportional difference in enplanements; thus, if enplanements were 25 percent greater at the larger hub, it might attract 10 percent more air travel from the community in which the trips originated.

Implications for the Role of Commuter Air Service

The results of this analysis have several important implications for the design and marketing of air service from small communities to large cities. First, the small aircraft typically flown by carriers serving these markets are evidently readily accepted by the traveling public, although travelers would certainly prefer equally frequent service on faster, larger aircraft. But when faced with the more realistic choice between several daily flights using 19- to 30-seat commuter aircraft and one or two daily departures of large propeller-driven or small jet aircraft—often entailing one or more stops en route to the final destination—travelers may actually prefer commuter service. Although larger aircraft do increase the probability of obtaining a seat at a specific departure time, more frequent service allows travelers to reduce the overall elapsed time and schedule disruption entailed in making a trip by air. Furthermore the availability of more frequent service makes earlier or later flights closer substitutes for the preferred departure time, thus partly offsetting the capacity disadvantages of smaller aircraft.

These results also suggest that in many small communities where jet carriers have withdrawn service (typically provided by using small jet aircraft with low seating densities) and have been replaced by commuter carriers, the overall quality of air service may have actually improved. In fact of the 30 nonhub cities affected by trunk and local service carrier terminations in the first year following passage of the Airline Deregulation Act, 20 began receiving more frequent service (generally provided by a commuter carrier) to the nearest medium or large hub within that period. The average frequency of departures from those 20 communities nearly doubled, with most of the increased flights scheduled during morning and evening commuting hours.[11] Although reliable data summarizing passenger travel on these specific routes are not available, passenger volumes in other markets often increased substantially when certificated carriers were replaced by commuter airlines.[12]

The more frequent service usually offered by commuters is important not only where they compete with or replace certificated carriers but also where automobile travel provides the major travel alternative. Again, because the availability of more frequent flights reduces schedule delays, the convenience of frequently scheduled air service can approach that offered by the automobile, while preserving the significant line-haul travel time advantage commuter aircraft can offer over even high-speed, direct highway routes.

Finally, the estimates of the sensitivity of air travel demand to fares in low-density markets suggest that some selective fare reductions could increase passenger volumes sufficiently to raise carriers' revenues. As will be discussed in chapter 8, some commuter carriers are beginning to offer limited fare discounts. The aggregate fare elasticity for all trips appears to be close to minus one, but this estimate is likely to include some types of trips for which demand is even more price sensitive. If carriers can offer selective fare discounts for those trips, while continuing to charge full fares for less price-sensitive travel, passenger volumes may rise enough to increase total fare revenues. Furthermore the types of trips stimulated by fare discounts may cost relatively little to accommodate, since they are likely to take place at times when excess seating capacity is often available even on smaller aircraft. Although these conclusions are somewhat speculative, the experience of the certificated jet carriers does provide a precedent for selective fare discounting.[13] In any case some careful experimentation with restricted fare discounts is likely to clarify the sensitivity of particular types of commuter air travel to fare variation in individual markets. By doing so, it should reveal some pricing strategies that may be effective in raising passenger volumes and fare revenues without requiring corresponding increases in capacity and expenditures.

Jet Service in Heavily Traveled Corridors

Another important segment of the short-haul air transportation market consists of heavily traveled routes connecting the nation's large cities. These routes are served primarily by certificated carriers using 100- to 200-seat jet aircraft.[14] Most of these routes are characterized by frequent departures, at least during morning and evening travel hours often by two or more competing carriers. In 1981 there were nearly 700 nonstop route segments connecting FAA-designated medium- and large-hub airports that were less than 1,000 miles apart. In comparison with those analyzed previously in this chapter, these routes were very heavily traveled, averaging nearly 20,000 passengers per month. They were also served by frequent departures: the average number of daily nonstop and multistop connecting flights on these routes was about 15.[15]

As chapter 7 will illustrate, virtually all of the city-pair markets entered by both new entrant jet carriers and former intrastate carriers expanding into interstate jet service have been these relatively short-distance, heavily traveled routes. Most of these routes already received frequent direct or nonstop jet service from at least one established carrier. Assessing the prospects for these new carriers requires some knowledge of the characteristics of demand for air service in heavily traveled short-haul markets, which are likely to differ from those in the commuter airline markets just examined for several reasons.

First, most of the trips between larger cities originate in and are destined for those cities, in contrast to commuter flights which are most frequently the initial or final link on a multiflight itinerary. Hence trips on route segments connecting large cities are generally themselves the transportation service demanded rather than a means of access to major onward transportation routes. Demand for these trips may thus be more sensitive to variations in fare levels, flying time, and departure frequency than on lower-density, hub-feeding routes, since fares and elapsed times on these high-density routes are inclusive rather than simply one part of more complex fare structures or total elapsed trip times.

Second, the fact that air service is already so frequent in heavily traveled short-haul markets suggests that traffic may be much less sensitive to variations in departure frequencies about their current levels than was the case in markets served by commuter carriers. When flights are infrequent, an additional daily departure can significantly reduce schedule delay and overall trip time, yet when flights are already numerous, additional departures are likely to represent a small improvement for most travelers. Compared to most commuter markets, therefore, fewer new trips seem likely to be induced, and fewer drawn from competing travel modes, when additional flights are offered between cities already receiving frequent service.

In addition the presence of many people traveling for nonbusiness purposes between larger cities suggests that aggregate demand for air travel may be more sensitive to price variation than was observed on the lightly traveled routes served by commuters. Social and recreational travel are commonly hypothesized to be more price elastic than business travel, primarily because alternate schedules, routes, travel modes, and even trip destinations are more easily substitutable for one another.[16] Moreover, because of tax deductions or reimbursement, business travelers may pay at most only a fraction of the air fare for their trips, whereas leisure travelers generally pay the full ticket price. Changes in airline fares may thus evoke a larger variety of responses by leisure travelers than among those traveling for business purposes, which generally entail fixed destinations and less flexible schedules.

Finally, the availability in more heavily traveled corridors of competing public or common carrier modes (bus and rail), in addition to private auto travel, may affect the sensitivity of air travel demand to variables such as travel time and departure frequency. The presence of other public modes broadens the range of combinations of price, travel time, and schedule frequency that are available to travelers, thus increasing the substitutability among them. At the same time driving may also represent a better substitute for air travel between large cities than it does in markets served by commuter airlines. Because the private auto can transport its occupants directly to the final trip destination without requiring them to transfer from the airport to a local distribution mode, the auto can often provide faster or more direct service, particularly for shorter trips between points not conveniently accessible to major airports.

Although the net effect of these differences on the characteristics of demand is difficult to anticipate, air service connecting larger cities has been the subject of considerable previous research. Table 3.1 reports empirical estimates of the sensitivity of demand for air travel between large cities to fare, flying time, and scheduled departure frequency. These estimates, drawn from a variety of research on the determinants of intercity travel demand, are presented in elasticity form, which gives the ratio of the percentage change in the number of air trips made in

Table 3.1 Demand elasticities for air travel in high-density corridors

Type of model and researcher(s)	Elasticity with respect to			Data source
	Price	Time	Departure frequency	
Airline demand functions				
Brown and Watkins	−2.1	−0.7	—	All U.S. short-haul markets
Straszheim	−1.5	−0.9	—	Toronto–N.Y.
Multimode demand models				
Baumol-Quandt	−2.3 to −3.2	−0.2 to −1.1	0.44	16 Calif. city pairs; 3 modes
Quandt-Young	−1.7 to −3.8	−0.4 to −1.0	0.8– .2	32 NE corridor city pairs
SARC	−0.9	−2.1 to −2.2		All NE corridor city pairs
Canadian Transport Comm.	−2.7	−0.6		Toronto–Montreal–Ottawa corridor; 3 modes
Mode choice models				
Stopher				
Business	−1.0	−0.1	0.3	2,085 trips in 22 city pairs
Nonbusiness	−1.9	−0.1	0.1	
Grayson				
NE corridor	−0.5	−0.2	0.1	1,458 NE corridor trips
Most heavily traveled routes	−0.6	−0.2	0.1	1,658 trips in 46 most heavily traveled city-pair routes

response to a given percentage change in fare, travel time, or frequency of departures. For example, a fare elasticity of -1.5 implies that a 10 percent increase in air fare on a particular route will lead to a 15 percent fall in the number of trips made by air. Most of the elasticities reported here generally capture both the diversion of travel from other modes and the generation of new trips not formerly made by any mode, although some measure only the former response.

As table 3.1 illustrates, air travel demand on relatively short routes connecting larger cities appears to be quite responsive to variation in the prevailing fare. The most common fare elasticity estimate appears to be in the neighborhood of -2.0, although the range of -1.0 to -1.5 may be more appropriate for business travel. While a few fare elasticity estimates are below 1.0 in absolute value, meaning that a given percentage change in fares results in a smaller percentage change in the number of air trips, most are considerably larger in magnitude than those previously estimated for commuter air service. This difference suggests that in markets where there is considerable nonbusiness travel, bus and rail services are available and air service is already frequent, price is a more important determinant of the number of trips made by air than in markets served by commuter carriers. Although business travel between large cities is probably less sensitive to fares than air travel in total, there is evidently a large segment of demand over which fare exercises a critical influence. Hence in these markets selective fare discounts offer the potential for significant increases in passengers and carrier revenues, particularly if, through restrictions on their use, they can be targeted at the most fare-sensitive travelers.

The consensus of the estimates reported in table 3.1 is that the demand for air travel is relatively insensitive to variations in flying time, although the range of estimates is quite wide. With only one exception the estimated flying time elasticities are below 1.0 in absolute value, although there appears to be little agreement about any single value within that range. Most of these estimates reflect travelers' response to scheduled flying time—a measure that varies less than total trip time—which would also include ground transport to and from passengers' actual origins and destinations. Even if air travel demand is more sensitive to total journey time than to its airborne component alone, its overall time elasticity is still likely to be fairly small in magnitude in these markets. Further, except by varying the number of stops per flight, air carriers have little direct control over improvement in either flying time or ground access times to and from airports. These are largely the product of technological developments and public investments in transportation facilities such as roads and airports, as well as the management of air and ground traffic congestion.

Table 3.1 also reports the few available estimates of the sensitivity of air travel to variation in the frequency of scheduled departures in major travel corridors. Again, the range of estimates is quite wide, although most of the estimates appear to cluster around the values of 0.1 and 0.4. Only one study reports higher values, but these were estimated from 1960 data, when air service among some larger cities may have been as infrequent as it now is on many of the routes served by commuter carriers.[17] The relative insensitivity of air travel to flight frequency in dense markets may occur because where departures are already closely spaced, an increase in their frequency does not significantly reduce overall trip time or schedule disruption for most travelers. For example, Eriksen estimates that once six daily departures are scheduled in a typical heavily traveled short-haul market, the addition of a seventh reduces passenger schedule delays (defined as the difference between actual and desired departure times) by only about 5 percent.[18]

Implications for Jet Carrier Market Development and Pricing

The available evidence on the characteristics of air travel demand among large cities has important implications for route development and pricing strategy by new entrant jet air carriers, as well as by existing carriers expanding service in short-haul markets. Most important is the critical role of price: virtually all of the estimates of fare elasticities indicate that discounting can be effective in increasing both passenger volume and revenues, at least within certain limits. Thus, if new entrant jet carriers can maintain fares below those previously charged by the established carriers, they may be able to operate profitably by inducing new air travel, even if they are unable to divert many passengers from the established carriers. Carriers that are unable to provide service at comparably low fares may still be able to use the sensitivity of air travel demand to fares in profitable ways, such as by offering discount fares for seats that are normally unoccupied. Although standby fares are probably the simplest way to accomplish this, restrictions on the use and availability of discount fares can also be effective in preventing their use by passengers who would have otherwise paid full fare. This strategy of market segmentation has been attempted by most established carriers in the wake of deregulation.[19]

The available evidence also suggests that new carriers may not necessarily have to offer frequent service in order to attract passengers and operate at profitable load factors. This conclusion contrasts sharply with the traditional theory of air carrier market share determination in the absence of price competition, whereby the share of passengers each competitor carried on a route would depend on the number of departures it offered.[20] In fact, in markets already receiving frequent service, new carriers relying on frequent departures rather than reduced fares to compete with established carriers may have considerable difficulty, unless they can differentiate their services in other ways from those already offered.

Offering service to a more conveniently located or less congested airport in the same metropolitan area may be among the most important product differentiation strategies available to new carriers. Examples of such airports include Newark Airport in the New York City area, Midway Airport in Chicago, Dallas's Love Field, and Houston's Hobby Airport, all of which are now used by new carriers. As noted in chapter 2, this strategy was originated prior to deregulation by intrastate carriers in Texas and California. Using these less congested and sometimes more conveniently located airports in major cities allows new entrants to offer some travelers important ground access time advantages over established airlines. At the same time, operating in the less congested air traffic conditions generally prevailing at these secondary airports can improve aircraft and crew utilization, a potential source of cost advantage. The evidence on fare and travel elasticities reported here suggests that both of these are likely to be effective competitive measures.

Summary

There do appear to be some important differences in the characteristics of demand for air travel between low-density short-haul markets served by commuters and the high-density short- to medium-haul markets served by jet carriers. In commuter markets the critical determinants are frequency of service and convenient scheduling, together with direct service to minimize flying time. On the other hand, price appears to be of only limited importance for determining commuter demand: although price cuts would probably stimulate some additional commuter traffic, the effect is not likely to be large.

On heavily traveled routes, by contrast, service frequency plays a decidedly secondary role to that of fare. In these markets travel appears to be nearly twice as sensitive to fare changes as in commuter markets and considerably less sensitive to frequency changes. In the more heavily traveled markets, of course, flight frequencies are already so high that an added flight makes little difference to the schedule delay experienced by most travelers. Yet the apparent sensitivity of demand to fare suggests that, within limits, fare discounts may increase passenger volumes sufficiently to raise carriers' total revenues.

Thus the differences in air travel demand characteristics between markets served by new entrant jet airlines and commuter carriers call for quite different route development, service scheduling, and fare-setting strategies. While the timing and frequency of departures are probably the most critical variables for commuter carriers, the capability to offer lower fares than established carriers is likely to be an important determinant of the success of new jet carriers competing in heavily traveled short-haul markets. The use of less congested airport facilities may also help the new jet carriers offer lower fares by reducing their operating costs, while at the same time allowing them to provide door-to-door travel time advantages over carriers using less centrally located and often more congested large airports.

Taken together, the results of these analyses clearly suggest that successful marketing strategies for commuter carriers will not necessarily succeed for the new jet carriers. Hence insofar as prior experience conditions or inhibits managerial perceptions about the likely success of particular marketing strategies, commuter air carriers may encounter competitive difficulties if they attempt to compete in markets usually served by jet carriers. Similarly, larger air carriers moving into less heavily traveled markets than they are accustomed to serving may find that their traditional market development strategies do not prove effective.

The longer-run competitive implications of these findings, however, are probably less rigid than this simple interpretation suggests. The determinants of demand in air travel markets could actually vary continuously across the whole spectrum of market densities; unfortunately this question is not fully illuminated by the separate analyses of extremely low- and high-volume markets presented in this chapter. Specifically, opportunities may exist for the commuter and new jet carriers to contest markets between the very different segments they have traditionally served. If the potential for commuter carriers' entry into larger markets combined with that of jet carriers' entry into smaller markets is sufficient to cover most of the range of market densities now lying between them, this could produce a reasonably competitive environment in the industry. Of course, insofar as the established jet carriers are already present in or available to enter these same markets, this conclusion would be strengthened.

In short, the dichotomy observable between the demand characteristics of markets served by commuter carriers, on the one hand, and the new jet entrants, on the other, must be interpreted cautiously in asserting whether these carriers can be expected to provide competitive checks on one another. At a minimum they may still provide such checks in certain other markets, particularly on short-haul medium-density routes traditionally served by the local service carriers prior to deregulation. Moreover this potential will be increased if the cost characteristics of short-haul airline operations vary continuously with regard to such determinants as passenger volume, length of haul, and total travel time elapsed. These cost issues are investigated in the next chapter, and their implications for prospective competition across the range of markets evaluated.

Appendix: Statistical Analysis of the Demand for Short-Haul Air Service on Low-Density Routes

This appendix describes the analysis of the demand for short-haul low-density air service on which conclusions about the development of commuter air service are based. The model focuses on the demand for air service connecting nonhubs to their respective nearest medium or large hub. The volumes of air travel between small communities and nearby hubs are hypothesized to depend on economic and demographic characteristics of both the origin and destination cities, as well as on the cost, elapsed time, schedule delay, and comfort levels entailed in travel by air and any other available modes. The variables used to measure each of these influences on air travel demand were discussed earlier in this chapter. Driving is considered the principal alternative to air travel on these routes since competition with other common carrier modes (bus and rail) is hypothesized to be of limited importance to potential air travelers in such markets.

Model Specification and Estimation Procedure
The basic specification of the demand and supply functions assumes both multiplicative interaction among their explanatory variables and a constant elasticity of response of air travel demand and supply to

each of these independent variables. Thus the mathematical form of the model is

$$\text{TRIPS} = a_0 \, \text{POP}^{a_1} \, \text{ENPL}^{a_2} \, \text{FARE}^{a_3} \, \text{FLYTIME}^{a_4} \, \text{FREQ}^{a_5} \, \text{SEATS}^{a_6}$$

$$\ast \, \text{DRIVCOST}^{a_7} \, \text{DRIVTIME}^{a_8} \, e^{\,a_9 \cdot \text{CERT}}.$$

After a logarithmic transformation the demand function can be readily estimated in the following form:

$$\ln \text{TRIPS} = a_0 + a_1 \ast \ln \text{POP} + a_2 \ast \ln \text{ENPL} + a_3 \ast \ln \text{FARE}$$

$$+ a_4 \ast \ln \text{FLYTIME} + a_5 \ast \ln \text{FREQ} + a_6 \ast \ln \text{SEATS}$$

$$+ a_7 \ast \ln \text{DRIVCOST} + a_8 \ast \ln \text{DRIVTIME} + a_9 \ast \text{CERT}.$$

The variables included in the demand function are defined as follows:

TRIPS is the number of one-way air passenger trips on an individual route connecting a community with a specific large- or medium-hub city during the third quarter of 1980.

POP is the population of the community in which those trips originate.

ENPL is the number of passenger enplanements at airports in the hub city at the route terminus.

FARE is the published air fare for the trip.

FLYTIME is the scheduled flying time.

FREQ is the number of weekly departures from the origin community to the major destination city, including nonstop and direct flights.

SEATS is the average seating capacity per departure.

DRIVCOST is the estimated out-of-pocket cost for travel by auto for the trip.

DRIVTIME is the estimated driving time for the trip.

CERT is a dummy variable equal to 1 if the route is served by a certificated air carrier and equal to 0 otherwise.

e denotes the base of the natural logarithms.

ln denotes the natural logarithm of a variable.

The supply function to be simultaneously estimated is of the form

$$\ln \text{FREQ} = b_0 + b_1 \ast \ln \text{TRIPS}_{ij} + b_2 \ast \ln \text{SEATS},$$

where the variables are as defined before.

Estimation Results

Table 3A.1 reports the results of two-stage least squares estimation of several variants of the basic demand function simultaneously with

Table 3A.1   Two-stage least squares estimates of demand function parameters (standard errors in parentheses)

	I	II	III	IV	V	VI
a_0	−0.2966	−0.2654	−0.4867	−1.782	−1.4408	−0.5166
a_1	0.0508 (0.1664)	0.799 (0.1635)	0.1094 (0.1653)	0.1030 (0.1684)	0.1486 (0.1630)	0.1084 (0.1622)
a_2	0.2785 (0.1278)	0.3769 (0.1264)	0.3567 (0.1275)	0.4509 (0.1241)	0.3705 (0.1226)	0.3581 (1.1212)
a_3	−0.8325 (0.4129)	−0.8764 (0.4216)	−1.0770 (0.4387)	−0.7906 (0.4279)	−1.1655 (0.4407)	−1.0512 (0.4383)
a_4	−1.4077 (0.4334)	−1.7840 (0.4334)	−1.8449 (0.4353)			
a_5	0.5601 (0.1404)	0.5656 (0.1415)	0.5815 (0.1420)	0.5658 (0.1398)	0.5554 (0.1415)	0.5809 (0.1403)
a_6		0.3557 (0.2290)	0.3168 (0.2783)		0.3478 (0.2181)	0.3165 (0.2768)
a_7	−0.0013 (0.0010)	−0.0010 (0.0011)	−0.0003 (0.0010)	0.0004 (0.0014)	−0.0009 (0.0013)	−0.0011 (0.0016)
a_8	1.7332 (0.5598)	1.7862 (0.5453)	1.8608 (0.5411)			
a_9			0.6070 (0.3458)			0.6019 (0.3154)
$a_4 = a_8$				−1.7674 (0.4392)	−1.9083 (0.4250)	−1.8484 (0.4219)
R^2 (adj.)	0.37	0.42	0.42	0.35	0.40	0.43
Standard error of estimate	1.128	1.183	1.182	1.236	1.191	1.176

this supply function, using data for a sample of 140 routes served by commuter air carriers during the third quarter of 1980. In general, the results are quite sensible, although the variables included in the demand function account for less than half of the observed variation in passenger volumes among specific routes. The estimates of the parameters of the demand function are fairly stable among the variations in its specification reported in the table.

Population of the communities in which air travel originates is apparently not an ideal index of their levels of travel-generating activities. Though somewhat unreliable, the best estimate of the effect of population seems to be that the proportional difference in the number of commuter airline trips originating in two identically served communities will be about one-tenth as large as the proportional difference in their populations. In contrast, passenger enplanements at airports in the destination city show a strong association with traffic volumes. The model suggests that if identical commuter air service to each of two equally distant major hubs is available from a community, 35 to 40 percent of the proportional difference in their passenger enplanements will be translated into a proportional difference in passengers traveling to each.

The elasticity of demand for commuter air travel with respect to the published fare is approximately -1; that is, within reasonable limits a given percentage change in the published fare is associated with an equal but opposite percentage change in the number of air passengers on that route. Passenger volumes are also apparently quite sensitive to flying time; for example, the model suggests that a given percentage difference in flying time to two otherwise comparably served major hub cities, such as might result where only one receives nonstop service, will be translated into a percentage difference in passenger volumes on the two routes that is nearly twice as large.

The frequency of scheduled flight departures also appears to exert a pronounced effect on the demand for commuter air service. For all specifications tested the elasticity of demand with respect to frequency is very close to 0.6, meaning that, for example, an increase in the number of scheduled departures on a route from 20 to 23 will be associated with a 15 percent increase in the number of passengers. In elasticity terms the effect of flight frequency appears to be about twice as large as that of average aircraft size: estimates of the elasticity of passenger demand with respect to aircraft size are consistently in the range of 0.3, although the estimate is subject to a considerably wider range of uncertainty than that for the frequency elasticity. One important implication of this finding is that, again within certain limits, a given number of seat departures per week will attract more passengers if provided in the form of more frequent departures using smaller aircraft, than if provided by large aircraft operating less frequently.

These results also suggest that air carriers that are certificated by the CAB attract slightly higher passenger volumes than do noncertificated commuter air carriers that provide identical levels of service between comparable city pairs, even when aircraft size is controlled for. This finding probably reflects a number of factors that distinguish the service provided by certificated carriers, the most important of which may well be that travel on a certificated propeller aircraft often allows a connection to that same carrier's jet aircraft at the hub airport, termed an "online" connection. In contrast, the flight connections afforded by uncertificated commuter carriers almost always require transfer to another airline, or an "interline" connection. Because passengers are usually thought to prefer online to interline connections, this result may simply reflect the wider availability of online connections that can be offered by certificated carriers serving such hub-feeding markets.

Another important factor seems likely to be that federal subsidies offered to certificated carriers that serve such small communities allowed them to provide more attractive service at comparable fares, including more elaborate passenger and baggage-handling facilities, higher on-board passenger service levels, or more attractive arrangements for ticketing and connection to onward flights. Among other possible ex-planations of the apparently greater attractiveness of certificated service are public perception that it is safer than service provided by noncer-tificated commuter carriers (a subject addressed in chapter 5) and greater public recognition of certificated carriers because of their considerably larger aircraft fleets and route networks. In any event it is important not to interpret these results as suggesting that commuter air carriers newly obtaining CAB certificated status, as many have done following deregulation, will necessarily experience passenger volume increases as a direct result.

Finally, the tests of the effect of modal competition from auto travel on the demand for commuter air service show mixed results. Driving time appears to have a pronounced effect on air travel demand. As an illustration, a reduction in driving time to a major hub city from five hours, the sample average, to four and a half hours (the average flying time for routes in the sample is approximately 90 minutes) might reduce the number of air trips by as much as 16 to 18 percent, judging from the results presented in the table. Presumably this reduction would be due to former air travelers switching to driving as a result of the closer time comparison between the competing modes. A particularly inter-esting aspect of the estimation results is that the coefficients for flying and driving time do not differ significantly (computed F-statistics for tests of the restriction that their coefficients are identical never exceed 0.01, regardless of the other variables included), which suggests that the ratio of flying to driving time is one important variable on which travelers base their choices between modes.

In most of the different specifications tested, driving cost has a weak negative association with air travel volumes, rather than the expected positive relationship. None of the results, however, allow one to conclude reliably that there is a significant relationship between air traffic and the measure of driving cost used here. Estimated driving cost in this analysis is a simple linear function of highway distance, which ignores any effects on operating costs of travel on different highway types, varying per mile operating costs of different automobiles, or parking charges. As a result variation in driving costs is only partly captured by distance so that its expected positive association with air traffic may be neutralized by the conventional "gravity" effect of larger city-pair separations, whereby longer distances tend to be associated with lower volumes of travel by all modes.

With this relatively minor exception these results accord reasonably well with a priori hypotheses about the generation of intercity travel as well as individual travelers' choices among modes. However, because well over half of the variation in commuter air travel volumes in the sample remains unexplained by the combinations of variables tested, it is clear that these basic theories and the measures of important variables used omit or improperly represent some important factors affecting air travel. Nevertheless, the results obtained do offer important insights into the determinants of demand for air service from small communities to large hubs, which represents an important segment of the market for short-haul air service.

Chapter 4

The Cost Structure of Short-Haul Air Service
by Clinton V. Oster, Jr., and Andrew McKey

A particular market or market segment is generally deemed to be more contestable, and therefore more subject to competitive pressures, if "surrounded" by potential suppliers who can enter and exit at relatively low costs. To provide effective competition, the potential entrants must also be able to supply the market at a unit cost not too much in excess of that incurred by those already in the market.

This chapter examines the comparative costs of providing short-haul air service with aircraft typical of those operated by new entrant jets and commuters. The focus is on the costs of matching or failing to match the characteristics of aircraft to those of specific markets to be served. First, the basic approach to modeling short-haul aircraft costs is described. Next, the structure and key parameters of the model utilized in these cost comparisons are reviewed, and the selection of aircraft types is discussed. The model is then used to compare the costs for single flights over various distances. Particular attention is paid to determining the conditions under which commuter aircraft offer cost advantages over jet aircraft and the sources of cost advantage a new entrant jet may have over an established jet carrier. Sensitivity of these results to changes in the cost components, such as fuel and labor, are also analyzed. The cost trade-offs between aircraft size and service frequency are then examined in light of the demand analysis reported in the preceding chapter. Finally, the model is applied to a specific comparison: the cost of "hedgehopping" jet flights to link several small communities to a large hub with the cost of direct commuter service between the hub and the same communities.

Modeling Short-Haul Air Service Costs

Short-haul airline markets range from some of the densest in the country to tiny markets enplaning only a few passengers per day. Thus it is hardly surprising that the aircraft used in providing short-haul flights also vary widely, from prop planes seating only 7 to 8 passengers to wide-body Airbus A300s seating upward of 250 passengers. The costs of providing air service with any size aircraft can be divided into three categories: (1) capacity costs, (2) traffic-related costs, and (3) overhead costs. Capacity costs are the costs of owning, flying, and maintaining a carrier's flight equipment. The major expense categories are flight crew (including both cockpit crew and attendants), fuel, maintenance, miscellaneous flying expense and oil, landing fees, and equipment costs (including any expense for depreciation, rentals, leasing, and hull insurance).

Traffic-related costs include costs of ticketing, baggage handling, and terminal, gate, and lounge facilities. Passenger food and beverage expense and aircraft handling are also considered part of this expense. Where aircraft handling is clearly integral to the operation of a flight, it is included as a traffic-related cost. Overhead costs include the expenses of maintaining the organization, such as personnel functions, planning, and general management.

In the initial analyses all routes are assumed to be served by turn-around flights. In other words, the service pattern modeled is a simple system consisting of aircraft flying back and forth between two points rather than an integrated hub and spoke route system. A simple turn-around route network facilitates high daily aircraft utilization and, as will be discussed in chapters 7 and 8, is characteristic of both new entrant jet and commuter operators. A further assumption is that the capital cost of the aircraft is assigned solely to peak-period service; the minimum service in any market is one round trip in the peak morning hours and a second round trip in the peak early evening hours. These assumptions greatly simplify the analysis and do not distort the central conclusions in any significant manner.

Neither traffic-related nor overhead costs (on a unit basis) are assumed to be directly linked to the type or amount of capacity provided. In fact many of the functions included in those categories can be contracted out; for instance, reservations passenger boarding, and aircraft handling. As a result economies of scale—if they exist at all—are expected to be insignificant in these activities. Efficient carriers specializing in stream-lined turnaround service should be able to achieve roughly equivalent levels of noncapacity costs per passenger. Comparisons of short-haul air transportation costs for various types of aircraft should therefore focus on variation in capacity costs.

Aircraft Types

Representative planes were selected from each of the major size categories used in short-haul service. For the commuters the categories used were the under 10-seat twin-engine piston planes, 15- to 19-seat turboprops, 30-seat turboprops, and 40- to 60-seat turboprops. The aircraft selected are typical of the best technology available in the first few years following deregulation in each category. In the smallest category the piston-powered Piper Navajo Chieftain seats 8 or 9 passengers, depending on whether it is operated with a single pilot or with two pilots. In the next group is the Swearingen Metro IIA, which seats up to 19 passengers, is pressurized, and has a higher takeoff weight (and therefore a longer range with full payload) than its predecessor the Metro II. The only aircraft in production immediately following deregulation in the 30-seat category was the Shorts 330, built in Ireland, which seats up to 30, is unpressurized and operates with a single flight attendant. (The actual Shorts model used in the cost analyses was the 330-200, which has a higher takeoff weight and a longer range than the earlier model 330; the older 330s incidentally can also be upgraded to 330-200s). Finally, for the 40- to 60-seat category, the four-engine pressurized de Havilland Dash 7 from Canada with 50 seats, operating with a flight attendant was chosen. Although the Dash 7 has short takeoff and landing (STOL) capability, the ability to use stub end runways was not incorporated in the analysis.

The twin-engine DC-9-30 (seating up to 115 passengers) was selected as the jet aircraft used most frequently by trunk and local service airlines in short-haul markets. Since this aircraft was still produced in the early 1980s and had also been purchased as a "used" aircraft by several new entrants, an analysis of both new and used DC-9-30s is included. Finally, a cost analysis is reported for the latest model of the DC-9 series, the DC-9-80; configured with 155 seats, this Super 80 represented the best narrow-body technology in use in 1982 by new entrant and former intrastate carriers.

All of the aircraft under consideration can be operated with two pilots—a captain and a first officer. FAA regulations require only a single pilot on the Navajo Chieftain, but many Navajo operators use two pilots to increase passenger confidence. Furthermore two pilots are required when providing subsidized essential air service. Consequently both one- and two-pilot operations were evaluated. The FAA also requires flight attendants on aircraft with more than 19 seats. Planes seating 20 to 50 passengers, such as the Shorts 330-200 and the Dash

7, must have a single flight attendant. Larger planes require one flight attendant for every 50 seats or part thereof; as a result the DC-9-30 is operated with three attendants, whereas DC-9-80s have four attendants.

Market Distances and Densities
The market distances examined are 50, 100, 150, 225, 300, and 500 statute miles. As will be seen in chapters 7 and 8, this range of distances encompasses most of the important markets served by entrepreneurial carriers. The market densities considered range from 10 daily one-way passengers, the level of demand required for economical Chieftain service at the minimum service frequency, up to 300 daily one-way passengers, the point where high-frequency jet service becomes economical.

Model Specification and Inputs
Aircraft operating costs consist of four major elements: flight crew, fuel, maintenance, and equipment. Also included are two smaller categories—miscellaneous flying expense and oil, and landing fees. Landing fees and a portion of maintenance costs are fixed per flight, whereas all other costs vary by the length of the segment. Also, not surprisingly, the costs incurred in each of these six categories vary with aircraft type. To analyze operating costs, then, block time and block fuel for each aircraft over each segment distance must first be specified.[1] These data were obtained from the FAA-approved flight manual for each aircraft. (For more detail, the model is described in depth in the appendix to this chapter.)

Using both block fuel and time to determine the values assignable to each category, the formula for segment costs for a given aircraft can be stated as follows:

$$\text{TOTSC} = \text{FUEL} + \text{CREW} + \text{MO} + \text{MAINT} + \text{EQUIP} + \text{LANDF}, \qquad (4.1)$$

where

TOTSC = total segment costs,

FUEL = fuel costs,

CREW = flight crew costs (including pilots and flight attendants),

MO = miscellaneous flying expense and oil costs,

MAINT = maintenance cost,

EQUIP = cost of owning and insuring flight equipment,

LANDF = landing fee.

Each of these elements except landing fee varies with the specific segment. Costs per passenger for a segment, PAXSC, are simply the result of dividing total segment costs by the number of passengers carried, PAX:

$$PAXSC = \frac{TOTSC}{PAX}.$$
(4.2)

Revenue passenger mile (RPM) costs on the segment, RPMSC, can then be calculated by dividing PAXSC by the segment distance, D:

$$RPMSC = \frac{PAXSC}{D}.$$
(4.3)

Available seat mile (ASM) costs, ASMSC, would equal:

$$ASMSC = \frac{TOTSC}{[D \times (\text{number of seats})]}.$$
(4.4)

Total costs for a market, TOTMC, are the product of the frequency of flights in the market, FREQ, and the cost per segment:

$$TOTMC = FREQ \times TOTSC.$$
(4.5)

Frequency is a function of the total passengers in a market, the assumed load factor, and the capacity of the equipment. Market costs per passenger, PAXMC, and per passenger mile, RPMMC, in a market are derived in the same fashion as segment costs.

Cost Inputs
The cost inputs for each cost category were selected to represent the experience of efficient low-cost operators. For example, all employees are assumed to be paid entry-level wages. Moreover cost inputs among aircraft were standardized where possible. The major sources of information were operators and manufacturers. The costs included in the model were tested for reasonableness by comparing them with the actual experience of operators.

Fuel was assumed to cost $1.08 per gallon for both the avgas used by piston planes and the jet fuel used by turboprops and jets. Pilot salaries varied somewhat according to plane type, ranging from $15 per block hour for the Chieftain to $40 per block hour for the jets. Block-hour salaries for first officers range from $10 to $20, while all flight attendants were paid $6 per block hour. In practice, many carriers pay flight personnel a fixed salary or a minimum guarantee per month. Since high utilization is the rule among entrepreneurial carriers, block-hour pay is a reasonable basis for determining flight crew costs. For all personnel, benefits, payroll taxes, and other personnel expenses were set at 30 percent of salaries.

For all aircraft except the Chieftain, maintenance costs were divided into cycle and flight-hour costs. Cycle-related maintenance accounts for the use of landing gear, brakes, auxiliary power unit, and takeoff thrust. Flight-hour maintenance is for normal engine operations and systems used during flights. For the Chieftain maintenance costs were treated as a cost per block hour as there was insufficient data to determine a division between cycle and flight-hour costs.

Equipment cost includes the expense for depreciation of the aircraft (the opportunity cost of the capital value of the asset) and the annual hull insurance premium. Residual values were assumed to be 15 percent for each plane, while useful lives were 7 years for the piston-powered Chieftain, 10 years for the three turboprops, and 12 years for the new jets. The useful life of the used DC-9-30 was assumed to be seven years. Based on the useful life of each plane and an opportunity cost of 5 percent (in real or inflation-free terms), a capital recovery factor was applied to the purchase price less residual value. Annual hull insurance premiums, based on a percent of the hull value which decreased with size of aircraft, were then added to arrive at a total annual equipment cost.

The ground time required before and after each flight to board and deboard passengers is an integral part of the flight. Therefore capital cost is allocated to ground time at the same rate as block time. For each aircraft, ground time is assumed to equal 15 minutes per flight. Maintenance activities are assumed to take place during off-peak hours, such as nights and weekends, when the aircraft would not otherwise be in use.

Implications and Qualifications of the Analysis
Several factors must be kept in mind when interpreting the results of this cost analysis. First, no provision is made for differences in consumer preference between aircraft, whether based on differences in speed or aircraft size. As the previous chapter demonstrated, all else being equal, most passengers prefer to fly in a larger or faster plane, but as also seen earlier, that is not always the choice facing consumers. Second, no provision is made for differences in load factors between various-sized

aircraft. Variation in demand may make it difficult to achieve high load factors with small aircraft without risking turning away some passengers on occasion. Conversely, since smaller aircraft enable capacity to be more closely matched to demand, smaller aircraft may achieve higher load factors in some markets.

Some biases may also have been introduced into the results through the treatment of capital costs. It is assumed that each aircraft can be turned around (boarded and unboarded) in 15 minutes. Since some airlines consistently are able to achieve 10 minute turnarounds (e.g., Southwest Airlines with a B-737-200 fleet), this time limit does not seem totally unreasonable. Since shorter turnarounds could probably be achieved with smaller planes, any bias introduced by using the same turnaround times for all aircraft would be to overestimate the relative costs of using smaller equipment.

Capital costs for new aircraft, especially the Dash 7 and the DC-9s, may be implicitly overstated because of additional benefits derived from using new aircraft. For example, manufacturers may provide extensive maintenance and training support, or more attractive payment terms or interest rates, which lower the total costs of operation for new equipment. Also the low purchase price of the used DC-9-30 relative to the new DC-9-30 may be accompanied by higher operating costs, such as maintenance or fuel consumption, due to differing age of the equipment. Since no provision is made for differences in operating costs between new and used DC-9-30s, the used DC-9-30 costs may be somewhat understated.

Finally, the model does not take into account some features that could operate in favor of particular planes. For example, jet costs may be understated since it is assumed that both jet and prop planes will travel the same distance in each market. In some markets, however, a shorter flight path can often be taken by a prop plane than by a jet since air traffic rules often force jets to take a more circuitous routing. Also some smaller aircraft can utilize their STOL capacity at some airports to land on a stub end runway and thereby lower airborne delays and taxi time relative to the use of normal runways.

Some Comparative Flight Costs

Total costs per flight for the eight aircraft analyzed are presented in figure 4.1 for distances ranging from 50 to 500 miles. Segment costs have a fixed component consisting of the time and fuel consumed in

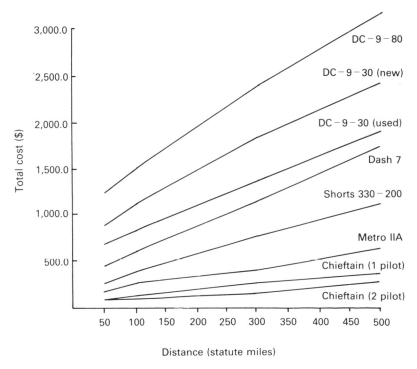

Figure 4.1   Operating cost vs. distance

the noncruise portions of each segment—time at the gate for boarding and deboarding, taxiing, takeoff, and landing. The cruise portion of each segment causes total costs to increase roughly linearly as distance increases.

The slopes of the cost curves in figure 4.1 for both the piston-powered and turboprop-powered commuter aircraft are roughly constant so that over the range considered, the marginal costs of flying these planes an extra mile are roughly the same at any of the distances analyzed. The gains in fuel efficiency and speed at the higher altitudes utilized for longer flights are largely canceled by increased fuel requirements for the longer climb portion, as well as from the weight of additional fuel carried for longer flights.

Not surprisingly, the total cost curves for each aircraft type align with the size of the equipment. The eight- or nine-passenger Chieftain incurs the lowest total cost over each segment, whereas the 155-passenger DC-9-80 has the highest total cost per segment. The total cost of op-

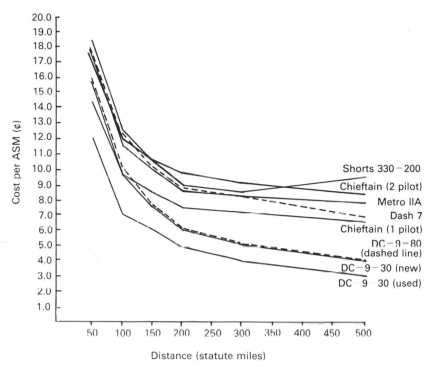

Figure 4.2   Short-haul aircraft operating cost per ASM vs. distance

erating a flight is of less interest to a carrier of course than are the costs of actually transporting each passenger on a flight. The lowest per passenger cost for an aircraft is achieved when all the available seats on a flight are filled, usually defined as the cost per available seat mile (ASM).

Costs per ASM, as seen in figure 4.2, generally fall with increasing distance as the fixed cost portion of each flight is spread over more miles. Improvements are most dramatic at short distances, and begin to flatten as stage lengths increase. Unlike the total segment costs, ASM costs are not clearly ranked by aircraft size. In fact the two-pilot Chieftain, the Metro, the Shorts, and the Dash 7 all display remarkably similar costs per ASM between distances of 50 and 150 miles. Moreover costs per ASM are almost identical for the new DC-9-30 and the DC-9-80 over the entire range of distances, despite the fact the Super 80 is a larger, newer, and more fuel-efficient plane. Exceptions to the close grouping of ASM costs are the single-pilot Chieftain, which is below all other propeller costs at each distance, and the used DC-9-30, the

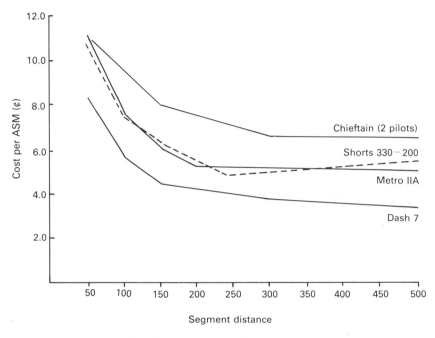

Figure 4.3 Commuter aircraft technical operating costs

costs of which are lower than for the other jets included in the estimates. Jet costs per ASM are clearly lower, as well, than for almost all commuter propeller aircraft.

The lack of any significant cost advantage for larger aircraft (of a similar technology) is at first surprising. Among aircraft of a given power plant—piston, turboprop, or fan-jet—planes are usually expected to show operating economies with increases in size. For example, larger planes should require relatively less fuel per seat for propulsion. Maintenance costs per available seat should also be relatively less expensive for larger planes since the number of engines, avionics systems, and the like, does not increase in proportion to capacity. Moreover the same number of pilots fly a greater number of passengers in the larger planes, so flight crew costs should also exhibit some economies of scale. In fact each of these hypothesized cost economies tends to be true, at least in part, as shown by comparing for large and small aircraft the costs per ASM for fuel, maintenance, and operating costs (assuming equally paid flight crews).[2] These costs are displayed in figure 4.3 for commuter aircraft and figure 4.4 for jets.[3]

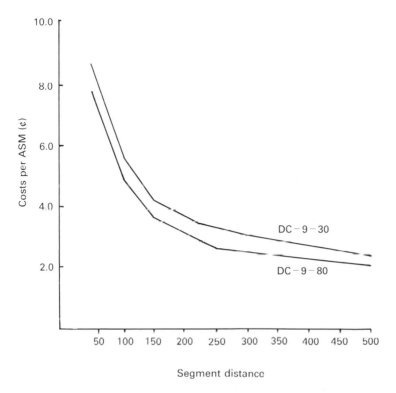

Figure 4.4   Jet aircraft technical operating costs

These "technical" operating economies do not carry over to total costs per ASM mainly because they seem to be largely "captured" by aircraft manufacturers in higher equipment prices and, to some extent, by pilots in the form of higher salaries.[4] The net result is that the equipment choices available to a carrier have very similar total ASM costs, regardless of the aircraft type selected. Whether this situation persists, or whether competition among manufacturers and flight crews eventually alters the situation, remains to be seen.

Another factor influencing aircraft operating costs is the limitation of range some aircraft encounter with a full payload. In this analysis range limitations constrained only the Metro IIA and the Shorts 330-200. Indeed, the Short's limited payload at 500 miles actually results in an increase in ASM costs at longer stage lengths.

The Potential Impact of Changing Fuel Costs
The airline industry has been shocked by rapidly escalating fuel prices twice in the past decade.[5] A third price change, say a doubling from

$1.08 to $2.16 per gallon or a halving from $1.08 to $.54, is not inconceivable. The impact on costs of any such doubling or halving fuel prices depends on two factors—the fuel efficiency of the aircraft and the percent of total costs attributed to fuel.

The impact of doubling the fuel price from $1.08 to $2.16 is illustrated in table 4.1 for three segments—50, 150, and 300 miles. The most severely impacted planes are the jets, particularly the used DC-9-30, due to the high percentage of total costs represented by fuel. Although the jets are still less expensive than the commuter aircraft (except for one-pilot Chieftains), a doubling of fuel prices would remove much of their cost advantage; conversely a halving of fuel prices would intensify the jet's advantage. To illustrate, if fuel rose to $2.16 per gallon, any jet cost advantage per ASM disappears almost entirely for 50-mile stage lengths. The commuter aircraft are all fairly evenly affected because of similarities in fuel efficiency and fuel cost as a percent of total cost.

The Impact of Crew Cost Changes
The flight crew costs used in the model represent entry level, nonunion wages with no added costs due to restrictive work rules or poor crew utilization. These costs were selected to represent the lowest crew costs a carrier could hope to achieve. As such, they are substantially below the average experience of established carriers. For example, the model used $101.40 as crew cost per block hour for a DC-9-30. Actually, the median flight crew cost experienced by an established carrier in 1980 for this aircraft was typically over $300.00 per block hour.

One major explanation of why actual crew costs are usually higher than a hypothetical minimum is seniority in the work force, since some airlines, like other enterprises, pay higher wages to more experienced workers. Higher wages may also result from unionization, depending on the nonunion wage level, and the emphasis of the union on wages in contract negotiations. A second factor is the relationship between work rules for the flight crews and crew scheduling. To the extent that flight crews are paid for nonflying hours, the crew costs per block hour may be higher than the simple wage rate would imply.

A question that naturally rises in examining new entrant jet carriers is how much lower crew costs help lower their total cost per segment. Table 4.2 examines the impacts of higher crew costs for jet segments of 300 and 500 miles. The table contains the percent increase in segment costs due to raising crew costs from the base model values to the median experiences of the established carriers. As can be seen, the increases

Table 4.1 Impacts of fuel price doubling

	$1.08 fuel price		$2.16 fuel price		Percent change in total cost per ASM
	Fuel cost as percent of total cost	Total cost per ASM (cents)	Fuel cost as percent of total cost	Total cost per ASM (cents)	
50-mile segment					
Chieftain (1 pilot)	22	13.9	36	17.7	28
Chieftain (2 pilot)	20	17.4	33	21.7	25
Metro IIA	25	17.7	40	22.6	23
Shorts 330-200	23	18.3	37	22.7	24
Dash 7	21	18.0	35	22.0	22
DC-9-30 (new)	39	15.4	56	21.6	40
DC-9-30 (used)	51	11.7	68	17.9	53
DC-9-80	31	15.8	47	20.8	31
150-mile segment					
Chieftain (1 pilot)	27	8.4	42	11.1	33
Chieftain (2 pilot)	24	10.5	39	13.6	29
Metro IIA	31	9.8	47	12.4	27
Shorts 330-200	28	10.2	44	13.3	31
Dash 7	27	10.0	42	12.9	29
DC-9-30 (new)	43	7.4	60	10.7	45
DC-9-30 (used)	55	5.7	71	9.1	60
DC-9-80	36	7.4	53	10.3	39
300-mile segment					
Chieftain (1 pilot)	29	6.9	45	9.4	36
Chieftain (2 pilot)	26	8.7	41	11.4	33
Metro IIA	31	7.9	47	10.6	34
Shorts 330-200	31	8.3	48	11.2	35
Dash 7	29	7.8	44	10.3	32
DC-9-30 (new)	44	5.1	62	7.5	48
DC-9-30 (used)	57	4.0	72	6.4	60
DC-9-80	38	5.1	55	7.2	41

Table 4.2   Impacts of changing crew costs on total jet costs

Aircraft	Percent increase in segment cost	
	300 miles	500 miles
Used DC-9-30	+13.5	+14.6
New DC-9-30	+10.5	+11.4
DC-9-80	+ 8.8	+ 9.6

Note: The crew costs were changed from the minimum costs used in the model to median costs of established carriers for the same aircraft.

are significant, ranging from an 8.8 percent increase for the DC-9-80 at 300 miles to a 14.6 percent increase for the used DC-9-30 at 500 miles. Nevertheless, as will be seen in chapter 7, the fare discounts offered by some of the new entrant jet carriers are greater than these differences, suggesting that low crew costs alone do not explain the new entrants' cost advantage.

Commuter pilot salaries have been low historically, so the base model crew costs may not understate typical commuter practice by as much as for jets. Commuters have often been viewed by pilots as a training ground for the major airlines. Many pilots have therefore moved from commuters to the majors with the result that seniority levels typically remained low for most commuter operators. Moreover few commuters are unionized, so there have been minimal union impacts on wages or work rules.

Increasingly, however, pilots have come to regard flying for commuter carriers as a career rather than as simply a stepping-stone to the majors. Thus for some commuters the average seniority of their crews may increase. Moreover, as some commuters continue to grow, they may present more attractive targets for unionization. For whatever reason, commuter crew costs may well increase relative to the other components of flying costs.

Table 4.3 presents an analysis of the percent increase in commuters' total costs for 150- and 300-mile segments that would result from a 200 percent increase in flight crew cost—approximately the same proportional increase as for the jets in table 4.2. The increases are substantial, ranging from 16.1 percent for the Dash 7 at 150 miles to almost 60 percent for the two-pilot Chieftain at either distance. Even the one-pilot Chieftain incurs increases of about one-third.

Other Sources of Cost Advantage
Differences in crew costs are obviously only part of the cost advantage the entrepreneurial carriers have over their more established compet-

Table 4.3   Impacts of changing crew costs on total commuter costs

Aircraft	Percent increase in segment cost	
	150 miles	300 miles
Chieftain (1 pilot)	+33.3	+32.3
Chieftain (2 pilot)	+49.9	+48.3
Metro IIA	+22.1	+25.2
Shorts 330-200	+21.4	+22.6
Dash 7	+16.1	+17.5

Note: Crew costs per block hour were increased by 200 percent.

itors. A CAB study has provided additional insight into the sources of entrepreneurial jet carriers' cost advantage by comparing Southwest Airlines' fully allocated cost of serving a 200-mile market using a B-737-200 aircraft with the costs of Piedmont and United using the same type of aircraft.[6] Table 4.4 reports results from this study. As the table demonstrates, Southwest's lower costs and different operating procedures resulted in a cost advantage per passenger of $23 over Piedmont and $34 over United.

Table 4.5 shows a breakdown of Southwest's cost advantage per passenger into its several components. Differences in crew costs, though significant, are not the major source of the cost advantage but account for only 13 percent of the advantage over Piedmont and 21 percent of the advantage over United. Rather, differences in flight-specific costs and passenger-specific costs account for most of the advantage. The differences in flight-specific costs, which include depreciation of the aircraft, fuel cost, landing fees, and aircraft servicing, stem largely from differences in daily aircraft utilization. Southwest concentrated on point-to-point turnaround service utilizing secondary airports to a much greater degree than Piedmont or United and as a result operated their aircraft an average of 9.5 hours per day compared with 7.3 hours for Piedmont and 5.2 hours for United. The differences in passenger-specific costs reflect Southwest's streamlined approach to reservations and sales, savings in baggage handling due to not interlining, and limited pre-flight and in-flight services to passengers.

Some of Southwest's operating procedures that contributed to lower cost could be emulated by the established carriers. Tables 4.4 and 4.5 also contain the results of a cost analysis that assumed Piedmont and United achieved the same crew complements, seating densities, load factors, landing fees, and aircraft utilization as Southwest. As these

Table 4.4 Comparison of airline costs for serving 200-mile markets

Cost category	Southwest	Actual Piedmont	United	Adjusted[a] Piedmont	United
Flight crew	$ 130	$ 251	$ 460	$ 251	$ 307
Aircraft, fuel, landing fees, and aircraft servicing	1,125	1,469	1,683	1,374	1,359
Cabin crew	70	86	149	72	124
Passenger specific costs	349	927	989	1,122	1,171
Overhead (excluding aircraft)	136	134	332	144	338
Fully allocated costs	1,900	2,867	3,613	2,963	3,298
Fully allocated costs per passenger	24	47	58	37	42
Seats per aircraft	118	110	103	118	118
Load factor	.67	.56	.60	.67	.67

Source: CAB, "Domestic Fare Structure Costing Program, Version 6, update." Data are for 12 months ending June 30, 1981, as reported in David R. Graham and Daniel P. Kaplan, "Competition and the Airlines: An Evaluation of Deregulation," Staff Report, Office of Economic Analysis, U.S. Civil Aeronautics Board, December 1982, table 4.1.

a. Adjusted costs assume crew complements, landing fees, load factors, and seating densities, and aircraft utilization are the same for United and Piedmont as are observed for Southwest.

adjusted cost figures show, although some of Southwest's advantage might be eroded by these operational changes, a substantial cost advantage would remain. Indeed, as can be seen in table 4.5, Southwest would still have an advantage of over $13 compared to Piedmont and over $17 compared to United with most (but not all) of the advantage coming from differences in passenger-specific costs.

Comparisons based on fully allocated costs, such as these, are instructive but must be interpreted with care. Whereas a new entrant carrier is likely to base its fares on fully allocated costs, an established carrier is far more likely to base a competitive response on its marginal cost. A perhaps more relevant comparison therefore may be the fully allocated cost of a new entrant with the marginal cost of an established carrier.

Table 4.5 Sources of Southwest Airlines' cost advantage

| | Cost difference per passenger | | | |
| | Actual | | Adjusted[a] | |
Cost category	Piedmont	United	Piedmont	United
Flight crew	$ 2.43	$ 5.80	$ 1.53	$ 2.24
Cabin crew	.51	1.52	.02	.68
Aircraft, fuel, landing fees, aircraft servicing	8.48	11.86	2.01	1.82
Passenger specific costs	10.64	11.59	9.78	10.40
Overhead	.45	3.65	.10	2.56
Total	$22.51	$34.42	$13.44	$17.70

Source: Derived from table 4.4.
a. Adjusted costs assume crew complements, landing fees, load factors, and seating densities, and aircraft utilization are the same for United and Piedmont as are observed for Southwest.

Unfortunately a meaningful measure of the established carrier's marginal cost is not available. In addition to severe data limitations there is a fundamental problem in deriving such a measure since in the airline industry marginal cost is an extremely complex concept. For example, if an established carrier has empty seats on a flight, then the marginal cost of accommodating a few additional passengers is quite low, little more than the few dollars it costs for ticketing and food service. Indeed, it was precisely the very low marginal cost to fill empty seats that attracted the established carriers to institute capacity-controlled discount fares in the late 1970s.

If, however, the load factors on a particular flight are relatively high, then the marginal cost of serving additional passengers would be much higher if another flight must be added. Even here, the marginal cost is not easily estimated since it depends on, among other factors, whether the carrier has an unused aircraft available at that time, how an additional flight affects crew and maintenance rotations and aircraft positioning, and whether adequate gate and terminal space is available. As can be seen easily upon reflection, the marginal cost can vary substantially from carrier to carrier, route to route, and flight to flight. Indeed, recognizing the true marginal cost of serving additional passengers in a market or of entering a new market is a critical element in successful airline management.

When carefully estimated, a new entrant may thus not have quite as large an advantage, at least in the short run, as the figures in tables

4.4 and 4.5 might imply. Still the magnitude of the advantage is enough that carriers such as Southwest can likely compete effectively with established carriers pricing on a marginal cost basis in many markets. And though Southwest is a model of low-cost operations, its performance is not unique. Indeed, People Express has achieved slightly lower costs, while operating, however, over slightly longer stage lengths.

Matching Aircraft to Markets

How can a short-haul operator choose among the various available aircraft for a market, given the similarity of potential costs per ASM? Moreover why are jets like the DC-9-30 not used in all markets, since their costs per ASM are much lower than commuter aircraft? The answer to both of these questions appears to be that the most suitable aircraft for a particular market depends on the size of a market, measured by the number of passengers, as well as on the ability to fill each flight for a given plane.

Operators generally attempt to minimize per passenger costs in each market while meeting the market's demand. The relevant consideration for a given market therefore is the lowest total cost sufficient to serve the demand in that market, rather than the aircraft exhibiting the lowest ASM costs for a particular segment. This can be modeled by specifying a minimum service level of two (round-trip) flights per day and assuming that though aircraft can operate with 100 percent load factors, all demand in a market must be accommodated, even if an additional flight must be added for a single passenger. An operator possessing perfect knowledge of the demand in a market would obviously not incur the expense of an extra flight for the revenue from a single passenger, except perhaps in special cases, such as the Eastern Shuttle. In short-haul markets, however, providing sufficient capacity to satisfy all demand is an important consideration, given the potential competition from auto travel. If passengers are turned away with any regularity, they may stop considering air transportation as a viable alternative. Unaccommodated demand thus acts as a signal to the operator to increase capacity in the market.

Selection of the least costly aircraft for a market rests on comparing the minimum-cost thresholds of each potential aircraft with the expected market characteristics. The minimum-cost thresholds for the eight aircraft in a 100-mile market are displayed in figure 4.5. To illustrate the concept of minimum threshold, consider the curve for the Shorts 330-

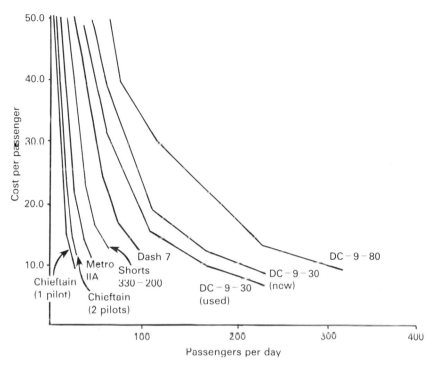

Figure 4.5 Minimum passenger cost thresholds (100-mile market, 2 flights per day)

200. The minimum cost per passenger is realized when all seats are filled. For two flights per day in this 30-passenger aircraft, filling all seats requires 60 passengers per day and results in a minimum cost of $12.33 per passenger. If, however, the market enplanes only 50 passengers per day, the same segment costs are spread over fewer passengers and the cost per passenger increases to $14.80. Similarly, if the market enplanes 38 passengers per day, the cost goes to $19.47. By contrast, at this 38 passenger per day enplanement level, a Metro IIA would be fully utilized and achieve its minimum cost of $11.48 per passenger.

As market densities increase beyond the point where minimum costs per passenger have been achieved with full loads on the initial two flights, additional flights must be considered. Adding flights to accommodate demand beyond the threshold load may result in increased total costs per passenger. As more passengers are added, costs again decline to the point where all seats on all flights are occupied and another flight has to be added. This results in a sawtooth patterned

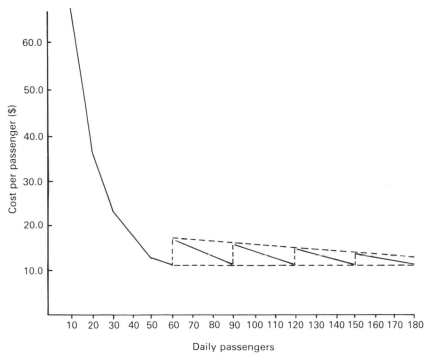

Figure 4.6   "Sawtooth effect": Shorts 330-200 cost per passenger (100-mile segment distance)

cost curve, as shown illustratively for the Shorts at a 100-mile segment in figure 4.6.

The threshold of daily passengers for which jet service is less expensive than commuter propeller service can be approximated by dividing the total cost of two daily jet flights by the minimum cost per passenger of the least expensive commuter for a particular segment. The level of traffic for this jet threshold and the change in that level with changing market distance are presented in figure 4.7.

The used version of the DC-9-30 has the lowest potential threshold, due to its lower ASM costs. Even for the used DC-9-30, however, markets enplaning fewer than 100 passengers per day are served more efficiently by commuter aircraft at all distances below 500 miles. The difference between the new DC-9-30 and the DC-9-80 is due to the larger capacity of the Super 80. As segment distance increases, the threshold for all three jets drops because of the greater ASM cost advantage for jets at longer distances.

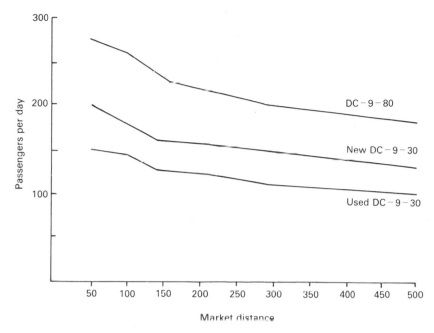

Figure 4.7 Threshold of lower jet costs by passengers per day

The threshold of passengers per day for which jet RPM costs are lower than commuter RPM costs is sensitive to assumptions about fuel price and flight crew expense. The overall impact of fuel price increases on the relative costs for each aircraft was discussed earlier. That analysis showed jet costs would increase faster than commuter costs in the event of a doubling of fuel prices, from $1.08 to $2.16 per gallon. Similarly, a doubling of fuel prices would result in a substantial increase in the passengers per day threshold. To illustrate, three segments are evaluated in table 4.6. The threshold for the used DC-9-30 would increase over 20 percent with higher fuel costs. The increase is less for the other two jets, although their thresholds were higher initially.

The impact of higher flight crew costs for jets—due to unionization and seniority—was also discussed earlier. The effect of these cost changes on the passenger threshold, holding commuter crew costs unchanged, is shown in table 4.7. In each case the threshold is at least 10 percent higher as a result of the higher flight crew costs.

Table 4.6 Impact of fuel cost increases on jet cost advantage

	Passengers per day		
	50-mile segment	150-mile segment	300-mile segment
DC-9-30 (used)			
Threshold before	156	136	118
Threshold after	190	170	142
Percent change	22%	25%	20%
DC-9-30 (new)			
Threshold before	205	175	151
Threshold after	229	199	168
Percent change	12%	14%	11%
DC-9 Super 80			
Threshold before	282	236	202
Threshold after	295	258	215
Percent change	5%	9%	6%

Note: The threshold is the minimum number of daily passengers for which jet service is less expensive than commuter service. Fuel costs are increased from $1.08 per gallon to $2.16 per gallon.

Table 4.7 Impact of increase in jet flight crew costs on jet cost advantage

	Passengers per day		
	100-mile segment	150-mile segment	500-mile segment
DC-9-30 (used)			
Threshold before	147	191	263
Threshold after	169	213	290
Percent change	15%	12%	10%
DC-9-30 (new)			
Threshold before	130	167	226
Threshold after	152	189	252
Percent change	17%	13%	12%
DC-9 Super 80			
Threshold before	108	137	183
Threshold after	127	157	205
Percent change	18%	15%	12%

Note: The threshold is the minimum number of daily passengers for which jet service is less expensive than commuter service. The crew costs were changed from the minimum costs used in the model to median costs of established carriers for the same aircraft.

Table 4.8 Klamath Falls–Redding–Chico–San Francisco routing

Origin	Destination	Actual miles	Equivalent segment
Hughes Air West jet routing			
Klamath Falls	Redding	118	100
Redding	Chico	54	50
Chico	San Francisco	145	150
Total route distance		317	300
Direct commuter service			
Klamath Falls	San Francisco	307	300
Redding	San Francisco	190	225
Chico	San Francisco	145	150
Total route distance		642	675

Hedgehop Analysis

A common routing for subsidized jet air service provided by local service carriers prior to deregulation was to connect a series of small communities to a hub airport along a linear routing. This type of flight is known as a "hedgehop" or "puddle-jump" flight. The rationale behind stops at several small points was to collect passengers at each point to try to minimize the handicap of the large capacity of jets. As seen in chapter 2, subsidy considerations also favored a hedgehop route.

The replacement of local service jets with commuter props in subsidized small community operations was therefore expected to result in more efficient and more convenient service for those points. That expectation can be tested using the short-haul cost model. As an example, three markets served by Air West were examined. Those markets are Klamath Falls, Oregon, Redding, California, and Chico, California—all flying to San Francisco. Air West's routing for Flight 931 based on the August 1, 1977, *OAG*, was Klamath Falls–Redding–Chico–San Francisco with a DC-9-30. The flight originated in Seattle and then stopped in Portland before continuing to Klamath Falls. The actual distances for Air West's routing, along with distances for direct commuter flights, are listed in table 4.8. Equivalent segments for use in the model are also listed. An element of conservatism is included in the test since the model understates the actual Air West routing distance while overstating the total commuter distance.

Each of the points was assumed to generate 70 passengers per day to San Francisco, or 35 per flight. The DC-9-30 load factor for the final segment is 91 percent, assuming seats were allocated equally between the three markets. It is also assumed that all three markets would be served by a single type of commuter aircraft. Table 4.9 compares the service provided by the various aircraft alternatives. In contrast to the two daily multistop flights of the DC-9-30, commuter service could offer 10 daily frequencies with two-pilot Chieftains, 5 flights with Metro IIA's, or 3 Shorts 330-200 flights, all nonstop. The Dash 7 would only allow two nonstop flights to be scheduled from each point, although Dash 7 service would also result in the lowest load factors in the market. Both Metro and Shorts service would also result in significantly lower load factors than jet service. But under conditions of variable daily demand, lower load factors also mean a smaller chance of having to turn away passengers seeking last minute reservations. In more than half the examples, moreover, the block time of direct commuter flights is less than the total trip time with the DC-9-30 routing. Although the jet can obviously operate at faster speeds, the multiple short hops and ground time requirements for each stop result in longer trip times at the two farthest points.

Total costs for the three markets are compared in table 4.10. Metro service with five flights per day is the least expensive alternative. The Metro total costs of $4,990 are less than both the used version DC-9-30, at about $5,020, and the new version DC-9-30, at $6,530. Total costs with each of the other three commuter aircraft are also less than service with a new jet. The Metro costs are also less on a per seat basis and, along with the other three commuter alternatives, are below both the new and used DC-9-30 seat costs. Moreover, although not included in this example, the higher commuter frequencies would probably stimulate additional traffic, thereby providing air service to more people.

In sum, comparing multistop jet service with direct commuter service shows that commuter aircraft can provide replacement service more efficiently and more conveniently for small communities. For this example, service with a Metro IIA is the lowest cost alternative and provides two and a half times as many flights as jet service, with lower load factors and faster trip times in two of the three markets.

Summary

Two principal conclusions emerge from the cost model developed in this chapter. The first is that lower flight crew costs of the new entrant jet carriers reduce segment costs by only about 10 to 15 percent. While

Table 4.9 Hedgehop analysis: market service by alternative aircraft

Market	Daily passengers	Daily frequency	Available seats	Load factor (percent)	Trip time (minutes)
DC-9-30					
Klamath Falls–San Francisco	70	2	76.7	91%	131
Redding–San Francisco	70	2	76.7	91	82
Chico–San Francisco	70	2	76.7	91	41
Chieftain					
Klamath–San Francisco	70	10	80	88	99
Redding–San Francisco	70	10	80	88	80
Chico–San Francisco	70	10	80	88	59
Metro IIA					
Klamath Falls–San Francisco	70	5	85	82	80
Redding–San Francisco	70	5	90	78	61
Chico–San Francisco	70	5	90	78	46
Shorts 330-200					
Klamath Falls–San Francisco	70	3	87	80	105
Redding–San Francisco	70	3	90	78	85
Chcio–San Francisco	70	3	90	78	62
Dash 7					
Klamath Falls–San Francisco	70	2	100	70	86
Redding–San Francisco	70	2	100	70	68
Chico–San Francisco	70	2	100	70	51

Table 4.10 Market cost by alternative aircraft

Segment	Jet routing Mileage	New DC-9-30	Used DC-9-30
Klamath Falls–Redding	100	$1,096	$ 842
Redding–Chico	50	888	675
Chico–San Francisco	150	1,281	991
Route total		3,265	2,509
× frequency		× 2	× 2
Market total		6,530	5,018
Cost per available seat		28.40	21.82

Segment	Commuter routing Mileage	Chieftain (2 pilot)	Metro IIA	Shorts 330-200	Dash 7
Klamath Falls–San Francisco	300	$ 209	$ 403	$ 724	$1,177
Redding–San Francisco	225	169	331	602	963
Chico–San Francisco	150	126	264	459	752
Route total		503	998	1,785	2,893
× frequency		× 10	× 5	× 3	× 2
Market total		5,034	4,991	5,354	5,785
Cost per available seat		20.97	18.83	20.05	19.28

these cost savings are not trivial, they by no means account for all of the cost advantage of the new entrant carriers. Indeed, according to a CAB study, flight crew cost savings account for less than one-fifth of entrepreneurial jet carriers' total cost advantage. Rather, most of the entrepreneurial jet carriers' advantage seems to come from higher aircraft utilization and streamlined ground operations.

The second principal conclusion is that among the 19-, 30-, and 50-seat turboprop commuter aircraft, the costs per ASM are virtually identical between 50 and 150 miles, and they are within 10 percent of one another up to 300 miles. The cost per ASM for the eight- to nine-seat piston-powered aircraft are similar to the turboprops, being somewhat higher if two pilots are used and somewhat lower if flown with a single pilot. Any scale economies one might expect from the larger aircraft seem to have been captured either by the aircraft manufacturer in the form of higher prices or by the pilots in higher salaries. In addition to the similarity of costs per ASM of the turboprops, the costs per ASM of the jets appear lower than the turboprops, with the used DC-9-30 the lowest and with the new DC-9-30 and DC-9-80 somewhat higher and virtually the same. Finally, and most important, there are only limited indications that unit costs, particularly costs per revenue passenger mile, decline with market density if plane type and schedules are reasonably well chosen.

Several implications flow from these cost relationships. First, since no aircraft has a uniform cost advantage, the key for commuter management is matching the aircraft to the market density and, to a lesser extent, the stage length. An obvious objective is providing enough capacity to meet the demand while keeping load factors high. As demonstrated in chapter 3, however, the demand is not independent of the service provided. In particular, demand responds positively both to frequency and aircraft size. For small changes around the mean of the sample used in chapter 3, the effect of frequency outweighs that of aircraft size, although it would be a mistake simply to maximize frequency at the expense of using larger, more comfortable aircraft. Beyond some point added frequency evokes less and less additional traffic, and a carrier would do better adding capacity in the form of larger aircraft. Balancing frequency and total capacity is thus an important element of successful commuter management.

The principle of matching the aircraft to the market also extends to the choice between jets and turboprops. Jets, with the lowest costs per ASM, have the lowest cost per passenger only if the larger number of seats can be filled. As the analysis of jet thresholds demonstrated, there are a broad range of density and distance combinations where the commuter aircraft are more efficient. As will be seen in more detail in chapter 10, most of the markets served by jet carriers under Section 406 subsidy were in the range where commuters with prop planes are much more cost effective. Thus it should come as no surprise that (and as chapter 10 will demonstrate) switching small community service from the jet-based Section 406 program to the commuter-based Section 419 program has resulted in substantial savings in subsidy cost to the government.

More important, the cost model provides insight into why the "small community problem"—one of the more hotly debated issues before deregulation—has proved to be not much of a problem. The concern was that jet carriers would withdraw from unprofitable low-density short-haul routes, leaving small communities with inadequate or no air service. As the model reveals, and as experience has demonstrated (see chapters 8 and 10), low-density routes that were unprofitable for jets are often profitable for commuters operating smaller aircraft at higher frequency. Moreover, because capital is quite mobile for commuters as well as for jet carriers, and because the commuter industry was accustomed to rapid growth, commuters were able to fill in quickly for terminating jet carriers with aircraft better tailored to the markets. As the hedgehop analysis demonstrated, commuter replacement could often result in profitable service with lower costs, higher frequencies, lower load factors (meaning greater last minute availability of seats), and comparable travel times.

Finally, these cost analyses make it very evident that short-haul air transport is a remarkably flexible, multioptioned activity. Although a particular aircraft will usually achieve the lowest costs for a specific service, other combinations of aircraft size and schedule frequency may have only slightly different cost characteristics. Furthermore changes in aircraft size and flight frequency combinations, which entail slightly higher costs, often may have a value that makes their use worthwhile. Perhaps the most obvious example is using a slightly larger plane than is optimal (at least initially) and thereby stimulating more traffic by avoiding overbookings and last minute unavailability of seats. The potentially effective combinations of service characteristics and costs are in fact almost endless. In a deregulated world of entrepreneurial experimentation many of these combinations will be explored, to the potential benefit of consumers and producers alike. Furthermore experimentation and exploration seem to be possible without incurring substantial cost penalties. As a consequence any laxity in providing service to these short-haul markets should be quickly contested and displaced.

Appendix: Description of the Short-Haul Air Cost Model

The short-haul cost model was designed to facilitate comparison of the capacity costs of operating several aircraft over a range of segment distances. This appendix describes the design of the model, and the performance and cost inputs. First, the calculation and sources of block time and block fuel performance are reviewed. Then, for each of the cost categories comprising total segment costs, the calculation and sources of each category are discussed.

The time and fuel required for an aircraft to fly a particular distance are determined by the performance characteristics of the aircraft. Additional factors influencing time and fuel are the speed and altitude selected by the aircraft operator. Moreover environmental factors such as temperature and winds also affect the time required and the fuel consumed.

Comparing performance between aircraft requires that conditions and variables be standardized insofar as possible to enable unbiased comparisons between aircraft. The time and fuel inputs calculated for this model rely on the experience of operators in selecting speed and altitude options. Moreover, in selecting specific speeds and altitudes within the range of those reported by carriers for representative operations, the criterion was to minimize total cost for each flight.

Environmental considerations can have a major impact on the performance characteristics of different aircraft. For example, hot temperatures and high runway altitudes require greater power or longer runways for takeoffs. Environmental factors were standardized, assuming the following for each segment distance:

1. No winds are present.
2. Temperatures are standard (ISA).
3. All runways are at sea level.
4. Runway lengths are sufficient to pose no constraint to any of the aircraft.
5. There are no geographic features requiring minimum enroute altitude.
6. No special air maneuvers are required.

7. All routings are straight-line between airports; the same routings are used for each aircraft type.

8. There are no air traffic control delays for either takeoff or landing.

Performance manuals prepared according to FAA specification by the manufacturer of each plane were the source of most of the data needed to calculate time and fuel performance. Telephone contacts with the manufacturers provided the additional information required.

The time and fuel performance inputs to the model are for block-to-block operations. Block-to-block operations encompass everything between the time the aircraft leaves the departure gate until it stops at the arrival gate. Therefore block time and block fuel include taxiing out from the gate, takeoff, climb, cruise, descent, landing, and taxiing into the gate. In general, the time and fuel for taxiing, takeoff, and landing of each flight are constant for a particular plane. The major portions of a flight—climb, cruise, and descent—can vary in terms of time and fuel depending on distance, altitude, payload, and speed.

Maximum takeoff weights prevented two of the aircraft—the Metro IIA and the Shorts 330-200—from carrying a full payload over the longer distance segments. Performance manuals were the source for both maximum takeoff weights and operating empty weights. Operating empty weight is the total weight of the aircraft, crew, and all systems and supplies, except fuel, required for passenger operations. Payload capacity is the difference between maximum takeoff weight less both operating empty weight and fuel.

In addition to block fuel, total fuel weight includes reserve fuel for holding and diversion to an alternate airport. FAA regulations govern holding and diversion to alternate requirements. For all the segments and aircraft in this analysis the alternate airport was assumed to be 100 statute miles (87 nautical miles) distant. The flight to the alternate airport is operated using minimum fuel consumption techniques. Holding time is set at 45 minutes for all aircraft and segments. For the piston and turboprop planes, holding altitude is assumed to be the cruise altitude on the main segment. Holding altitude for the jets is assumed to be cruising altitude to the alternate. Fuel weight for the avgas used by the piston-powered Chieftain is 6.0 pounds per gallon, whereas the jet fuel (Jet A) used by the other aircraft has a weight of 6.7 pounds per gallon.

Payload in the model is composed of passengers and baggage. On average, each passenger is assumed to account for 190 pounds, 165 of which is the average passenger weight with the remaining 25 pounds for baggage. This average weight is 10 to 20 pounds less than the average often used in estimating payloads for long-haul or international schedules. The lower weight for short-haul flights is due to the majority of passengers being on short duration trips and consequently requiring less baggage.

Actual practices of operators provided the basis for determining aircraft altitudes over the different segment distances. However, subject to the constraints of the options available in the performance manuals, at least one-third of the distance for each segment was operated in the cruise position. Nonpressurized aircraft were assumed to operate at below 10,000 feet.

Cost Categories

Total segment costs are the sum of six separate cost categories:

$$\text{TOTSC} = \text{FUEL} + \text{CREW} + \text{MO} \quad\quad (4\text{A}.1)$$
$$+ \text{MAINT} + \text{EQUIP} + \text{LANDF},$$

where

TOTSC = total segment costs,

FUEL = fuel costs,

CREW = flight crew costs including pilots and flight attendants,

MO = miscellaneous flying expense and oil costs,

MAINT = maintenance cost,

EQUIP = cost of owning and insuring equipment,

LANDF = landing fee.

All the cost categories vary by aircraft type. Except for landing fees all categories are also at least a partial function of segment distance, as measured by block time and block fuel. The following sections review each of the six categories.

Fuel Costs

Each segment consumes a fixed amount of fuel for taxiing, takeoff, and landing. Moreover each flight requires at least some climbing and descending. The remainder of fuel consumption varies by the distance flown. The fuel cost for a segment (FUEL) is then simply:

$$\text{FUEL} = \text{FUEL}_P \times \text{FUEL}_B, \quad\quad (4\text{A}.2)$$

where

FUEL$_P$ = price of fuel per pound,

FUEL$_B$ = block fuel consumption (pounds).

The fuel price per gallon is assumed to be constant for all carriers at $1.08 per gallon for either avgas or Jet A. The constant price per gallon represents purchase of a large enough scale to secure long-term fuel contracts. The avgas used by piston planes weighs 6.0 pounds per gallon, resulting in a price per pound of $.18. Jet A—used by turboprops and fanjets—with a weight of 6.7 pounds per gallon, results in a $.16 per pound price.

Flight Crew Cost
Flight crew cost includes all the personnel required to fly a plane in passenger service. The formula for the calculation of segment flight crew costs (CREW) is

$$\text{CREW} = \text{T}_B \times (1 + \text{EBR}) \tag{4A.3}$$
$$\times [\text{PILOT}_W + \text{COPILOT}_W + (\text{FA}_N \times \text{FA}_W)],$$

where

T_B = block time,

EBR = employee benefits and taxes ratio,

= 0.3 (constant),

PILOT_W = pilot salary per hour,

COPILOT_W = copilot salary per hour,

FA_N = number of flight attendants required,

FA_W = flight attendant salary per hour.

The cost of flight crews can vary a great deal between carriers. In part, differences reflect factors such as the seniority of crew members and varying policies toward pay and benefits. Also crew costs can be higher if a carrier is forced to provide overnight accommodations for crews at an airport other than their home base, thereby incurring hotel, meal, and transportation costs. Furthermore, scheduling to minimize paid duty time relative to actual flying time can lower costs.

Crew costs for the model have been standardized to the extent possible. First, to factor out seniority effects, all salaries are based on starting salaries. In the case of pilots the starting salary is based on starting as a pilot in that aircraft type, rather than a new hire to the firm. The variation between salaries for different aircraft types is explained by a tendency for salaries to reflect the productivity of the equipment. The productivity basis for salaries is carried over from the certificated jet industry, where pilot unions negotiated higher wages for the newer, larger, and faster aircraft based on the plane's increased productivity.

Except in the case of the Chieftain, the size of the flight crews for each plane is determined by FAA regulations. The Chieftain, with fewer than 10 seats, can be operated with a single pilot. However, many carriers choose to use two pilots in an effort to improve the public's acceptance of flying on a small plane. In fact the CAB usually requires two pilots to be used in providing essential air service to small communities under the Section 419 program. All the larger planes must include both a captain and a first officer. Flight attendants are required for planes with 20 or more passenger seats. Moreover, a second flight attendant is mandated for equipment seating over 50 passengers, and for each additional 50 seats or part thereof. Flight attendant salaries were set at a constant $6.00 per hour for each aircraft type. Although this amount is low for established airlines, it is the amount actually paid by several new entrant jet carriers.

Most airline cost models treat flight attendant expense as an indirect cost. However, since flight attendants are required by the FAA for passenger operations to be conducted, the model includes them with other costs of providing capacity.

Total crew costs are set at 130 percent of crew salaries. By adding employee benefits and taxes, the ratio of employee benefits and taxes (EBR) to salaries of 0.3 is representative of commuter and new entrant jet carriers.

Maintenance Costs

Maintenance costs are the most difficult cost component to estimate. Airlines report direct maintenance costs which vary as much as 200 percent for the same aircraft. According to Douglas Aircraft Corp., "airline factors—not aircraft design characteristics—contribute most to the dispersion of reported costs and the estimating model results."[7]

Among the "airline factors" considered in Douglas' maintenance cost model are operators' in-house labor rate, labor rates for subcontracted maintenance, operators' labor productivity and accounting differential ratio (relative to the average for U.S. trunks), operators' material usage factor ratio, percent of maintenance to be subcontracted by the operator, subcontract material premium, subcontracted administration factor, anticipated aircraft utilization, and estimated aircraft average flight length.[8]

Each of the major jet manufacturers has performed comprehensive studies of maintenance costs for their own and for competitive aircraft. In simple form the two major parameters of maintenance costs have been identified as a cost per cycle (taxiing, takeoff, and landing) and as a cost that is a function of flight time which excludes taxiing. The formula to calculate maintenance cost for the model using the cycle/flight hours division is

$$\text{MAINT} = \text{CYCLE} + (T_B - T_G) \times \text{FLTHR}, \tag{4A.4}$$

where

> CYCLE = maintenance cost per cycle,
>
> FLTHR = maintenance cost per flight hour,
>
> $(T_B - T_G)$ = flight time,
>
> T_G = ground or taxiing time.

Manufacturers' data on cycle and flight hour costs was available for the DC-9-30, DC-9-80, and Dash 7. However, the jet data indicated costs well below the costs experienced by U.S. operators. Therefore the DC-9-30 maintenance cost per cycle and per flight hour was inflated to reflect the average level for New York Air as reported in CAB Form 41. The DC-9-80 costs were inflated by the same ratio as the smaller jet.

The manufacturers' data on maintenance costs for the Metro and Shorts did not separately identify cycle and flight hour components. Therefore the Air Transport Association (ATA) maintenance costing formula, modified for commuter aircraft by Simat, Helliesen and Eichner, Inc., was utilized for the Metro and Shorts.[9]

The maintenance costing formula was not considered applicable to small piston planes. Therefore for the Chieftain maintenance cost was treated simply as a cost per block hour. The resulting formula is

$$\text{MAINT} = T_B \times \text{BLKHR}, \tag{4A.5}$$

where BLKHR = maintenance cost per block hour.

Despite the uncertainties in estimating input costs for maintenance, the costs included in the model are well within the ranges of costs reported by the operators of each aircraft type. The maintenance costs used in this basic model do not include an allowance for maintenance burden (management, utilities, facilities rent, unallocated supplies and labor, etc.). Maintenance burden is assumed, like other overhead costs, to be determined independent of aircraft type.

Equipment Cost
Equipment cost includes the costs of the depreciation of the aircraft and the cost of hull insurance. The formula for equipment cost over a segment (EQUIP) is

$$\text{EQUIP} = (\text{T}_B + \text{T}_T) \times \left[\frac{(\text{AO} + \text{HI})}{\text{PH}} \right], \tag{4A.6}$$

$$\text{AO} = \text{PRICE} \times [(1 - \text{RV}) \times \text{CRF}], \tag{4A.7}$$

$$\text{HI} = (\text{RATE} \times \text{PRICE}), \tag{4A.8}$$

where

T_T = turnaround time = 15 minutes (constant),
AO = annual aircraft ownership cost,
HI = annual hull insurance cost,
PH = annual peak hours = 2,080 (constant),
PRICE = aircraft price,
RV = residual value = 0.15 (constant),
CRF = capital recovery factor = 0.05 (constant),
RATE = annual hull insurance rate.

Manufacturers were the source of aircraft price data, except for the price of the used DC-9-30 which was based on data published in the AVMARK Newsletter. Hull insurance rates were determined through interviews with aviation insurance suppliers and with operators.

Miscellaneous and Oil
Miscellaneous flying expense (charts, other cockpit supplies, etc.) and oil expense both represent very small portions of total segment costs. For simplicity, the two are combined. The formula is

$$\text{MO} = \text{T}_B \times \text{MOEXP}, \tag{4A.9}$$

where

MOEXP = combined miscellaneous and oil expense per block hour.

Manufacturers' and CAB Form 41 data were the sources for miscellaneous and oil expense for each aircraft type.

Landing Fees

Landing fees are set by individual airports. They are based on the assumed landing weight of each aircraft. The formula for each aircraft landing fee is

$$\text{LANDF} = \text{FEE} \times \text{LANDWT}, \tag{4A.10}$$

where

> FEE = landing fee rate per 1,000 pounds landing weight
>
> = 0.30 (constant),

LANDWT = aircraft landing weight.

Although landing fees vary considerably between airports, the model uses an average of $.30 per 1,000 pounds based on a survey of landing fees across the country.[10] Therefore for each plane landing fees are consistent for each segment in the model.

Chapter 5

Commuter Airline Safety
by Clinton V. Oster, Jr., and C. Kurt Zorn

How safe is commuter airline travel? The popular perception is that it is not nearly as safe as travel on the large established jet carriers. Indeed, considerable media attention has also focused on the safety issue, especially since deregulation. A December 1979 article in *The Washington Monthly* entitled "Travelers' Advisory: The Commuters Are Coming" stated, "The accident frequency of commuter lines is about three times that of the major carriers, and the number of commuter fatalities has been rising rapidly."[1] In another article in *The Washington Monthly* Robert Kaus also questioned the acceptability of commuters, "The commuters do have a reputation of unreliability. . . . When they do fly, the commuter planes are often unpressurized, their rides are bumpy, and—well, there's always that factor they don't talk about in the airline ads. People, it seems, just do not think the little planes are as safe as the big jets, and the existing statistics on accidents per mile don't do a very good job of dispelling those fears."[2]

If commuters really are not as safe as other airlines, the implications for the future development of a deregulated airline industry could be serious. To start, safety considerations can have important implications about the competitiveness of different segments of commercial aviation. If, for example, commuters are perceived by the public to be considerably less safe then larger jet carriers, the commuters will be less able, all else equal, to enter into competition with jet carriers. Similarly, if newly formed commuter carriers are believed to have an emphatically poorer safety record than the older and more established commuter airlines, the latter may be under somewhat less competitive pressure than would otherwise be the case. Safety considerations can also pose a direct threat to the future vitality and growth of the commuter airline industry. If commuters are seen as deficient in terms of safety, potential customers may choose ground transportation or forgo a trip rather than fly commuters. The perception of safety differences could thus reduce the competitiveness and profitability of commuter airlines, especially newly formed commuter airlines. This effect could be important in an industry like commercial aviation in which safety considerations have historically received substantial media and public attention.

Eventually, the public's perception of commuter airline safety will be shaped by the actual safety record the commuters amass. In the interim, however, as commuters enter markets in which passengers have had little or no prior experience with commuter airlines, the perceptions may lag behind the reality of commuter airline safety. To assess how the perceptions of commuter safety are likely to evolve as communities gain more experience with commuter carriers, this chapter presents an analysis of the historical record. The chapter begins with a comparison of the safety records of the commuter airlines and the certificated jet carriers. The validity of commonly cited safety measures is discussed, and alternative safety measures are introduced that provide a more appropriate means of making comparisons between commuters and other segments of the airline industry and comparisons among different segments within the commuter industry. The limited literature on commuter airline safety is reviewed, and those factors thought to affect safety are examined. Finally, since the commuter industry encompasses a wide variety of carriers, a cross-sectional analysis of safety in different segments of the industry is presented.

Comparing Safety: Commuters and Jets

Statistics clearly give some credence to the belief that commuters are less safe; it has often been stated that the commuter airline accident rate is many times that of the certificated air carriers.[3] A former chief administrator of the FAA, Langhorne Bond, once told a gathering of commuter operators and other airline officials that, "no matter how you cook or juggle the statistics on commuter accidents, they add up to a safety record that is unacceptable . . . and we are not comparing apples and oranges here . . . we're comparing one apple with another, and yours doesn't look so good."[4] Indeed, as table 5.1 indicates, using a distance-based measure, commuters were 10 to 30 or more times less safe than certificated jet carriers over the 1977 to 1980 period (although even on this basis, commuters have a record about equal to that of the private auto).

Major differences in flight lengths, however, make such comparisons quite misleading. A typical jet, a B-727-200, flying full on an average jet flight of 730 miles will amass approximately 105,850 passenger

Table 5.1 Passenger fatalities per 100 million passenger miles: domestic scheduled service

Year	Commuter carriers	Certificated jet carriers
1977	2.463	0.244
1978	2.463	0.077
1979	1.694	0.154
1980	1.141	0.000

Source: Federal Aviation Administration, *FAA Statistical Handbook of Aviation* (Washington, D.C.: Government Printing Office, assorted years); Civil Aeronautics Board, *Commuter Air Carrier Traffic Statistics, Twelve Months Ended December 31* (Washington, D.C.: CAB, assorted years); National Transportation Safety Board, *Briefs of Accidents Involving Commuter Air Carriers and On-Demand Air Taxi Operations* (Washington, D.C.: NTSB, assorted years).

miles, yet will take off and land only once. For a typical commuter aircraft (e.g., a Swearingen Metro) to accumulate a similar number of passenger miles flying the industry average of 120 miles per flight with all seats occupied, it would have to make over 46 flights (thus landing and taking off 46 times). Since the greatest risk of accident occurs during takeoff and landing, commuters should appear less safe than certificated jet carriers when distance-based measures are used.

A potentially more appropriate safety measure—one based on departures, for example—would remove, or at least reduce, the bias reflected in distance-based measures by taking into account that the major risk of accident is on takeoff and landing. Table 5.2 compares commuters and jet carriers in terms of passenger fatalities per 100,000 aircraft departures. Relying on this measure, commuters had lower accident rates than the large carriers in three of the six years, and for the overall period 1975 to 1980 they had an average fatality rate of 1.1 while the certificated jet fatality rate was 3.4. By this measure commuters thus appear to be safer than certificated jet carriers.

But this departure-based measure is also seriously deficient as it fails to account for the different size of the aircraft used by the carriers. The seating capacity of the average jet aircraft is significantly greater than that of the average commuter aircaft; a B-727-200, for example, seats about 10 times as many passengers as a Beech 99. Thus a typical jet carrier departure represents many more passenger departures than does a typical commuter departure. As an extreme example, it would take about 20 crashes of Beech 99s to produce the same number of passenger fatalities as a single DC-10 crash.

Table 5.2 Passenger fatalities per 100,000 aircraft departures: domestic scheduled service

Year	Commuter carriers[a]	Certificated jet carriers
1975	0.081	2.536
1976	1.452	0.848
1977	1.360	7.961
1978	1.393	2.893
1979	1.128	6.156
1980	0.828	0.000
Average 1974–78	1.089	3.399

Source: Civil Aeronautics Board tapes and Federal Aviation Administration, *FAA Statistical Handbook of Aviation* (Washington, D.C.: Government Printing Office, assorted years); Civil Aeronautics Board, *Commuter Air Carrier Traffic Statistics, Twelve Months Ended December 31* (Washington, D.C.: CAB, assorted years); National Transportation Safety Board, *Briefs of Accidents Involving Commuter Air Carriers and On-Demand Air Taxi Operations* (Washington, D.C.: NTSB, assorted years).
a. Commuter departure data are not available for prior years.

A more useful statistic therefore might be passenger fatalities per one million enplanements.[5] Passenger fatality rates per one million enplanements for commuter carriers and certificated jet carriers are presented in table 5.3 for the years 1970 through 1980. Although commuters are less safe by this measure, the difference is substantially less than that suggested in table 5.1. For the entire period the overall fatality rate per one million enplanements was 3.04 for commuters and 0.91 for certificated jet carriers.[6]

Clearly the safety record of commuter carriers is not as good as the excellent safety record of certificated jet carriers. The difference, however, is not nearly as great as is popularly perceived. Although there is a higher probability that a person boarding a commuter will experience a fatal accident, reliance on statistics based on passenger miles greatly exaggerates the danger. Thus the criticisms of the safety record of the commuter airline industry by the public, government officials, and media are only partially justified; the safety problem is real, yet the degree of the problem is often overstated.

Moreover assessing the safety of commuters relative to jet carriers is more complex than simply comparing the safety measures cited here. Although a passenger departing on a jet flight faces, on average, a smaller risk than one departing on a commuter flight, the larger size of the jet aircraft usually dictates operating flights with more intermediate

Table 5.3   Passenger fatalities per one million enplanements: domestic scheduled service

Year	Commuter carriers	Certificated jet carriers
1970	4.43	0.47
1971	6.39	1.11
1972	5.32	0.92
1973	1.56	1.07
1974	5.12	2.21
1975	1.63	0.59
1976	1.90	0.20
1977	1.76	1.72
1978	1.88	0.56
1979	4.59	1.11
1980	1.29	0.00
Average 1970–80	3.26	0.91
Overall rate 1970–80	3.04	0.91

Sources: Civil Aeronautics Board, *Commuter Air Carrier Traffic Statistics* (Washington, D.C.: CAB, 1980); Federal Aviation Administration, *FAA Statistical Handbook of Aviation: Calendar Year 1980* (Washington, D.C.: Government Printing Office, 1981); National Transportation Safety Board, *Briefs of Accidents Involving Commuter Air Carriers and On-Demand Air Taxi Operations* (Washington, D.C.: NTSB, assorted years).

stops so that the actual risk a passenger faces for the total trip may in fact differ very little between jets and commuters.

Research on Commuter Safety

Despite the concern over the safety of commuter airline travel, literature on the subject has been confined to a handful of government studies, congressional hearings, and journal articles. Initial investigation into the safety of commuter airlines did not commence until 1971 with a study by the National Transportation Safety Board (NTSB).[7] This investigation, prompted by concern over a series of commuter accidents in 1971, reached the conclusion that the safety of commuter airlines could be improved by revising the standards set by the FAA. Suggested amendments included recognizing that commuter air carrier operations are distinct from air taxi operations; improving the training of pilots, operations, and maintenance personnel; improving the quality of the airport and airline equipment available to commuter operators; insuring adequate maintenance and operations procedures; and finally, increasing FAA surveillance of commuter airlines. The FAA, recognizing the growing role of commuters, revised the regulations pertaining to commuter airlines, but these revisions were not adopted until 1978. Not surprisingly, a second study conducted by the NTSB in 1979 concluded that the issues raised in the 1972 report were still relevant during the 1972 to 1979 period.[8]

Several congressional hearings have been held since 1977 on the safety of the commuter airline industry. These hearings have run the gamut of safety issues, from broadly considering all the issues related to commuter airline safety to examining in detail specific areas such as the impact of deregulation on safety.[9] While the hearings have been useful in recording the opinions of prominent people in the industry on the subject of safety, the testimonies have rarely included concrete, systematic statistical evidence.[10]

A review of the literature, examination of NTSB accident reports, and discussions with commuter operators and FAA officials all lead to the conclusion that there is no single determinant of safe operations in the commuter airline industry. At least five major factors can be identified from the available testimony and research: (1) the commuter airline pilots' level of proficiency, (2) the adequacy of commuter airport facilities, (3) the effectiveness of commuter maintenance and operation procedures, (4) the adequacy of FAA surveillance, and (5) the financial health of the commuter airline.

Training of commuter pilots has on occasion suffered from the high cost involved to the operators, the lack of training standardization within the industry, and the lack of flight simulators for most commuter aircraft.[11] Before the 1978 revision of commuter safety regulations, pilots could operate commuter aircraft with either an air transport pilot's (ATP) rating, or a commercial rating—with the former requiring a greater knowledge of aeronautics, higher proficiency, and more flight time. Since the 1978 revisions the pilot in command must have an ATP rating. Similarly because flight experience in a specific aircraft type seems important to safety, standards for flight experience are set for different aircraft in a vein increasingly similar to that required for certificated jet carriers.[12]

Pilot work load is also often cited as a factor affecting safety. Because of shorter flights the average commuter pilot must execute more takeoffs and landings per hour of flight time than the average jet pilot. In addition the pilot or copilot may assist in such activities as refueling and cargo and passenger loading.

The adequacy of airport facilities may also be a determinant of commuter airline safety. James King, former NTSB chairman, testified at a hearing on commuter airport safety that the NTSB "is deeply concerned that, at present, there is a significant gap between the facilities and equipment available at airports serving certificated air carriers and those serving commuters."[13] Of the 362 airports served exclusively by commuters in 1979, only 23 percent had a control tower, 12 percent terminal radar service, and 33 percent a precision approach system.[14] Moreover many of these control towers were closed following the PATCO strike in August 1981. Both pilots and commuter operators maintain that these inferior facilities are detrimental to the industry's safety record.

The effectiveness of commuter maintenance and operation procedures, a third factor often cited as critical to safety performance, is conditioned by regulations that require commuter airline companies to have only a director of operations, a director of maintenance, and a chief pilot. As a result work loads and responsibilities for a commuter's employees can often be ill-defined and the operation and maintenance of the airline can suffer, directly affecting safety. For example, proper weight and balance calculations are crucial to the safe operation of commuter aircraft. If the dispatcher in charge of doing these calculations is overworked or his role unclear, the probability is heightened of a miscalculation or oversight that could result in an accident.

Adherence to the safety regulations established by the FAA is believed essential for a good safety record within the commuter industry. To insure that operators comply with these safety regulations, surveillance by the FAA is necessary. Both congressional hearings and reports by NTSB have suggested that such surveillance is presently inadequate. Low staffing levels, reduced travel budgets, high work loads, and a lack of standardization of surveillance procedures at the FAA's General Aviation District Offices (GADO) are common criticisms.[15]

With regard to the financial health of commuter carriers as a determinant of safety, the NTSB concluded in 1972 that "the financial condition of air taxi/commuter air carriers is very closely related to the level of safety at which they operate."[16] The NTSB further stated that "to survive . . . management may compromise safety when company personnel, maintenance work, and training programs are reduced to subminimal standards."[17] In 1980 the NTSB concluded much the same thing; there is a relationship between the financial situation of the airline and its level of safety.[18] In neither study, however, was any systematic evidence presented on the magnitude of this relationship. Such investigations are all but precluded by a lack of public financial data on commuter airlines.

Another factor not discussed in the literature, but at least indirectly related to all of the determinants of safety already cited, is the role of top management. Management's attitude is one of the first things mentioned by most commuter operators when the topic of safety arises. Defining management's attitude with any precision is difficult, and measuring it objectively is impossible. Obviously no carrier wants to have an accident. Beyond the potential human tragedy, a commuter's traffic usually drops sharply for up to two quarters after an accident, a drop in traffic that can tip a marginal airline into bankruptcy.[19] There are, however, varying degrees to which management can pursue safe operations. Some carriers, for example, exceed FAA regulations whereas others merely meet them. It may never be possible to analyze quantitatively the impact of differing managerial attitudes, but the impact is undoubtedly important.

Statistical Analysis of Intraindustry Safety

By no stretch of the imagination can the commuter airline industry be considered a homogeneous industry. Operators vary widely in terms of size, experience, managerial sophistication, route network, aircraft fleet, and financial condition. Concluding that commuter carriers are less safe than certificated jet carriers tells little more than what occurs, on average, in both industries. It is important to look at intraindustry safety by asking the question: Are there differences in safety among various segments of the commuter industry? By dividing the commuter industry into segments based on specific operational characteristics and examining differences in the safety performance of these segments, a better understanding can be gained of the role these characteristics play in contributing to safe operations and of the role of safety as a barrier to entry and a partial determinant of commuter growth.

The difficulty with such an approach is that, despite what some critics of the industry suggest, a commuter accident is a rare event. By dividing the industry into segments based on some characteristic (or a combination of characteristics), it can only be observed that for the time period covered by the data, these rare events were less rare in some

Table 5.4 Passenger fatalities per one million enplanements: top 20 commuters vs. rest of industry

Year	Top 20 commuters	Other commuters
1970	1.05	11.05
1971	0.61	24.15
1972	2.52	17.06
1973	0.00	4.12
1974	1.21	12.20
1975	2.48	0.37
1976	1.36	4.40
1977	0.20	5.57
1978	1.76	3.15
1979	0.33	3.50
1980	1.11	1.53
Average 1970–80	1.15	7.92
Overall rate 1970–80	1.12	5.91

Source: Rene Riecke, "Commuter Airlines: Impact of Carrier Size and Rate of Growth on Safety," honors thesis, Indiana University, Bloomington, 1981, table V-2.

segments of the industry than in others. Such a finding does not prove that the characteristics used to divide the industry contribute to safer or less safe operations, nor does it in any sense mean that all carriers in the less safe segment are conducting unsafe operations. Rather, these findings must be used in combination with observations of commuter management and pilots, and other research into the determinants of airline safety, to draw even tentative conclusions.

Carrier Size

In 1980 commuter airlines differed significantly in terms of size. For the 12-month period ending June 30, 1980, enplanements ranged from as few as 514 for Cape Smythe Air Service to as many as 761,447 for Puerto Rico International Airlines, Inc.[20]

As table 5.4 indicates, size does seem related to the safety record of commuters, as a significant difference exists between the safety record of the largest commuters and that of the rest of the industry. On average during the 1970 to 1980 period the top 20 commuters (measured in terms of enplanements) were over five times safer than the rest of the industry. As a group the top 20 carriers carried over half of all commuter passengers. Referring back to table 5.3, it is evident that the top 20 carriers have a safety record only slightly worse than the certificated jet carriers' safety record. At the same time the rest of the commuter industry had a significantly less safe record than the jet carriers. Hence, although the overall safety record of the commuter industry is worse than the jet carriers' record, a passenger on one of the large commuters faces about the same small risk of being killed on a flight as a passenger on a jet carrier.

One hypothesis as to why size might contribute to safer operations is that a larger carrier can afford greater specialization in maintenance, training, and operations. By allowing each individual in the organization to concentrate on a narrower range of responsibilities, it may be possible for these responsibilities to be discharged more competently. There may be other ways, as well, in which size makes some functions easier. For example, maintaining an aircraft requires a substantial inventory of spare parts. A larger carrier with more aircraft may find it easier to maintain the necessary inventory, both financially and in terms of space and organization. Although the size and depth of inventory should not matter too much for scheduled maintenance overhauls, it may matter, on occasion, for marginal unexpected repairs; if a part shows wear or slightly diminished performance, it might be replaced quickly if the part is on hand, while replacement might be postponed if the part has to be ordered.

The Allegheny Commuters
The Allegheny Commuter System has been a special subset of the commuter industry since the first Allegheny commuter started operations on November 15, 1967. USAir, formerly Allegheny Airlines, has had contractual arrangements with several commuter operators to provide feeder service from small communities to larger cities served by USAir jets. In return USAir provides assistance in marketing, ticketing, reservations, and scheduling—and in some cases financial guarantees. In order to qualify as an Allegheny commuter, an operator must meet operation and maintenance standards set by USAir that are more stringent than those required (by the FAA) for non-Allegheny commuters.

As can be seen in table 5.5, Allegheny commuters have amassed a significantly better safety record over the 1970s (0.12 passenger fatality per million enplanements) than either the top 20 non-Allegheny commuters (1.40) or the rest of the industry (3.96). In fact the Allegheny commuters outperformed the certificated jet carriers during this time

Table 5.5 Passenger fatalities per one million enplanements: Allegheny, top 20 non-Allegheny, rest of industry

Year	Allegheny	Top 20 non-Allegheny	Rest of industry[a]
1970	0.00	1.08	4.60
1971	0.00	0.62	6.93
1972	0.00	2.63	8.18
1973	0.00	0.00	1.76
1974	0.00	1.27	6.61
1975	0.00	3.00	2.01
1976	1.36	1.54	2.87
1977	0.00	2.45	2.91
1978	0.00	0.78	2.93
1979	0.00	0.60	2.34
1980	0.00	1.47	2.44
Average 1970–80	0.12	1.40	3.96

Source: CAB data tape.
a. Industry minus Allegheny commuters.

period by a substantial margin. Furthermore, while some of the Allegheny commuters are very large, others are small with quite limited operations. It would seem that the more stringent standards imposed by USAir, coupled with the generally high quality of management in the commuters they select, have had a significant impact on safety. The record of these carriers may provide support for the argument that the 1978 revisions in commuter safety regulations, which bring maintenance and operation requirements more in line with those for certificated carriers, should improve safety in the commuter industry.

Aircraft Type
Commuter operators utilize a wide variety of aircraft, ranging from small piston-engine craft originally designed as corporate or general aviation aircraft to large 55- to 60-seat turboprops designed as commercial passenger-transport aircraft, with a few air boats for water-based operations mixed in as well. Turboprop aircraft use turbine engines, operating with the same basic mechanism as large fan-jet engines found on such aircraft as B-747s. Although the propeller appears much different to passengers than the fan portion of a high bypass fan-jet, in reality the difference is more one of degree than basic approach. Turbine engines, with or without props, offer advantages over piston engines

Table 5.6 Interaction of carrier size and fleet type, 1974–1980

	Passenger fatalities per million enplanements	
	Top 10/20	Remainder
Piston only (top 20)	1.66	3.73
Turbine only (top 10)	1.60	0.11
Combined (top 10)	0.59	6.34

(e.g., far fewer moving parts and greater simplicity of operation) and therefore easier maintenance and greater reliability.

There is no reason to believe that the apparent impact of carrier size on safety performance operates independently of impacts of other operational characteristics. To examine the influence of the type of aircraft fleet operated, it is also necessary to control for the effect of carrier size. Table 5.6 presents the results of an analysis of the interaction of carrier size and the type of fleet operated. For carriers operating only piston-engine aircraft, the top 20 piston carriers, as expected, had a better safety record than the remaining piston carriers. Also, perhaps somewhat surprisingly, the top 20 piston carriers had about the same safety record as the top 10 carriers who operated only turbine-engine aircraft (which carried about the same number of passengers); this result suggests that among the larger carriers both piston and turbine aircraft can be operated with the same degree of safety. It may be that the managerial, maintenance, and financial capability of the larger carriers is sufficient to ensure safe operations with either type of aircraft.

Operating a combined fleet of both piston- and turbine-engine aircraft might be expected to pose added difficulty over either purely piston or purely turbine fleets. Mechanics, for example, might be split between the two types of aircraft and thus not be able to "master" either type. Similarly, it might be more difficult to maintain an adequate spare parts inventory for two types of engine than for a single type. As the table indicates, small carriers do seem to have difficulties with combined fleets and have a safety record far worse than any other type of carrier. Somewhat surprising is that the top 10 carriers operating combined fleets had a better safety record than either piston-only or turbine operators. Apparently, arguments about the increased difficulty of operating a combined fleet are less applicable to a large carrier than to a small.

Of particular interest is the observation that both large and small turbine operators seem to be able to operate safely. Such a finding is perhaps not unexpected given the relative simplicity of turbine-engine maintenance and operation. Among both piston and combined operators the large carriers operate more safely. Indeed, the very poor safety performance of the smaller combined-fleet carriers is particularly disturbing and suggests that a phased transition from piston to turbine operations may be particularly difficult for a small operator. It would seem that the poorer safety record of the smaller piston and combined carriers was largely responsible for the impact of carrier size on safety seen in table 5.4.

Landing Aids
An assertion often made is that part of the difficulty commuters have in operating as safely as larger jet aircraft stems not from the commuters themselves but rather from the nature of the airports they serve. Many commuter flights are made into airports that are not equipped with the array of landing and navigational aids found in the airports served by the larger jet carriers. A major difference in airports is the provision of an electronic glide slope (precision approach). The availability of a glide slope to aid in landing puts fewer demands on the pilot, particularly in marginal weather conditions. In interviews, commuter pilots have usually maintained that a precision approach is an important aid to safe operations. The counter argument, however, is that the minimum landing conditions for each airport account for the presence or absence of such landing aids and that it should not be more hazardous to operate in unequipped airports.

It is certainly true that many of the airports served by commuters do not have a glide slope, and an analysis of accidents occurring during the landing phase reveals that passenger fatality rates are, indeed, higher on flights into airports not equipped with glide slopes than into airports so equipped. However, it must be recognized that airports not equipped with glide slopes are more frequently served by smaller commuter carriers which have worse safety records.

Table 5.7 presents the results of an analysis of the interaction of carrier size and the presence of a glide slope. Only accidents occurring during the landing phase of flight were included; thus the fatality rates are somewhat lower than in the previous tables. The table indicates that the presence of glide slopes at airports does not affect the safety records of commuters landing at these airports. Instead, large commuters are seen to operate equally safely into airports equipped or not equipped with this landing aid. Likewise, small commuters have similar safety

Table 5.7 Interaction of carrier size and glide slope, 1970–1980

| | Passenger fatalities per million enplanements | |
	Top 20	Remainder
Airports with glide slopes	0.89	3.72
Airports without glide slopes	0.66	4.24

Source: Derived from Civil Aeronautics Board, Form 298, Schedule T-1, National Transportation Safety Board Accident Briefs, and Federal Aviation Administration, Master File of Airport Facilities Information.

records whether they are operating into airports equipped with glide slopes or not.

These results further strengthen the conclusion that the size of the commuter carrier is a critical determinant of safety performance. They also imply that service to small community airports not equipped with the latest landing aids is not inherently less safe than service to the larger, better equipped airports. Of course, though the absence of a glide slope need not result in less safe operations, it may well result in more flights being canceled due to an inability to land in poor weather.

Summary

Two major observations emerge from a systemwide examination of commuter safety. The most important is that when appropriate measures of safety are used—those not strongly biased either for or against commuter carriers—commuters are found to have a worse safety record than certificated jet carriers, but one that is perhaps only three times worse rather than the more commonly cited 10 to 30 times worse.

The second observation is that safety performance varies widely and systematically within the commuter industry, with carrier size being an important determinant of safety. For example, the top 20 carriers, which carry about 58 percent of commuter passengers, have a safety record much better than the rest of the industry. In fact the record of the top 20 carriers is about the same as the excellent safety record of the certificated jet carriers. And another subset of the industry, the Allegheny commuters, has a safety record even better than that of the jet carriers.

Two conclusions flow from these observations. First, since a major segment of the commuter industry has demonstrated an ability to operate with safety virtually equal to that of the jet carriers, safety should not hamper commuters' ability to enter into competition with jet carriers in markets where their cost and service characteristics are comparable. Thus safety differences need not present commuters with an insurmountable barrier to entry in markets that they are otherwise well equipped to serve.

The second conclusion is that within the commuter industry, safety differences between large and small carriers may provide an edge to the large carriers in battles for commuter markets. Indeed, the superior safety performance of the larger carriers may hamper new entry by small commuters. An exception may be for those small commuters who chose to operate turbine rather than piston aircraft.

Thus the safety record of the industry as a whole, when properly measured, does not seem so bad as to preclude commuters from playing an increasingly important role in the nation's air transportation system. At a minimum, safety considerations should not keep the larger and better established commuters from replacing or otherwise challenging the established jet carriers, if and when market opportunities present themselves.

Part **III**

MANAGEMENT STRATEGIES

Chapter 6

Financial Strategies for the New Entrepreneurs
by Marni Clippinger

The fundamentals of costs, demand, safety, and other considerations were obviously propitious for entrepreneurial activity in the airline industry after deregulation. It remained, however, to translate these fundamentals into the creation of new carriers or a substantial expansion of activities by small carriers already on the scene. This translation required in turn that explicit financial and operational strategies be formulated by the new entrant jet and commuter carriers, as they pursued their entrepreneurial opportunities.

The operating strategies with which the new entrant jets utilized their cost advantage to lower fares are evaluated in the next chapter. Following that, chapter 8 examines how the commuters' rapid growth after deregulation was based on their ability to offer frequent, well-timed service on short-haul low-density routes. As chapters 7 and 8 will illustrate, although the low-fare strategies of the entrepreneurial jets largely dictated the routes they chose to serve, the commuters' service advantage on certain types of routes drove their fare policies. But before their fare and route strategies are assessed, the mechanisms used by the new entrepreneurs to finance their expanding activities are explored in this chapter, since proper financing is an obvious prerequisite to implementing almost any business strategy.

The Financial Risks

Historically, the major carriers have been able to finance most of their capital requirements by means of debt instruments and leasing transactions. Commercial lenders have generally been receptive to requests for equipment financing from the trunks and local service airlines because the risk of carrier bankruptcy was effectively eliminated by the CAB. The airline industry was viewed as a safe, if not highly profitable, area for investment.

In contrast to the established major carriers, the commuter industry has never enjoyed the insulation from downside risk that regulation offered the trunks and local service airlines. Unsheltered against competitive entry, the commuters have always had to fend for themselves and, as such, have generally been considered high-risk loan recipients. The impact of deregulation on these carriers' access to capital was, if anything, slightly positive. As discussed in chapters 2 and 10, passage of the act scheduled the phaseout of the Section 406 subsidy program and made it easier for local service and trunk carriers to terminate service in small communities. At the same time the act called for the introduction of the Section 419 subsidy program, which entitled commuters to receive subsidy for the first time for providing essential air service to small communities. The anticipated need for replacement service in communities where larger carriers were terminating air service, in conjunction with the availability of subsidy in some markets, offered an opportunity for considerable market expansion by commuter carriers.

Although commercial lenders have maintained a skeptical view of the commuter industry even after deregulation, an absence of financing has not constituted an insurmountable barrier to entry for commuter carriers. Between 1971 and 1981 the number of aircraft operated by commuter carriers grew from 782 to 1,463—an increase of 87 percent.[1] This expansion was financed by a combination of aircraft leasing, domestic government loan guarantee programs, foreign government subsidized loans, private equity investment, and, in a few instances, successful public stock offerings.

The new entrant jet carriers have been fueled financially by many of the same sources of capital tapped by commuter carriers, with the addition of venture capital and more extensive use of public offerings. The capital requirements of these carriers have been far greater than those of the commuters, and their growth since deregulation reflects their success in raising healthy initial capitalization.

The first part of this chapter focuses on the effects of leasing, commercial loans, federal loan guarantee programs, and foreign government subsidized financing on entrepreneurial carriers' ability to acquire aircraft. The chapter then turns to a brief exploration of the organizational structures adopted by some of the carriers to attract investment and the use of public offerings to raise equity capital. Finally, the future prospects for availability of capital to new entrant jets and commuter carriers are discussed, along with the possible impacts of various modes of financing on future industry growth.

Table 6.1   Leased aircraft by carrier type

Carrier group	Total in-service fleet (number of aircraft)[a]	Number leased	Percent leased
Trunks	1,722	368	21%
Local service airlines	449	70	16%
Top 50 commuters[b]	369	134	36%
New entrants	135	46	34%

Sources: CAB Form 298 computer tape and Aviation Data Service, Inc. (AvData), Wichita, Kansas, *Air World Survey*, supplement to vol. 33, No. 2 (1981).
a. As of June 30, 1981.
b. Measured by enplanements.

Debt Finance for Aircraft Acquisitions

Leasing

Table 6.1 shows the percentage of leased as opposed to owned aircraft in service as of June 30, 1981, for trunk and local service airlines, the top 50 commuters, and the new entrant (including former intrastate) jet carriers. The percentage of leased aircraft in the latter two categories is considerably higher than for the established carriers. Although data are not available on the remaining 200 carriers in the commuter industry, the percentage leased probably increases as the size of the carrier diminishes.[2]

The leasing transactions used most frequently in the airline industry are tax-oriented leases, sometimes called "true" leases for tax purposes. Under such an arrangement the lessor (frequently a leasing company, bank, or private investor) purchases the equipment and claims the Investment Tax Credit (ITC) and depreciation, while generally passing through some of these tax benefits to the actual user in the form of lower rental fees. The lessee in turn considers lease payments as an operating expense. At the end of the lease term the lessor retains title to the equipment.[3]

Three different kinds of aircraft-leasing transactions are commonly arranged for commuter and new entrant jet carriers. The largest, most profitable commuters, as well as some of the new entrant jet carriers have obtained direct "dry" leases (in which warranties remain with the aircraft operators) from the leasing subsidiaries of major corporations such as General Electric and Greyhound. As the lessor corporation assumes the risk of carrier default, the aircraft being purchased is selected very carefully, as are the carriers who are selected as lessees.

Another type of leasing arrangement is transacted by leasing companies that act as brokers ("independent lessors"). In such cases the carrier approaches the leasing company with a purchase proposal, and the leasing company arranges for financing by a bank, insurance company, or industrial investor. The leasing company is paid a commission and assumes no risk. In the commuter industry the carriers involved in these transactions are often considered slightly riskier than those financed by leasing subsidiaries of major corporations; as such, their lease payments tend to be somewhat higher.

The third kind of leasing arrangement is one in which the leasing company again acts as a broker, but in this case the actual lessor is either a wealthy individual looking for a tax shelter, or a group of such individuals (most often a limited partnership). Unlike banks and institutional lessors, these leasing companies are primarily concerned with the marketability of the aircraft in the event of carrier default. In a case where a lessee does default on lease payments, it is the responsibility of the leasing company to find a new lessee to assume the payments and make use of the equipment. By selecting planes for purchase that are believed to be good future investments, the investor is better able to hedge against the risk of default in the transaction.

As is the case with other leasing arrangements, planes are purchased for the carrier by the investor. The lessor takes advantage of all tax benefits and receives a positive cash flow from the carrier for the duration of the lease term (usually five years, in keeping with the usual depreciable life of aircraft). The carrier receives the right to operate the aircraft for the duration of the lease (frequently an operating lease), usually with the option to purchase the plane at the end of the term at fair market value (unless some other value has been established). Lease payments for the carrier can run as low as $15,000 per month per $1 million of aircraft. The leasing company is paid a percentage commission for its efforts, for example, 10 percent of the purchase of the aircraft.

Leasing is likely to remain an important source of aircraft for small entrepreneurial carriers. Of course, if several major carriers were to become bankrupt, the used aircraft market could be flooded (at least temporarily) with an excess of planes, thus placing a damper on the profits of companies leasing equipment to new entrant carriers. From the carrier's perspective, however, leasing companies will need lessees more than ever in such a situation, which should result in the continued availability of aircraft on attractive lease terms.

Commercial Loans

Much of the equipment financing available to established commuter carriers seeking to expand their fleets since deregulation has come through local banks in small communities where there is strong interest in maintaining or extending air service. As long as commuters continue to expand by acquiring more small planes (as opposed to moving into larger aircraft), financing on the local level will probably continue to meet some or most of the capital needs of many small commuters. Carriers expanding into larger aircraft, however, frequently run up against the limitations of local banks and are obliged to seek financing from larger capital markets.

Of the estimated 250 commuter carriers in the United States, it is often said that one-quarter, at most, might be considered credit worthy by conventional standards, with net worths in excess of $500,000. Table 6.2 shows the debt-to-investment ratios and net worths of the 19 certificated commuter carriers (within the 48 contiguous states) for whom financial data were filed with the CAB in 1981. As the table demonstrates, these carriers are heavily leveraged, with more than half of their debt-to-investment ratios in excess of 100. Although the certificated commuters are not necessarily representative of the commuter industry as a whole, these figures do give some idea of the range of financial conditions extant among commuters.

Additional perspective on these figures can be found by contrasting them with the majors and new entrant/former intrastate jet carriers (tables 6.3 and 6.4). Although many of the larger carriers are also highly leveraged, no carrier's debt exceeded investment in the third quarter of 1981.

In view of the "highly leveraged" financial status of most commuters, commercial lenders have been forced to look beyond the balance sheet in evaluating the potential ability of fledgling carriers to support debt service. Most frequently, management, route structure, market, and equipment of the carrier are examined closely, in addition to attempting to insure that cash flows will be sufficient to cover debt payments. The degree of flexibility in making these assessments varies widely; for example, some lenders are willing to accept considerable risk to maintain air service into their communities.

The risky nature of the commuter industry has been reflected in the interest rates on debt available to commuters. It would be difficult to characterize any set of terms as typical for the industry. However, most loans made during 1981 for the purpose of purchasing aircraft had

Table 6.2 Debt-to-investment ratios and net worth of certificated carriers (third quarter, 1981)

Carrier	Net worth (net stockholders' equity)	Debt-to-investment ratio
Sky West	$ 1,179,495	48.15
Air Wisconsin	23,449,288	52.64
Empire	3,924,032	55.08
Aspen	509,030	79.22
Wright	880,484	80.52
Altair[a]	6,986,643	84.42
Big Sky	583,065	84.78
Mississippi Valley	7,180	99.96
Air Midwest	− 177,971	101.18
New Air	− 23,638	101.34
Cascade	− 321,636	108.20
Great American	− 337,748	110.39
Golden West	− 5,274,384	111.15
Swift Aire[a]	− 2,218,865	111.57
Mid South	− 295,030	124.22
Air North	− 1,304,459	124.43
Air New England	− 815,841	125.89
Cochise	− 347,222	143.19
Imperial	− 3,073,413	667.60

Source: CAB Form 41.
a. Second quarter, 1981.

floating interest rates, running from one to two and a half points over the bank prime rate. The term of such loans has varied with the size and age of the aircraft, ranging from 7 to 12 years for new planes and 5 to 7 years for used aircraft. Financing is generally available for up to 80 percent of the purchase price of the plane, and more when the loan is guaranteed by the FAA Aircraft Loan Guarantee Program.

For the most part major institutional lenders such as insurance companies, pension funds, and national banks have not developed an expertise in commuter aircraft and have been less than enthusiastic about the prospect of financing commuter acquisitions. Many large institutional investors have not considered it worth their while to invest the time and effort necessary to develop the knowledge required to make sound judgments in such a high-risk, low-return industry. As such, a small core group of banks and financial institutions has emerged that specialize

Table 6.3 Debt-to-investment ratios and net worth of new entrant and former intrastate jet carriers (third quarter, 1981)

Carrier	Net worth (net stockholders' equity)	Debt-to-investment ratio
Southwest	$169,196,148	27.43
Midway	22,133,328	38.50
Air California	60,635,885	48.60
Pacific Southwest	184,223,000	60.99
New York Air	18,198,116	62.94
People Express	17,444,384	71.21
Air Florida	74,556,649	75.17
World	85,171,364	81.37
Capitol International	1,987,045	90.89

Source: CAB Form 41.

Table 6.4 Debt-to-investment ratios and net worth of major carriers (third quarter, 1981)

Carrier	New worth (net stockholders' equity)	Debt-to-investment ratio
Northwest	$ 839,931,000	8.20
Delta	1,040,271,000	18.02
US Air	340,941,000	39.92
United	877,281,141	55.49
Pan Am	869,494,000	57.38
American	863,606,000	65.27
TWA	551,111,191	69.33
Western	178,316,053	72.18
Eastern	516,219,359	75.79
Continental	144,316,543	77.05
Braniff International	108,102,000	83.89
Republic/Hughes	109,020,000	87.38

Source: CAB Form 41.

in commuter loans and aircraft-leasing arrangements. Carriers are frequently referred to these institutions by other banks and leasing companies not familiar with the industry's technology and market structure.

Federal Loan Guarantee Program

One of the by-products of deregulation that has helped to lower financial barriers to entry, at least temporarily, for new entrants and commuters was the act's revitalization and expansion of the FAA Aircraft Loan Guarantee Program. In an effort to quell fears that air service in small communities would suffer with the passage of the Airline Deregulation Act, the Aircraft Loan Guarantee Program was extended to include eligible commuters, intrastate, and charter carriers. In addition the maximum loan amount was increased to $100 million per carrier, with a maximum term of 15 years.

Under the Aircraft Loan Guarantee Program, the FAA, acting for the secretary of transportation, was authorized to guarantee a loan only if the carrier could demonstrate that it had been unable to obtain uninsured financing elsewhere on reasonable terms. The aircraft to be purchased also had to be shown to improve the service and efficiency of the carrier. Before granting the loan guarantee, the FAA assessed the intention and ability of the carrier to (1) repay the loan during the established term, (2) continue its operation as a commuter or intrastate air carrier, and (3) continue operating the same routes in the future as those operated at the time of the loan. The loan guarantee has insured loans on up to 90 percent of the purchase price of the aircraft, spare parts and engines, and guarantees 90 percent of the loan and 100 percent of the interest outstanding. Loan guarantee terms have been up to 15 years for new jets and 12 years for new turboprops. There has been an annual guarantee fee (0.25 percent in 1981) on the unpaid balance of the guaranteed portion of all loans.

Once granted, the loan guarantee insured the lender against the possibility of the carrier's defaulting on loan payments, thereby reducing the risk involved in the loan and enabling lenders to offer carriers financing at lower rates and longer terms than would otherwise be possible. An FAA loan guarantee often reduced interest rates to carriers by as much as four percentage points. Overall, loan guarantees reduced the debt service drain on cash flow by lowering interest rates, extending the loan terms available, and, most important, making financing possible where it had previously not been available.

Table 6.5   Summary of FAA Loan Guarantees (October 24, 1978, through January 15, 1982)

Carrier	Amount of loans	Number of aircraft
Commuter carriers	$100,036,305	61
Other carriers[a]	583,975,745	64
Total	$684,012,050	125

Source: Federal Aviation Administration, Office of Aviation Policy, Loans Executed as of January 15, 1982.
a. Include new entrant and former intrastate jet carriers and one local service airline.

Table 6.5 shows the loan amounts guaranteed for commuters, new jet entrants, and former intrastate jet carriers between deregulation and January 15, 1982. The number of aircraft purchased under the Aircraft Loan Guarantee Program's 20 years prior to deregulation totaled 149 planes for loans granted to 20 certificated carriers in amounts totaling $300 million. In the first three years following deregulation and the liberalization of the loan guarantee program, the loan amount guaranteed totaled about $685 million, or more than twice the amount guaranteed in the preceding 20 years.

New entrant and former intrastate carriers have received more than 85 percent of the total amounts guaranteed. Indeed, only four such carriers—New York Air, People Express, Midway Airlines, and Muse Air—have received guarantees for loans equal to 23 percent of the total amount guaranteed to all carriers since deregulation. Although the number of planes purchased by commuter carriers is roughly equal to the number purchased by the new entrant and former intrastate carriers under the loan guarantee program, it is evident from the dollar amounts guaranteed that the jet carriers have taken greater advantage of the program. In fact many commuters have complained of difficulty and confusion in attempting to file for loan guarantees. The application process is lengthy (three to four months) and sufficiently complicated so that carriers frequently have had to seek external help in completing the forms. Many commuters have also expressed reluctance to open their financial records to government officials, preferring the more personal and less bureaucratic assistance of local commercial loan officers.

To determine whether any particular biases have appeared in the granting of FAA loan guarantees to commuters, tables 6.6 through 6.8 examine the types of aircraft purchased with guaranteed loans and the relative size of the carriers that have received loan guarantees.

Table 6.6 lists the number of each commuter aircraft purchased since the passage of the act using FAA guaranteed loans. It is not surprising

Table 6.6 Manufacturers and seating capacities of planes purchased with FAA Loan Guarantees (October 24, 1978, through January 15, 1982)

Manufacturer and model	Number of planes purchased	Seating capacity
Fairchild Swearingen Metro	16	19
Shorts 330	13	30
Nihon YS-11	6	60
Beech Model 99	6	15
Handley Page Jetstreams	6	17
Fokker F-27	4	50
de Havilland Twin Otter	2	19
Cessna 402	2	8
British Aerospace HS-748	2	50
de Havilland Dash 7	1	50
Embraer Bandeirante	1	18
CASA 212	1	27
Gulfstream American	1	24
Total	61	

Source: Federal Aviation Administration, Aircraft Loan Guarantee Programs, Loans Executed as of January 15, 1982.

that the most frequently purchased 19- and 30-seat aircraft—the Swearingen Metro and the Shorts 330—were also the most widely used aircraft in the industry in their respective size categories.[4] In addition 41 of the 61 planes purchased were models that ranked among the top 10 commuter passenger aircraft in 1981; collectively, they accounted for more than 60 percent of the 1981 commuter seat capacity.[5]

Table 6.7 contrasts the 1980 to 1981 changes in industrywide fleet structure (in terms of aircraft seating capacity) with the aircraft purchased using FAA loan guarantees. Carriers using FAA loan guarantees again seemed to follow industry trends, buying the highest proportion of planes in the 10- to 19-seat category and few planes in the 1- to 9-seat category.

Table 6.8 compares the distribution of loan guarantees by size of carrier with the distribution of passengers carried. The top 50 commuter carriers in the contiguous United States carried more than 82 percent of the 1980 commuter traffic yet received only 69 percent of the total amounts guaranteed to commuters.

The established trunk and local service carriers have criticized the loan guarantee program, claiming that the program amounts to overt

Table 6.7   Analysis of changes in commuter aircraft fleet

Total commuter industry

Multiengine (seating capacity)	Fleet in 1980	Fleet in 1981	Percentage change in commuter aircraft fleet
1–9	548	541	(9.5)
10–19	410	470	81.1
21–30	102	108	8.1
31–60	100	115	20.2
Total	1,160	1,234	100.0

Aircraft purchased by commuters with FAA loan guarantees (through 1/15/81)

Multiengine (seating capacity)	Number of aircraft	Percentage of total purchased
1–9	2	3.4
10–19	31	50.8
21–30	15	24.6
31–60	13	21.3

Sources: Total industry figures were derived from the 1980 CAAA Annual Survey as reported in the *1980 CAAA Annual Report*, pp. 120–121, and the 1981 RAAA Annual Survey as reported in the *1981 Annual Report of the Regional/Commuter Airline Industry*, Regional Airline Association, Washington, D.C., February 1982, pp. 128–129. Data on aircraft purchased by commuters with FAA Loan Guarantees from the Federal Aviation Administration, Aircraft Loan Guarantee Program, Loans Executed as of January 15, 1982.

government subsidy of their new entrant competitors. (The only established carrier to have made use of the program is Piedmont.) These complaints, in combination with budgetary considerations, led to the imposition of a $100 million budget ceiling in fiscal year 1982, as well as a new restriction limiting participation to carriers purchasing aircraft with less than 60 seats and payload limits under 18,000 pounds. This restriction effectively eliminates the availability of additional loans for the new entrant jet carriers.

The FAA Loan Guarantee Program is not the only federally guaranteed loan program to have been instrumental in financing commuter aircraft acquisition. On a smaller scale the Business and Industrial Loan Program, administered by the Farmers Home Administration, has operated a similarly structured regional loan guarantee program, aimed at upgrading the economic quality of rural life. Since the program started in 1974, seven commuter carriers in the 48 contiguous states have received a total of $10,323,000 in loan assistance for the purchase of equipment.

Table 6.8 Commuter carriers: share of passengers carried and dollar amounts of FAA Loan Guarantees, 1980

Carriers	Number of passengers carried	Amount of FAA Guaranteed Loans	Percentage of total commuter passengers carried	Percentage of total amount of FAA Guaranteed Loans
Top 10	5,461,796	$ 24,004,674	36.9	24.0
11–20	2,781,594	25,923,806	18.8	25.9
21–30	1,785,311	1,761,494	12.1	1.8
31–40	1,316,037	10,885,500	8.9	10.9
41–50	822,335	6,431,674	5.5	6.4
Total top 50	12,167,073	69,007,148	82.2	69.0
Below 50/other	2,642,929	31,029,157	17.8	31.0
Total all commuters	14,810,002	100,036,305	100.0	100.0

Sources: Federal Aviation Administration, Aircraft Loan Guarantee Program, Loans Guaranteed since Deregulation (as of January 15, 1982), and CAB Form 298 Computer Tape.

Foreign Government Financing

Foreign governments have made generous contributions toward sub-sidizing the purchase of their manufacturers' aircraft by U.S. carriers. Many of the foreign manufacturers that produce aircraft for the commuter market have been able to offer government-guaranteed financing at considerably lower rates than those available through domestic alternatives.

As a consequence there is increasing pressure from U.S. manufacturers to negotiate multilateral agreements on minimum interest rates to be allowed on aircraft sales. American manufacturers of smaller planes have advocated an expansion of the Common Line Agreement negotiated in August 1981 between the United States and those European nations selling large air transport planes. This agreement attempts to limit "predatory" financing practices and government subsidy for commercial aircraft sales by establishing a minimum interest rate on export sales of large aircraft and a maximum term on government loans.

Unlike their foreign counterparts, the U.S. Export-Import Bank (ExIm Bank) has not been involved in financing smaller commuter planes in export sales, beyond guaranteeing loans made by commercial banks. By contrast, foreign companies such as the Brazilian manufacturer, Embraer, have been able to offer financing through their government's export bank to U.S. buyers at interest rates as much as 10 percentage points lower than commercial rates available for the purchase of aircraft made in the United States, while at the same time restricting imports of U.S. aircraft to Brazil.

Although U.S. aircraft manufacturers may have suffered at the hands of their foreign competitors, the U.S. commuter industry has thrived on the magnanimity of foreign suppliers and their export banks. The details of individual arrangements between U.S. buyers and foreign manufacturers are not publicly available, but ranges of terms have been reported. For example, in 1981 Embraer was reported to have offered interest rates of 7.5 to 9 percent on 85 percent financing of Bandeirantes, at the same time that Piper Aircraft was arranging financing for carriers purchasing Navajo Chieftains at 15 to 19 percent (the rate depended largely on whether or not the carrier had obtained an FAA loan guarantee) for 90 percent of the purchase price. Embraer's ability to offer such interest rates was the result of the Brazilian government reimbursing the bank involved in the transaction for the difference between the prime lending rate and the interest rate negotiated with the buyer.

Brazil is frequently cited as the most generous foreign benefactor of the U.S. commuter industry, but other countries are not far behind. Manufacturers of commuter aircraft made in Canada, Spain, and Great Britain have also been able to offer U.S. buyers financing through their government export banks at terms far more attractive than those available from U.S. financial sources. Most frequently, the foreign export bank structures leasing transactions through U.S. financial intermediaries (i.e., a major leasing company or private partnership established to take advantage of investment tax credits or accelerated depreciation deductions). In 1981 the interest rates reported to have been offered to these intermediaries by foreign export banks were between four and eight percentage points lower than the financing available to intermediaries buying American-made aircraft. Although the intermediaries in turn structure longer-term wraparound leases for the commuter carriers at varying rates (depending on the perceived degree of risk) that are higher than what they are paying, the rates available to commuters on foreign aircraft leases have been considerably lower than those on U.S.-manufactured planes.

The domestic manufacturers of commuter aircraft have been forced to become increasingly involved in the financing of their sales and to experiment with a variety of methods in order to compete with the terms offered by foreign manufacturers. For example, Cessna has assisted domestic buyers in financing aircraft through its own internal resources. Piper has employed an outside consultant to help carriers complete loan guarantee application forms. Fairchild Swearingen Aviation Corporation has become instrumental in matching up investors seeking tax advantages with commuters seeking aircraft. All of the domestic manufacturers benefited from the Safe Harbor leasing provisions of the Economy Recovery Tax Act of 1981, which allowed many of the smaller carriers to arrange attractive sale and leaseback transactions with entrepreneurs and private investors seeking tax advantages.

Equity Financing: Venture Capital, Public Offerings, and Corporate Structures

Venture capital's role in airline growth since deregulation has been more apparent in financing new entrant jet carriers than commuters. It is not surprising that prior to deregulation, venture capitalists had little involvement in the airline industry. Although the risks of airline investment had been limited by regulation, the potential for high returns on investment were similarly stunted.

The new entrepreneurial opportunities that emerged following passage of the deregulation act caught the attention of several venture capital groups, but it took some time and effort on the part of the entrepreneurs to stimulate any investment. The founders of Midway Airlines spent three years attempting to raise what they considered to be sufficient capital to get the airline started. The first round of financing was obtained in July 1979 when, with the help of Shearson Loeb Rhoades, Inc., almost $6 million was raised from the sale of convertible preferred stock to more than a dozen professional venture capitalists. When the company commenced operations five months later, the founders had been able to retain between 30 and 40 percent of the stock. Since then, Midway has had two public offerings and raised over $17 million for aircraft acquisition and operational expansion. Midway has also received FAA loan guarantees totaling $24.1 million to finance the acquisition of four DC-9-30s and one DC-9-15.

Midway's success in obtaining sufficient financing undoubtedly helped pave the way for the emergence of subsequent new entrants. People Express received $200,000 of first-stage equity financing from FNCB Capital Corporation (Citicorp Venture Capital), in exchange for almost 13 percent of the stock, and raised an additional $800,000 from its founders and directors. Six months later the company raised more than $25 million through a public offering underwritten by Hambrecht & Quist. When the airline became operative at the end of April 1981, it received FAA loan guarantees for over $12 million and soon thereafter obtained guarantees for an additional $46 million to finance the acquisition of fourteen B-737-100s.

The timing of the first new entrant jet carriers was an essential element in their ability to raise public equity financing. The new issues market that welcomed Midway, New York Air, People Express, and, later, Muse and Jet America appears to have subsequently sated its appetite for new airlines, at least temporarily. In late 1981 at least two fledgling airlines (Air Chicago and Columbia Air) tried to make public offerings and failed. In general, the second round of would-be new entrant airlines found a less receptive new issues market, and financial institutions that have loans outstanding to carriers teetering on the edge of bankruptcy have been less than enthusiastic about financing new competition.

The role of venture capital in helping the new entrants has spilled over into the commuter market in only a few isolated instances. Despite the added opportunities for growth that deregulation presented to commuter markets, venture capital financing has not been a frequent phenomenon. In those rare instances where venture capital has entered the commuter industry, it has generally done so with the purpose of taking over an existing carrier, replacing the management team, and replacing the turboprops with jets, while maintaining the infrastructure and identity of the old commuter (e.g., Pacific Express).

Venture capital's lack of involvement in the commuter industry, both before and after deregulation, is probably based on the perceived limited appeal of commuter carriers in the public equity markets. Although a small number of commuter carriers have made successful public offerings (e.g., Empire, Metro, Suburban, and Air Wisconsin), such successes have not been common. From the venture capitalist's perspective, an ideal investment has been an equity position in an undiscovered but up-and-coming company, and a subsequent public offering as quickly as possible, in order to recover the initial investment and realize high returns within a year or two. As this is hardly a frequent scenario in the commuter industry, it is understandable that venture capitalists have not been too active there. Although commuter carriers can be quite profitable, the magnitude of gain that typically attracts venture capital is difficult to project among commuters.

In the absence of venture capital the Subchapter S corporation has been a popular method among commuters of attracting equity capital from private investors. Simply stated, a Subchapter S corporation is one that has elected not to be subject to federal income tax but to pass its income (or losses) along to be taxed to its shareholders at their applicable personal income tax rates. The appeal of the Subchapter S election is greatest in cases where the company is experiencing losses or minimal profits, and its stockholders are in high tax brackets. The Subchapter S election has been used as a means of attracting wealthy individuals to invest in new commuter ventures because it offers shareholders the advantage of using their pro rata share of corporate losses to offset additional personal income from other sources. The election also allows for the pass-through to shareholders of tax benefits such as investment credits. Examples of carriers that have made Subchapter S elections are Mississippi Valley Airlines and Air Oregon.

The 1981 Tax Act liberalized eligibility for the Subchapter S election, making the election that much more accessible to small companies such as commuter airlines. The maximum number of shareholders was increased from 15 to 25, losses were allowed to be carried back 3 years and carried forward 15 years, and rules governing the distribution of corporate stock were relaxed.

Summary

Since the passage of the Airline Deregulation Act, a remarkable array of financing sources and techniques have been used to bring new entrant jet carriers into the industry and commuter and former intrastate jet carriers into new markets. The act provided for loan guarantees on aircraft purchases by commuters, new jet entrants, and former intrastate carriers. By early 1982 loans on purchases of close to $685 million of aircraft had been guaranteed under this program.

Aircraft leasing has proven to be a major factor in the ability of commuter and new entrant jet carriers to finance fleet expansion. As of mid-1981, 34 percent of the aircraft in both new entrant and the top 50 commuter carriers' fleets were leased planes. The highly leveraged financial status of many commuters meant that additional debt financing was available only at particularly high interest rates, so that leasing has frequently been the only viable avenue for fleet expansion. As commuter aircraft become more expensive and commuters move into larger planes, leasing will probably become an increasingly prevalent method of financing fleet expansion and modernization.

Foreign governments have also played an important role in making commuter aircraft available to U.S. carriers on attractive terms. Through arrangements ranging from foreign government guaranteed loans to direct subsidy of interest rates, governments of aircraft manufacturing countries including Brazil, Canada, the United Kingdom, and Spain have contributed significantly to the accessibility of new equipment for commuter carriers. The contrast between financing terms offered by foreign manufacturers and those available in the U.S. market has resulted in increasing pressure on U.S. manufacturers to become involved in assisting carriers to finance aircraft purchases.

Despite the fact that the commuter industry has always been viewed as a risky area for investment, it managed to expand operations at a rapid clip and financed a 22 percent increase in the number of aircraft in domestic service in the first three years after deregulation. Combining private investors with penchants for flying planes, sweetheart deals from foreign and domestic aircraft manufacturers, local (private and commercial) debt financing in communities where air service has been cut back or terminated, government loan guarantees, and extensive use of aircraft leasing, the commuter industry has not apparently suffered for lack of funds.

The new entrant and former intrastate jet carriers have used most of the same financing techniques as the commuters as well as venture capital and public equity to finance their start-up operations. Ongoing access to financing as the industry continues to adjust to deregulation could prove, however, more difficult for those carriers than for commuters. Banks with loans outstanding to any of the financially distressed majors might be less receptive to financing new competition than in the past. The imposition of limitations on the Aircraft Loan Guarantee Program and on the tax savings obtainable from leasing provisions could have a significantly adverse impact on the availability of financing for equipment acquisition. On the other hand, the new entrant and former intrastate jet carriers may serve an important function in taking used aircraft off lenders' hands in the event that any of the majors fail.

Ultimately the availability of financing to the new entrants and commuters may depend as much on general economic and financial conditions as on the particular circumstances of the industry. It is nevertheless impressive how much financing the new airline entrepreneurs have been able to garner during the financially troubled years just after deregulation. Despite the fact that these were years characterized by historically high interest rates and much discussion of "crowding out" and "capital shortages," the new entrants and commuters have gained considerable access to the capital markets.

Chapter 7

Competitive Strategies of New Entrant Jets

The route and fare freedoms ushered in by deregulation allowed carriers of all types to take advantage of their particular strengths to seek special niches in the marketplace. As seen in chapter 4, the main advantage of the intrastate and new entrant jet carriers was a cost advantage stemming mostly from efficient utilization of low-cost nonunion employees, streamlined no-frills operations, and high daily utilization of relatively fuel-efficient, but older (and therefore initially cheaper), twin-engine jet aircraft. Moreover excellent opportunities for new entry existed in short-haul markets that had not been highly profitable for the established carriers under CAB regulation and often were made even more costly to serve by the sharp rise in fuel prices that began in mid-1979.[1]

New Entrant Jet Carrier Fares

Several possible competitive strategies were available to the new entrant carriers because of their lower cost structures. One approach would be to enter a market with roughly the same fare and service offerings as the incumbent established carrier and exploit the lower cost structure by accepting lower break-even load factors. With aggressive marketing and scheduling, the new carrier could hope either to gain enough market share to become profitable with the incumbent still in the market or take traffic away from the incumbent, thereby forcing the incumbent to abandon the market. To force the incumbent out, the new carrier would seek to add enough capacity to break even or make a small amount of money, while the incumbent with a higher break-even load factor was losing money. A major drawback to this approach was that the new entrants would have to beat the incumbent at the incumbent's own game—conventional service at standard fares. Additionally, the new entrant essentially tied "one arm behind its back" in that only added frequency would be used to stimulate market growth rather than both added frequency and lower fares. And as seen in chapter 3, added frequency in medium- and high-density markets seemingly has a very limited ability to stimulate traffic.

An alternative strategy for a low-cost new entrant would be to use its cost advantage to charge much lower fares. Although low fares, particularly very low fares, may require consistently high load factors to be profitable, they may also attract enough media attention that less money need be spent on advertising. Low fares have also proven effective in stimulating entirely new airline traffic. Some passengers may be attracted from other modes—mostly from private autos but in some cases intercity bus or train. Other travelers, particularly those on vacation, may be diverted from one destination to another. Still other passengers may be induced by the low fares to make trips they otherwise would not have made. From whatever source, new passengers attracted by lower fares, coupled with those diverted from the incumbent carrier, can make the achievement of break-even loads possible even if the incumbent carrier lowers its fare in response.

An approach emphasizing low fares based on low costs can also help differentiate a new service from that which existed in the market previously. Of course, to the extent that lower costs are derived from lower labor costs or from leasing used rather than new aircraft, passengers may become concerned about the safety and reliability of the operation and may be reluctant to take advantage of the lower fares. But if the cost advantage also derives from simplified operations, fewer in-flight amenities, no interlining, and the use of secondary airports, then the lower fares can easily be justified in a manner unlikely to alarm most passengers.

Still another strategy for exploiting low costs would be to provide amenity-laden first-class service at standard coach fares. This approach, essentially an "upmarket" variant of the low-fare strategy, aims directly at diverting business travelers from the incumbent carriers. Although business travelers, whose travel costs are either fully reimbursed or at least tax deductible, are not thought to be highly sensitive to fares, they may be sensitive to the level of amenities. Less dense seating and first-class service, for example, may facilitate working in flight. Established carriers with limited first-class seating could find it difficult to match these new entrant fare and service offerings. A serious drawback to this approach is that it does little to stimulate the market other than by adding frequencies. To get passengers, therefore, the new entrant must rely almost entirely on drawing them away from an incumbent carrier, rather than also stimulating new trips and diverting passengers from other modes or other destinations. Moreover business travelers are particularly sensitive to convenient scheduling so that the new carrier might be faced with difficult choices between scheduling flights conveniently and achieving high aircraft utilization.

Given these considerations, it is not surprising that most new entrant jet carriers have used low fares as an important part of their development strategies. Determining the extent to which fares were lowered, however, is often difficult. A new entrant to a market may use a limited-time introductory fare that is lower than any possible cost advantage could justify. Such fares can be used as a substitute or supplement for advertising, and they may not be an accurate long-term indication of the extent of fare cutting by the carrier. Fares in new entrant markets may also change frequently, particularly as incumbent carriers adjust their fares in response, so that it is sometimes difficult to determine what is actually being charged. A symptom of this instability is that since deregulation the *OAG* has often published only a range of fares in many markets for each fare category, rather than the specific fare charged by each carrier.

Despite measurement difficulties the extent to which new entrant carriers were cutting fares below previous levels can be approximated. A baseline for comparison is provided by the CAB's Standard Industry Fare Level (SIFL). The SIFL formula, by which trunk and local service airline fares are often computed, consists of a terminal charge applied to all flights and a mileage charge based on flight length (as shown in table 7.1). For example, the formula values for coach fares as of May 1, 1980, were: $25.14 for the terminal charge, plus 13.75 cents per mile for the first 500 miles, 10.49 cents for the next 1,000 miles, and 10.08 cents for all additional miles. Since April 1975 the CAB has made adjustments in SIFL by changing each component of the formula by the same percentage as airline costs have risen.

The SIFL, incidentally, was not the maximum fare that could be charged. During most of the time since deregulation, carriers have been allowed to charge up to 130 percent of SIFL plus $16 without special CAB approval. Indeed, as of June 15, 1981, the average coach fare for markets less than 850 miles was about 8 percent above SIFL.

To analyze the fare policies of the new entrant jets, all nonstop markets for Midway, New York Air, and People Express were examined, as were the domestic interstate nonstop markets of Air Florida, Pacific Southwest Airlines (PSA), and Southwest. Fares as listed in the June 15, 1981, *OAG* were compared to the SIFL then in effect.

Table 7.1 Standard industry fare level

Effective date	Base fare (dollars)	Per mile charges (cents)			Percent change
		0–500 miles	501–1,500 miles	Over 1,500 miles	
5/1/78	17.37	9.50	7.24	6.96	—
11/15/78	17.93	9.80	7.48	7.19	3.2
5/15/79	18.65	10.19	7.78	7.47	4.0
7/1/79	19.86	10.86	8.28	7.96	6.5
9/1/79	21.73	11.89	9.06	8.71	9.4
11/1/79	22.54	12.33	9.40	9.04	3.7
1/1/80	23.27	12.73	9.71	9.33	3.2
3/1/80	23.85	13.05	9.95	9.57	2.5
5/1/80	25.14	13.75	10.49	10.08	5.4
7/1/80	25.92	14.18	10.81	10.39	3.1
1/1/81[a]	24.97	13.66	10.41	10.01	(3.7)
3/1/81	26.39	14.44	11.00	10.58	5.7
5/1/81	28.45	15.56	11.86	11.41	7.8
7/1/81	28.80	15.75	12.01	11.55	1.2

a. SIFL formula reduced on January 1, 1981 (carriers not required to lower fares).

Two of these carriers, People Express and Southwest, adopted almost identical pricing strategies by using deep fare cuts and simple fare structures with peak and off-peak differentials. Peak weekday fares averaged 53 percent of SIFL for People Express and 60 percent of SIFL for Southwest. Off-peak weekend fares averaged only 34 percent of SIFL for People Express and 42 percent of SIFL for Southwest. These carriers also priced markets of similar distances identically. Three of People Express's five markets had fares of $35 peak and $23 off-peak. All of Southwest's interstate markets were either $40 peak and $25 off-peak or $60 peak and $45 off-peak, depending on the length of the flight.

Two other carriers, New York Air and PSA, also adopted similar strategies but made more moderate fare cuts. New York Air's peak fares averaged about 75 percent of SIFL and PSA's interstate fares averaged about 79 percent. New York Air's off-peak fares averaged about 45 percent of SIFL.[2]

Midway Airlines made only modest cuts in fares, with peak fares averaging 96 percent of SIFL and off-peak fares averaging 75 percent of SIFL. In two markets where only a single fare was offered, fares averaged 83 percent of SIFL. Although Midway's fare cuts appear slight (at least in comparison with other new entrant carriers), two of Midway's eight markets involve New York's La Guardia Airport and Washington's National Airport—two of the most congested airports in the United States. As discussed in detail in chapter 9, operating in these airports can entail higher than average costs, and fares in markets involving these airports are typically above average.[3]

Midway's fare cuts in uncongested markets were, though, less deep than those made by most other new entrant carriers. Midway offered service to Midway Airport with better access to downtown Chicago and less congestion than the major Chicago airport, O'Hare. Fare competition thus played less of a role in Midway's strategy than it did for the other new entrant carriers.

Air Florida seemed to tailor its fares closely to the specific characteristics of each market, so that its fares bore no consistent relationship to SIFL. For example, in its two markets involving White Plains, New York (to Chicago's O'Hare and to Washington's National) where it faced no direct competition, the fares were above SIFL. On the other hand, in interstate markets involving a Florida city at one end and competition from another carrier, Air Florida fares were below SIFL and in some cases substantially below. Thus Air Florida seemed to be pursuing a dual strategy of being a low-fare competitor when faced with competition, and charging roughly average fares in noncompetitive markets.

To a large extent, the depth of the fare cuts by these carriers was related to their cost advantage over the competition. A CAB study comparing airline system costs and controlling for average stage length reveals that the two carriers shown to have had the deepest fare cuts, Southwest and People Express, also had by far the lowest costs.[4] Once adjustments were made for the effect of stage length on cost, Air Florida and PSA had the next largest cost advantage, whereas New York Air and Midway had about average costs. The only exception seems to be New York Air whose fare cuts may have been deeper than their cost characteristics would suggest. It should be noted, however, that the CAB compared costs on an ASM basis. Thus, to the extent the entrepreneurial carriers have higher load factors than the established carriers, their cost advantage per RPM may have been greater than the CAB data indicated.

New Entrant Route Strategies

The route strategies of the new entrants were strongly influenced by their fare and equipment strategies. A low-fare strategy is most effective if fares are low enough to attract considerable attention so as to establish an identity in the marketplace and thus lessen required expenditures on advertising, promotion, and so forth. Keeping costs and fares low also usually required keeping load factors high. Thus the low-fare new entrants concentrated on medium- or high-density markets between large hubs or connecting large hubs to medium hubs.

The new entrants also emphasized short- and medium-haul markets. Most of their flight segments were less than 500 miles, with very few over 750 miles, reflecting among other considerations the range limitations of the twin-engine jets available in the used aircraft market. The new entrants were further discouraged from entering longer-haul markets by the excess capacity in long-haul wide-body aircraft owned or operated by the trunks. A clear symptom of this excess wide-body capacity was the frequency and intensity of the fare wars in long-haul markets, particularly transcontinental markets.

The new entrants' emphasis on low fares and no-frills service generally attracted a higher proportion of nonbusiness travel than was typical for the established trunk and local service airlines. Indeed, in medium- and high-density markets, low fares could often stimulate enough additional nonbusiness travel to allow new entrants to achieve acceptable load factors without diverting substantial business traffic from established carriers.

Satellite or secondary reliever airports also commonly played a major role in the operations of the new entrant carriers. As intrastate carriers, PSA and Southwest emphasized the use of satellite airports in large hub cities and thus turned quite naturally to secondary airports in San Francisco, Los Angeles, Dallas, and Houston from which they expanded their routes after deregulation. Midway, as mentioned earlier, used Midway Airport in Chicago for its hub instead of the more popular and more congested O'Hare. Similarly People Express based its operations in Newark rather than La Guardia. Again, with the exception of Air Florida, the new entrants also operated outside the conventional airline networks by not interlining with established jet carriers. Most new entrants had interline agreements only with commuter carriers that could provide feed traffic and were not competitors. And of course the absence of interline agreements was less of an inconvenience in secondary airports where connection opportunities with other carriers were limited at best.

Types of Route Structure

Route networks can be classified as being of four general types: (1) turnaround, (2) single hub, (3) multiple hub, and (4) independent markets. In a turnaround route structure a carrier simply flies to a city, turns around, and flies back. The service is aimed at travelers whose original and final destinations are the two cities involved, rather than passengers who wish to connect to onward flights. Both PSA and Southwest started as predominantly turnaround carriers but evolved into operating more complex route systems. Turnaround markets can also play an important role in the route structures of the trunks, as the Eastern Air Shuttle illustrates, because they greatly simplify scheduling and operating procedures and facilitate achievement of high daily aircraft utilization. A major disadvantage of course is that a turnaround route offers a very limited service and thus may appeal to only a small fraction of the total market. For this reason turnaround jet operations are usually restricted to very dense markets between large metropolitan areas.

A single-hub network is the simplest application of the hub and spoke approach (as pioneered by trunks such as Delta and Eastern in Atlanta and United in Chicago). A hub operation can attract not only passengers whose final destination is the hub but also passengers traveling to another city (e.g., via a connecting flight at the hub or on the same flight continuing on through the hub to other locales). Most travelers prefer single-plane service to connections and, failing that, online connections to interline connections. A hub and spoke system with many flights converging on a single hub at the same time and with flights continuing on through the hub to other places will offer attractive service to a wide number of passengers. Midway, People Express, and New York Air have all become predominantly single-hub carriers. A single-hub operation may also incorporate turnaround flights on dense spokes or overflights between two cities also served through the hub. New York Air, for example, offered nonstop turnaround service between Boston and Washington, and it also offered connecting service through its hub at La Guardia.

A multiple-hub system, such as those of PSA and Southwest, operates on the same principle as a single-hub system. Southwest, for example, uses both Love Field (Dallas) and Hobby Airport (Houston) as hubs.

Characteristic of multiple-hub systems, Southwest also offers frequent service between its two hubs.

An independent market system characterized Air Florida's domestic network of jet routes. Air Florida treated its markets as largely separate entities and made little, if any, effort to link these markets. The distinction between independent markets and turnaround markets is that independent markets are served infrequently as part of multistop flight itineraries, whereas turnaround markets are served with frequent nonstop flight itineraries.

Route Structure Development

Analysis of how the new carriers have developed their route strategies can be divided into two time periods, pre- and post-PATCO strike. In this chapter only the pre-PATCO period is examined. The post-PATCO period is considered in chapter 9 as part of a general analysis of the effects of airport congestion.

Midway not only took its name from its hub at Chicago's Midway Airport but used that single hub as either an origin, destination, or intermediate stop for every flight. In 1981, about 70 percent of Midway's flights were turnaround flights, with the remaining 30 percent flowing through Midway Airport to offer single-plane, one-stop service between two spoke cities. Midway had interline agreements only with commuter carriers. Service was mostly to large hubs and some medium hubs. As of January 1, 1982, the cities served to the east were Boston, Detroit, Cleveland, Philadelphia, Washington's National, and New York's La Guardia; to the west the carrier served Kansas City, St. Louis, Omaha, and Minneapolis–St. Paul; to the south the carrier served Tampa.[5]

People Express has also operated out of a single hub, Newark Airport. Newark has been relatively uncongested, especially compared to La Guardia, while still offering good access to New York City; Newark also offers low-cost terminal facilities. Although Newark has some connecting possibilities, People Express had no interline agreements with established jet carriers. As with Midway, People Express has used its single hub intensively, with, at first, every flight originating, terminating, or making an intermediate stop at Newark. People Express has also served a mixture of large and medium hubs, with 50 percent of its flights (as of July 1, 1981) operating between two spoke cities as one-stop flights through Newark and the remainder as turnarounds. People Express tried and withdrew from service to Cleveland and Indianapolis, but otherwise its coverage of cities has expanded steadily. By January 1,

1982, People Express had begun to overfly its hub and provide limited nonstop service between two spoke cities (e.g., Columbus to Palm Beach and Buffalo to Sarasota). People Express also represented the extreme in no-frills service, charging extra for checked baggage, food, and beverage service—but reflecting this lack of frills, as seen previously, in exceptionally low fares.

New York Air has differed from Midway and People Express as a single-hub carrier in that its single hub, La Guardia, is in no sense a secondary airport. La Guardia offers excellent access to New York City, but it is also heavily utilized by other carriers and suffers from frequent congestion delays (see chapter 9). New York Air has therefore overflown La Guardia with service from Boston to Washington and offered service from Washington to Newark. New York Air has also competed head to head with established carriers in several of its major markets. Prior to PATCO it competed with the Eastern Air Shuttle in both Boston–La Guardia and La Guardia–Washington, with both Delta and Eastern in Boston–Washington, and with United from La Guardia to Cleveland. Of New York Air's flights involving La Guardia as of July 1, 1981, 60 percent were turnaround and 40 percent were single-plane through flights (usually involving Boston at one end and one of New York Air's other spoke cities at the other). New York Air had interline agreements only with commuter carriers.

Pacific Southwest Airlines (PSA), when deregulation began, had a well-developed network of service to California points with hubs at secondary airports in both San Francisco and Los Angeles. In San Francisco, PSA served both the San Francisco and Oakland Airports; in Los Angeles, PSA served Los Angeles International, Burbank, and Ontario. Thus PSA used both primary and secondary airports in these cities with the secondary airports serving as connecting hubs and the primary airports as destinations.

Prior to deregulation PSA had been excluded from serving non-California points. With the passage of the Airline Deregulation Act PSA moved immediately into service beyond the boundaries of California. The airline did so with great care, however, using a strategy of linking its new points to several of its California cities. The first move was into Reno, Nevada, where nonstop service was initiated to its Oakland hub and with the plane continuing as a one-stop flight to either San Diego or Burbank. PSA subsequently linked Reno to other California cities, replacing the one-stop Burbank service with nonstop Ontario service and adding service to San Francisco. PSA followed a similar pattern with Phoenix, Las Vegas, Salt Lake City, linking them first with nonstop service to one of its existing California hubs and one-stop service to several other California points. PSA typically followed up with nonstop links to other California points for its new non-California cities. PSA moreover did not establish any nonstop service among any of its new non-California points but remained closely tied to its California bases.

PSA has altered the specific links of its new and out-of-state destinations to California cities with surprising frequency, apparently experimenting to find the most productive patterns. PSA thus served its system—both California and non-California—with a mixture of nonstop and multistop flights averaging 0.3 intermediate stop per flight as of July 1, 1981. As a point of contrast, United Airlines had a domestic system average of 0.7 intermediate stop per flight and Delta Airlines had an average of 0.9. PSA has also operated with high flight frequencies and high station utilization with an average of 18.3 weekday departures per station as of July 1, 1981; again, as a point of comparison, the corresponding values for United and Delta were 15.4 and 19.1, respectively.

Southwest Airlines, confined to intrastate Texas markets prior to deregulation, also moved quickly into interstate service after passage of the Airline Deregulation Act. Southwest followed a pattern of service extensions that was similar to PSA's. The first move was into New Orleans, which was linked to the Texas network with nonstop service to Houston; one-stop service to Dallas, San Antonio, Austin, and Lubbock; and two-stop service to El Paso. Southwest used a similar pattern in extending service to Tulsa and Oklahoma City. In all cases Southwest would link the new city to either its hub at Dallas's Love Field or its hub at Houston's Hobby Airport with nonstop service, and to the other hub and other Texas cities via one-stop or multistop single-plane service. As the market developed over time, Southwest would often replace one-stop service with nonstop service, thus overflying the hub on some flights. Southwest used a mixture of nonstop and multistop flights with a system average of 0.5 intermediate stop per flight as of July 1, 1981. At that time Southwest operated with very high average frequencies and intense station utilization with average weekday departures per station of 23.6—higher than any trunk or local service airline.

The three route strategies of turnaround, single hub, and multiple hubs represent evolutionary steps in a carrier's growth and development. In starting up, a new entrant may begin with turnaround service to one or two cities from its chosen base of operations. As the traffic builds and additional aircraft are acquired, routes will usually be added from the base to additional cities. At some point the carrier will begin to schedule flights from the spoke cities to arrive at the base or hub at about the same time to facilitate online connections; the carrier will then effectively operate a single-hub network.

When a large number of connecting passengers develop between a specific pair of cities, a carrier's response is to route aircraft from one city through the hub and on to the second city, thereby providing one-stop single-plane service within the hub and spoke system (instead of only connecting service). If sufficient traffic develops on the one-stop service, the first departure from a hub and spoke system is usually simply to bypass (or overfly) the hub and offer nonstop service between the two cities.

As expansion continues, a second hub may be developed. As of January 1, 1982, only PSA and Southwest had established multiple hubs, but it would not be surprising to see other successful new entrants eventually establish additional hubs.

The new entrants' route strategies and tactics have also shown that many airline markets have two basic characteristics essential for contestability. The first, easy entry, has been amply demonstrated by the rapid expansion of the new entrants into new city-pair markets following deregulation. The second necessary characteristic is easy exit, as high exit cost can deter entry. As People Express, New York Air, and PSA have shown, the costs of exiting an airline market are not prohibitively high and can be borne even by an airline in its early stages.

The growth and expansion of the route networks of the new carriers has raised a concern in some circles that the integrity of the interline system may be threatened. One of the great virtues of the interline system of the established jet carriers is the ease with which a passenger can plan and execute a complicated trip involving flights on several carriers. Such a trip can be planned with a single reservation and taken with a single ticket incorporating such conveniences as automatic baggage transfers. Although the convenience of such arrangements is undeniable, the costs of the interline system are spread across the tickets of all travelers, whether or not they make use of these features. The new entrants have lowered their costs in part by avoiding interline agreements. To the extent that new entrants are successful in driving established carriers from some city-pair markets, passengers may lose the option of easily arranging trips involving these city pairs as links in more complex trips, though at some saving in fares paid.

While participating in interline agreements with established carriers and making more use of primary airports might increase the appeal of new entrant carriers to some passengers, such steps would also increase costs and fares, thus blurring the distinction between new entrants and the established carriers. It is not at all obvious that such moves would be in the new entrants' interests. Moreover, if and as new entrant route networks grow, the disadvantage to passengers of not having interline agreements with other carriers would diminish, since the new entrants would themselves serve a broader range of destinations.

Established Carriers' Responses to the New Entrants

Entry by one of the new carriers into a market has usually provoked some sort of a response by the incumbent carriers. The specific responses have differed depending on the market and the incumbent, but one or more of three strategies has generally been used: (1) introducing a new matching low-fare category, (2) adjusting the range of an existing fare category, and (3) streamlining the fare offerings.

The most common response by incumbent carriers to new low-fare competition has been to add a capacity-controlled discount fare that matched the fare of the new entrants. Eastern Airlines, for example, introduced a supercoach fare at the same level as People Express's standard fare in the Boston–Newark market. Texas International added a jet thrift category to match Southwest's fare in the New Orleans–Houston market, while Braniff added an off-peak fare on the same route. All of Midway's major competitors in the Chicago–Washington market added supercoach fares to match Midway's fares, even though their service was to O'Hare rather than Midway Airport.

Carriers that already offered capacity-controlled discount fares in a newly entered market have often extended the range of the discount to include the new entrant's fare. Occasionally, an incumbent carrier would respond by altering its standard coach fare, but it was far more common for the changes to be confined to discount fares. Sometimes these responses have been used in combination. For example, Western Airlines, competing with PSA in the Los Angeles–Las Vegas market, increased its coach fare, added a first-class fare, and added a jet thrift fare that matched PSA.

Finally, several incumbent carriers have streamlined their fare and service offerings by dropping fare categories when confronted by competition from new entrants. Braniff, for example, eliminated first-class fares and service in Dallas–Tulsa and Dallas–Oklahoma City when faced with competition from Southwest. Similarly, Republic-West eliminated its business coach fare and retained only standard coach and discount fares in the Los Angeles–Las Vegas and San Francisco–Las Vegas markets when these were entered by PSA.

The common thread in virtually all of the incumbent responses to the new entrant carriers has been to counter with some kind of capacity-controlled fare that allowed sufficient flexibility for the incumbent to match the new fare with a minimum dilution of existing fares. With capacity controls, the incumbents have attempted to offer only as many seats at the low fare as necessary to counter the new entrant. An incumbent also need not offer the same number of discount-fare seats on every flight but can alter the number of seats on a seasonal, daily, or even hourly basis, depending on demand and the offerings of the new entrant. Indeed, carriers with a sophisticated computerized reservation system could even alter the number of seats on an individual flight basis, perhaps even making fewer discount seats available on a particular flight in response to a higher than normal number of advance full-fare bookings, and vice versa.

Both the low-fare entry by new carriers and the incumbents' response of lowering fares have provoked occasional claims of predatory pricing. Identifying predatory pricing in practice is difficult in any industry, and perhaps particularly so in the case of airlines.[6] One suggested definition is that a price is *potentially* predatory if it is set below the firm's own short-run marginal cost, or where those costs are not observable, below average variable or short-run average cost.[7] However, such prices might not always be deemed predatory if, for example, learning curve or scale economies were present, or if higher load factors were expected to reduce costs in the near future and lower current prices were needed to develop the market. Some would also take a broader view by suggesting that average total costs or long-run marginal costs be considered as well.[8]

Neither the fares of the new entrants nor the responding fares of the established carriers seem to have been below short-run marginal costs. The relationship between some of these fares and short-run average variable cost or long-run marginal cost is less clear, however. Such comparisons are complicated by large differences in the cost structures of the carriers and in the nature and amount of service provided and by rapidly changing prices of the factors of production. Moreover the issue of predatory pricing has arisen as often in discussions of competition among established carriers (e.g., Braniff and American) as in examining competition involving new entrants. Still the introduction of price competition in the airline industry accompanied by substantial variations in fares makes predation an issue likely to persist in response to continued growth of low-cost airlines. Unfortunately, an accurate assessment of the claims of predation would seem impossible with publicly available data.

The combination of the low fares of the new entrants and the established carriers' response has markedly reduced average fares in markets served by new entrants. A study by Graham, Kaplan, and Sibley found that average fares in markets served by new entrants were 19 percent lower than otherwise comparable markets in 1980 and 26 percent lower in 1981.[9] The larger effect in 1981 was the result of both increased market share of the new entrants and the fare response of the incumbent established carriers.

Although the most direct response of the established carriers to the new entrants has been greater use of capacity-controlled discounts, a more subtle response, and potentially more important from the standpoint of assessing the competitive potential of airline markets, is the pressure placed on the established carriers to reduce their costs. Most of this pressure has come from the realization that with deregulation very low fares based on very low costs are no longer confined to the intrastate markets of Texas and California and are certain to spread eventually to many or even most markets.

The new entrants' emphasis on low fares based on low costs has thus provided an important check on the fares the established carriers have been able to charge in short- to medium-haul markets. Through the end of 1982, of course, the effect of the new entrants on the practices of the established carriers has been limited by air traffic control restrictions in the aftermath of the PATCO strike, by the recession, and by the small size of the new entrant carriers in relation to the rest of the industry. However, the new entrants have grown rapidly since deregulation and have proved profitable despite PATCO and the 1980 and 1981–82 recessions (at least relative to the established carriers).

The limited number of markets served by the new entrant carriers has led to some fare distortions. Examples abound of two markets of similar length and density but with widely different fares because one has been "blessed" by a new entrant's presence whereas the other has not. These situations may be regretable from the point of view of communities without a new entrant, but they are unlikely to persist over time. Not only are new entrants likely to grow and expand; but as established carriers lower their costs in response to new entrant pressures, they will likely keep their fares down even in markets without new entrants so as not to attract new entrant attention.

Some Concluding Observations

The new entrant and former intrastate carriers have featured low fares as their primary means of exploiting their cost advantage over incumbent carriers. Most of the low-fare jet carriers seem to have evolved into a hub and spoke route strategy, with the post-deregulation new entrants operating mainly out of a single hub and the former intrastates, PSA and Southwest, out of multiple hubs. New entrant jet carrier routes have also been concentrated in short- to medium-haul markets of medium to high density. Finally, the new carriers have made extensive use of secondary airports as their bases of operation. The use of secondary airports and the general pressure to keep costs low in pursuit of low fares have allowed the new entrant jet carriers to operate largely independent of the trunk and local service carriers and to maintain interlining agreements with commuter carriers only.

An important unresolved issue is the eventual share of the air transportation market that the new entrant carriers will garner. The cost advantage of the new entrants will lessen over time as the established carriers bring their costs under better control and otherwise provide more effective competition. Furthermore the new entrants may see their cost advantages wither with age as their work forces acquire seniority and become more expensive. As explained in the next chapter, the new entrants may also find their markets challenged from "below" as commuter carriers grow and develop regional route networks, using their low costs to enter some of the very short-haul markets now served by the new entrants. In short, the new entrant jets' long-term growth may be inhibited as they are "squeezed" from both above and below by increasingly effective competitors, but the industry structure that emerges from that configuration of events (see chapter 11) remains to be determined.

Chapter 8

Competitive Strategies of Commuters
by Clinton V. Oster, Jr., and John Strong

For the new entrant jet carriers, low fares determined their niche in the market and thus drove their route strategies. For commuters, the situation was reversed; the commuters' market niche was largely determined by the routes their aircraft were suited to serve and the choice of routes largely dictated fare policy. Moreover, while new entrant jets purposely avoided interlining and other interaction with the trunk and local service airlines, commuters aggressively sought close relations with established carriers since their primary role was to feed passengers from small communities to the ongoing longer-haul flights of the jet carriers. Thus, though both new entrant jets and commuters shared common entrepreneurial characteristics and low costs relative to trunk and local service carriers, their roles in the air transportation system were much different, and their competitive strategies differed accordingly.

The long-term influence of the commuters and new entrant jets on the competitive structure of the industry may not, however, be all that different. Both, in the long run, can and probably will pose competitive threats to the established carriers, albeit from somewhat different departure points. Indeed, as seen in the previous chapter, the new jet carriers constitute a direct and immediate competitive challenge to the established carriers. By contrast, though the commuters initially offer feeder services complementary to the large airlines, as they grow and become better established, they could move "up scale" into services more directly competitive with the established airlines, especially the local service carriers on short- to medium-length and medium-density routes. Under the contestability doctrine, in fact, this plausible possibility could be enough to discipline some established carriers' competitive practices.

Since the dominant strategic choice for commuters has been which routes to serve, this chapter begins with an examination of commuter route policies. The chapter then turns to the subject of commuter fares and the concern that since most commuter markets are served by a

Table 8.1 New routes as a source of growth (48 contiguous state operations)

	1976–78[a]	1978–80[b]
Base-year passengers on original routes	4,341,648	5,015,934
End-year passengers on original routes	5,562,726	5,399,387
End-year passengers on new routes	1,078,824	1,919,114
Total annual growth rate	23.7%	20.8%
Original route annual growth rate	13.2%	3.8%
New routes as a percent of total growth	46.9%	83.3%

Source: Derived from CAB Form 298, Schedule T-1.
a. Based on carriers operating under Part 298 exemption for four quarters in both 1976 and 1978.
b. Based on carriers operating under Part 298 exemption for four quarters in both 1978 and 1980.

single carrier, excessive fares may be charged in certain monopoly situations.

Patterns of Commuter Growth

The most striking feature of commuter airline development has been the heavy reliance placed on new markets and new routes as a source of growth in enplanements. As can be seen in table 8.1, between 1976 and 1978 commuter enplanements (in the 48 contiguous states for carriers operating during the entire period) increased 23.7 percent per year. Growth on those routes served in 1976, however, was only 13.2 percent per year. Thus new routes accounted for almost half—46.9 percent—of the growth for these carriers.

Between 1978 and 1980 new routes played an even larger role in commuter growth. As the rate of total airline traffic growth began to slow because of recession and increasing fuel prices, growth on those commuter routes served in 1978 dropped to 3.8 percent per year. Because of new routes, however, total growth remained high at 20.8 percent per year, with new routes accounting for 83.3 percent of total growth.

The apparent increased reliance on new routes after deregulation was due both to opportunities presented by deregulation and other factors. As certificated carriers began to withdraw from small communities, commuters were able to enter these markets as replacements. As seen in chapter 4, though these low-density markets were typically unprofitable for the large jets of the certificated carriers, commuters with smaller aircraft could often establish profitable service. Still other markets were entered by the commuters as an indirect result of the traffic downturn in late 1979 and early 1980. As traffic declined, some commuters found that their existing routes could be adequately served with fewer aircraft. Aircraft released by such service reductions, coupled with deliveries of new aircraft ordered prior to the recession, made it easy, perhaps even necessary, to seek new markets.

Examining route changes in an industry with over 200 participants serving over 500 airports is a formidable task. Fortunately the analysis can be simplified, without too much loss of insight, by focusing on the largest carriers and those for which data are readily available: specifically, 38 of the largest 40 commuters in the 48 contiguous states in 1980.[1] During 1980 these 38 carriers carried 80 percent of commuter passengers enplaned in the 48 states. Generally, these 38 carriers also included the most profitable and successful airlines in the industry.

As a group these airlines experienced a high rate of growth in both number of markets served and passengers carried. Between 1976 and 1980 the number of markets served grew at an annual rate of 22.2 percent, while passengers carried increased at the almost identical rate of 22.8 percent. During the first half of the period (1976 to 1978) passengers increased at a faster rate than markets, whereas in the second half (1978 to 1980) markets increased at a faster rate than passengers. This pattern suggests that some of the route expansion in the latter period may have been with aircraft made available by slower than expected traffic growth on existing routes.

Table 8.2 shows how service by these 38 large commuters were distributed among city-pair markets by hub size in 1976, 1978, and 1980.[2] As shown, their operations were concentrated in markets involving nonhubs. A most important trend, however, is the decline in relative importance of nonhub markets. Between 1976 and 1980 the share of markets involving nonhubs dropped from 87.2 to 75.6 percent. This drop was the result of large declines in the relative share of nonhub markets involving large hubs and other nonhubs whereas those markets involving small hubs and medium hubs increased in share.

Despite the sharp drops in nonhub–nonhub and nonhub–large-hub markets, these nevertheless remained the two most prevalent types of markets for commuters. Moreover, although these markets declined in relative importance, they nevertheless increased in absolute numbers.

Table 8.2 Percent distribution of city-pair markets (38 large commuters in contiguous 48 states)

	1976	1978	1980
Nonhub–nonhub	26.4	27.4	19.3
Nonhub–small hub	12.4	11.7	14.3
Nonhub–medium hub	13.1	15.4	16.4
Nonhub–large hub	35.3	31.8	25.6
Small hub–small hub	1.2	1.0	2.0
Small hub–medium hub	2.5	2.7	5.1
Small hub–large hub	4.4	4.9	7.5
Medium hub–medium hub	0.2	0.5	2.4
Medium hub–large hub	2.9	3.0	4.9
Large hub–large hub	1.7	1.6	2.4

Source: Derived from CAB Form 298, Schedule T-1, and CAB Form 41, table 10.

Commuters were thus not abandoning their traditional markets as much as they were expanding into other types of markets at a much faster rate. While nonhubs and large hubs were decreasing in relative importance between 1976 and 1980, small hubs were increasing their share from 20.5 to 28.9 percent, and medium hubs were increasing their share from 18.7 to 28.8 percent.

Table 8.3 displays the percent distribution of passengers (enplanements) by market type. The reason for the decline in relative importance of nonhub–nonhub markets becomes clear when these data are compared with the market distributions shown in table 8.2. While nonhub–nonhub markets represented 26.4 percent of the markets served in 1976, they accounted for only 2.1 percent of the passengers enplaned. Obviously, these markets were not very productive, enplaning an average of just over 10 passengers per week. By contrast, nonhub–small-hub markets and nonhub–medium-hub markets enplaned just over 35 and 62 passengers per week, respectively. The commuter airlines thus had an incentive to shift priority to denser markets, especially as they took delivery of newly available and larger 30- and 50-seat aircraft.

The shift in the relative importance of nonhubs compared to small and medium hubs is also apparent in table 8.3. Between 1976 and 1980 the share of passengers enplaned in markets involving nonhubs declined from 83.2 percent to 70.5 percent, whereas the shares in small and medium hubs increased from 12.5 to 21.1 percent and from 10.9 to 16.2 percent, respectively.

Table 8.3 Percent distribution of passengers by market type (38 large commuters in contiguous 48 states)

	1976	1978	1980
Nonhub–nonhub	2.1	1.6	0.7
Nonhub–small hub	3.4	3.5	2.7
Nonhub–medium hub	6.4	7.5	8.0
Nonhub–large hub	71.3	67.4	59.1
Small hub–small hub	0.6	0.4	0.3
Small hub–medium hub	2.1	2.6	2.8
Small hub–large hub	6.4	8.7	15.3
Medium hub–medium hub	*	*	0.3
Medium hub–large hub	2.4	3.0	5.1
Larbe hub–large hub	5.2	5.3	5.7

Source: Derived from CAB Form 298, Schedule T-1, and CAB Form 41, table 10.
Note: An asterisk appears where the value is less than 0.05.

Commuters' reliance on feeding passengers to connecting airlines is evident in the very high share of passengers in nonhub–large-hub markets. This traditional role has declined in relative importance, although the number of passengers in these markets increased throughout the period. New market opportunities and a decreasing reliance on the traditional feeder role might have been expected as a result of deregulation, and indeed, such a trend did accelerate after 1978. But as can be observed in the tables, these trends were well underway during the two years before deregulation as well.

A move by the commuters to longer hauls is another trend apparent both before and after deregulation. The share of commuter markets with a nonstop distance of 150 miles or more increased from 41.8 percent in 1976 to 55.8 percent in 1980. Similarly, the share of passengers carried in these longer hauls increased from 26 percent in 1976 to 36.9 percent in 1980. Even in 1980, however, these 38 commuters remained predominantly short-haul carriers with only 14.4 percent of their markets, enplaning only 2.1 percent of their passengers, involving distances of 300 miles or longer.

Terminations as a Source of Growth

The opportunities presented by deregulation for commuters to fill in for terminating jet carriers have certainly stimulated commuter growth, but assessing the magnitude of the contribution to growth is at best tenuous. In some cases the termination simply opened up a market to a commuter it would not otherwise have served. In other instances a commuter may have served the terminated point for several years before deregulation, on occasion competing head to head with the terminating certificated carrier but more often serving different markets out of the same point. In still other cases, although one trunk or local service airline withdrew from serving a community, others remained, still providing jet service.

Many terminations moreover have no potential to influence commuter traffic. For example, when Allegheny (now USAir) transferred points to Allegheny commuters prior to deregulation, those points usually remained on Allegheny's certificates even though service was no longer provided by Allegheny itself. After deregulation USAir removed those points from its certificates, but those terminations had no effect on commuter growth since the points continued to be served by the same commuter carriers. Besides these Allegheny commuter points, there were 23 airports "terminated" after deregulation where the terminating carrier was not providing service at the end of 1978 because service had previously been suspended. In addition there were three other locations where no commuters entered following termination because another established jet carrier entered the market. Obviously any changes in traffic carried by commuters in these situations could not be reasonably attributed to deregulation. With these cases excluded, there were 70 nonhubs where commuters provided service after a termination by a trunk or local service airline. Of these 70 points, 42 had service by one or more of the top 38 commuters.

In estimating the contribution of terminations to commuter traffic, all traffic from that point was attributed to a termination if the commuter entered the "terminated market" any time after late 1978. The entry was considered to have been "termination induced" even if it was prior to the certificated carrier formally filing with the CAB.[3] In those cases where a commuter served the market prior to late 1978, any increase in the commuter's traffic after the termination seems attributable to the termination.

About 27 percent of the growth in the number of city-pair markets served between 1978 and 1980 by commuter airlines was termination induced.[4] In other words, slightly over one-quarter of the new markets served by these carriers were entered in response to the termination in a nonhub by a trunk or local service airline. In terms of passengers carried, about 23 percent of the growth in enplanements between 1978 and 1980 can be attributed to deregulation in the form of terminations.

In total about 7.5 percent of the total passengers carried by these commuters in 1980 was apparently the result of terminations.

These figures, though, probably overstate the contribution of terminations to commuter growth. The commuter airlines would have used the aircraft assigned to termination-induced markets to add frequencies in markets already served, to enter other new markets, or in some instances to compete head to head with certificated carriers. Any of these courses of action would have given commuters some growth in enplanements, although probably less than actually achieved under deregulation.

The size distribution of termination-induced city-pair markets is much more uniform than the distribution of all markets for these carriers. Nonhub-nonhub markets account for 33 percent of termination-induced markets, whereas nonhub–small-hub, nonhub–medium-hub, and nonhub–large-hub markets account for 22, 23, and 22 percent, respectively. Indeed, without terminations, nonhub–nonhub markets would have declined as a share of the commuters' market even more dramatically than they did and would have actually fallen in absolute numbers. It appears that terminated nonhubs were often incorporated into commuter route networks as part of multistop flight itineraries. The share of nonhub–large-hub markets would have held about the same had there been no terminations, although obviously the number of those markets would have been smaller. Terminations added significantly to growth in the share of nonhub–small-hub and nonhub–medium-hub markets. In the case of nonhub–medium hub, almost all of the increase in share is attributable to terminations.

Commuter Route Strategies
Individual commuter airlines pursued varied route development strategies, ranging from simple turnaround service in one or two markets to much more complex route patterns covering broad geographic areas. The essential differences in route strategies can be summarized by examining three basic characteristics of commuter route networks: (1) percentage of passengers in large-hub markets, (2) daily aircraft departures per station, and (3) intermediate stops per flight itinerary.

Table 8.4 shows the 1980 values for these three characteristics and the changes in those values since 1976 for three groups of carriers: (1) the Allegheny Commuter System, (2) those non-Allegheny top 38 commuters that are predominantly large-hub oriented, and (3) the remaining top 38 commuters. The top line in the table reports the percent of

Table 8.4 Characteristics of commuter route networks, 1980

	Allegheny commuters	Large-hub oriented	Non-large-hub oriented
Percent passengers in large-hub markets	99%	91.4%	24.9%
Change from 1976	0	− 0.5	+10.6
Departures per station	19.9	11.4	9.1
Change from 1976	+ 7.0	+ 1.5	+ 2.7
Intermediate stops per flight	0.5	0.5	1.2
Change from 1976	− 0.2	− 0.3	+ 0.03

Sources: CAB Form 298, CAB Form 41, and *Official Airline Guide.*

passengers carried to or from large hubs—the basis for dividing the carriers into large-hub oriented and non-large-hub oriented. Of the 29 non-Allegheny commuters in the sample of 38 top commuters, 22 had a percentage of passengers in large-hub markets greater than 75, while the remaining 7 all had fewer than 43 percent of large-hub passengers.[5]

Even the seven carriers that were not large-hub oriented did, though, serve one or more large hubs. On average these non-large-hub-oriented carriers each served 1.7 large hubs, whereas the large-hub-oriented carriers served an average of 2.4 large hubs each. The Allegheny commuters and the large-hub-oriented commuters have changed very little since 1976 in terms of hub orientation, whereas the remaining carriers have substantially increased their large-hub orientation.

The third line in table 8.4 contains the average weekday aircraft departures per station in 1980 for each of the three groups of carriers, and on the fourth line is shown the change in this measure since 1976. The Allegheny Commuter System had the most departures per station, with the large-hub-oriented carriers somewhat lower and the remaining carriers lowest of all. But all three groups recorded increases in departures per station between 1976 and 1980. A high value of departures per station would indicate that a carrier was better able to spread station costs, which are largely fixed, over a greater number of flights. Higher departures per station also would be preferred because of the traffic stimulation often made possible by higher flight frequencies, as reported in chapter 3.

Although the large-hub-oriented carriers have more departures per station on average than those that are not large-hub oriented, the averages conceal considerable variation within each group. Although most large-hub-oriented carriers had more than 10 weekday departures per station, 3 carriers (with more than 94 percent of their passengers in large-hub markets) had fewer than 7 weekday departures per station. Similarly, although 6 of the 7 carriers who were not oriented toward large-hub service had fewer than 9 weekday departures per station, the seventh carrier, Cascade, had over 17 weekday departures per station. Thus, although the tendency of the two groups is quite clear, several carriers stand out as exceptions.

The final two lines in table 8.4 report the average intermediate stops per flight and the change in this since 1976. Since a low value is associated with a high proportion of nonstop flights, and passengers typically prefer nonstop flights to multistop flights, lower values are usually associated with better service. As would be expected, the Allegheny Commuter System and the large-hub-oriented carriers had many fewer average intermediate stops per flight than did those carriers that were not large-hub oriented. The large-hub markets are typically higher-density markets, and in such markets the aircraft can more easily be filled to acceptable load factors with nonstop service. In low-density markets, by contrast, stops at several small communities may be needed to collect enough passengers to achieve break-even or profitable load factors.

Competition among Commuters
The majority of markets served by commuter carriers are served by a single carrier (since they do not have sufficient traffic to support competitive service). Commuters have expanded most frequently by entering markets previously without service or recently exited by certificated jet carriers. As the industry has grown, however, commuters have increasingly found that expansion brings them into competition with other commuters and thus an increase has occurred in the number of city-pair markets in which two or more commuters provide competitive service.

Figure 8.1 shows the growth in competitive commuter markets between 1976 and 1980. Because of data limitations the figure is based on a very narrow definition of commuters.[6] Thus the figure understates, possibly to a significant degree, the number of competitive markets, with the understatement becoming greater in 1980. Even with this understatement a strikingly rapid growth in competitive markets has happened since 1977; specifically, between 1977 and 1979 the total number of competitive markets almost tripled.[7]

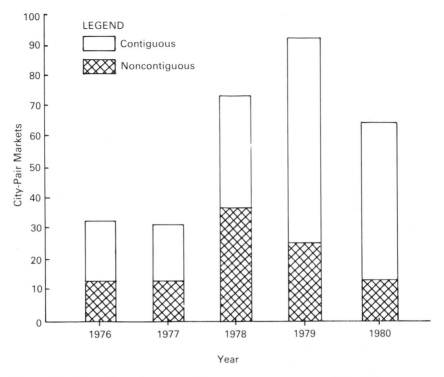

Figure 8.1 City-pair markets served by two or more commuters (Part 298 commuters only). Source: CAB Form 298.

As also shown in figure 8.1, the growth in competitive markets has been most rapid in the contiguous 48 states. The growth in competitive markets parallels to some extent the growth in passenger enplanements. Commuter markets in the noncontiguous regions and states developed earlier and are more mature; thus the proportion of these markets that are competitive is probably greater, and so their recent growth in competition has been less. In the contiguous 48 states, on the other hand, many commuter airlines are still rapidly expanding their geographic coverage. The typical pattern in the contiguous area was a competitive battle for a market, with one carrier eventually dropping out, whereas in the noncontiguous areas it was more often the case of two or more carriers sharing a market throughout the period. On average 58 percent of the competitive markets in the noncontiguous area remained competitive throughout the period examined, whereas only 45 percent remained competitive in the contiguous 48 state area.

As might be expected, the markets in which commuters competed tended to be denser than the average commuter market. For example, in 1976, 81 percent of competitive markets involved a large hub whereas only 44 percent of all commuter markets involved a large hub. The trends in the mix of competitive markets are similar to the trends in the mix of total markets. Nonhub–large-hub markets—the single most important market in both cases—were declining in relative importance between 1976 and 1980. Markets involving small and medium hubs were becoming relatively more important, both in competitive markets and in total.

Although some commuters clearly aspire to become regional and, perhaps, following an earlier pattern of Local Service Airlines (LSAs), jet carriers, others recognize the substantial and potentially profitable market for short-haul low-density feeder service. Since deregulation, moreover, conditions have been far different from those when the LSAs began feeder service. When the LSAs were formed, CAB policies made becoming an LSA the only way to enter into certificated scheduled service. That the LSAs would use feeder service as a stepping-stone to achieving "larger ambitions" was therefore not surprising, as no other possibility was available. Since deregulation, however, carriers wishing to enter into point-to-point jet service can do so directly, as the new entrant jets have demonstrated. Thus, although the route policies of many current commuters parallel the early development of the local service airlines in the move to nonstop service in more dense markets using larger aircraft, the commuter industry is unlikely to follow closely in the footsteps of the LSAs.

Commuter Airline Fares

To study commuter fare policies, a sample of 50 commuter airlines operating in the 48 contiguous states was selected.[8] The sample included a broad cross section of the industry and was evenly distributed both geographically and with regard to size of operations. These 50 airlines carried over 8.4 million passengers in 1979, which represented about 75 percent of contiguous 48 state commuter airline enplanements.

To examine the relationship between flight length and fare, the standard one-way coach fare as listed in the August 1, 1980, *OAG* was plotted against distance for each of the 694 nonstop markets served by these 50 carriers. The analysis was confined to nonstop flights, the most prevalent form of commuter service. The standard coach fare was used because, unlike the established jet airlines, commuters have not made widespread use of discount fares.[9]

Figure 8.2 shows the composite plot of these standard commuter coach fares against distance. The SIFL is included in the figure as a point of reference. Two aspects of the plot are of particular interest. First, for flights longer than about 80 miles, fares seem to increase uniformly with distance. Second, for very short flights, particularly those under 60 miles, there is a distinct falling off of fares, apparently in response to potential competition from the automobile. Indeed, in field interviews several commuter carriers commented that fare increases in very short markets had not kept pace with rising costs, as measured by changes in the SIFL, because auto competition effectively imposed a fare ceiling.

Comparisons with Major Airlines
Figure 8.3 presents a plot of actual fares against fares calculated using the SIFL formula. If actual fares were equal to those under the SIFL formula, the points would lie along the line marked "SIFL" in the figure. The "130 percent of SIFL" line provides a measure of what local service carriers have traditionally been permitted by the CAB to charge in similar markets.

As seen in the figure, most commuter fares in the sample fall between 100 and 130 percent of SIFL. Those few markets where fares were found to be significantly less than the SIFL were generally characterized by substantial competition (e.g., from the automobile in very short-haul markets or from jet carriers or other commuters in longer-distance markets). Specifically, although 55 percent of the airline markets in the sample were served by a single carrier, in those markets where commuter fares were lower than the SIFL fare, only 47 percent were in single-carrier markets. Conversely, of those fares that exceeded 130 percent of the SIFL-based fare, 65 percent were in single-carrier markets.

Commuters sometimes compete head to head with jet carriers (usually local service airlines) in low- to medium-density short-haul markets. In a sample of markets served by both jet and commuter carriers, the commuter's fare was lower than the certificated carriers' fare in 56 percent of the markets and equal in another 9 percent. In these markets, fares for the jet carriers tended to be at or very close to 130 percent of the SIFL. As seen in chapter 4, jets are poorly suited to low-density short-haul service. Using smaller aircraft better tailored to the size of the market gives commuters an opportunity to provide higher fre-

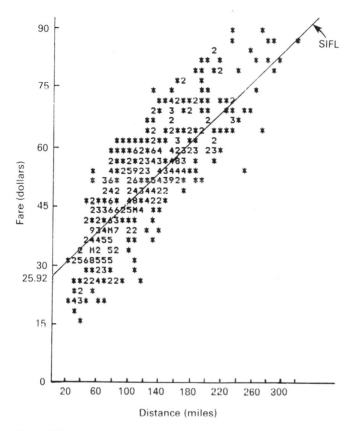

Figure 8.2   Commuter fares vs. distance. (Note: Numbers give total observations at that point; *M* indicates more than nine observations.)

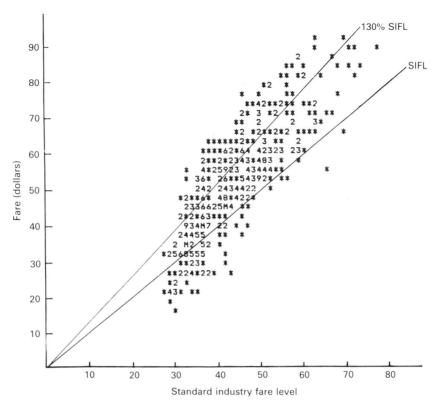

Figure 8.3 Commuter fares vs. SIFL (130 percent SIFL). (Note: Numbers give total observations at that point; *M* indicates more than nine observations.)

quencies and a cost advantage that frequently can be translated into lower fares. Since, all else equal, passengers usually prefer larger and more comfortable jets, lower commuter fares may be necessary to induce passengers to select commuters when both are available. In markets where commuter fares were equal to or higher than the jet fares, the commuters seemingly attracted passengers with more frequent and more conveniently scheduled service.

Replacement Service
Opponents of deregulation have asserted that commuter replacement service generally has been rendered at substantially higher fares than the prior jet airline service. To assess this claim, a sample of 120 city-pair markets where replacement service has occurred was investigated. The sample was evenly divided between commuter replacement of a

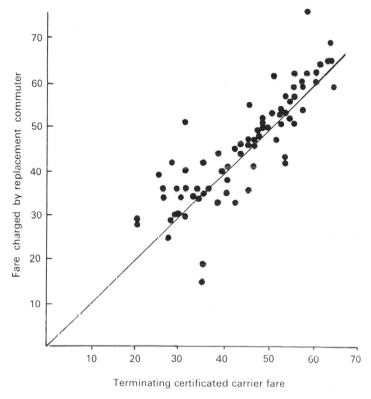

Figure 8.4   Commuter replacement service fare levels

certificated carrier and replacement of another commuter. The fare of
the original carrier for the six-month period prior to termination of
service was compared with the fare charged by the new commuter
carrier.

The previous fare was found to be closely related to the replacement
fares. For those commuters replacing local service carriers, as seen in
figure 8.4, approximately two-thirds charged the same fare as the departing local service carriers. Only 25 percent of commuter replacements
charged higher fares, with the average premium being 15 percent.

Where one commuter replaced another, however, replacement fares
were higher in slightly over 80 percent of the cases. Presumably a
commuter leaving a market generally did so because it was unable to
make money in the market. Under these conditions it is not surprising
that most replacement commuters, with similar costs, would raise fares.

Moreover raising fares in these situations probably made sense, given both the limited fare response observed in the demand analyses of chapter 3 and the recognition by many travelers that the previous commuter with lower fares had been unable to sustain service.

To evaluate the possibility that initially low fares quoted by replacement carriers were later supplanted by much higher fares, commuter replacement fares were compared not just to the last fare charged by the carrier terminating service but to what that fare would have been had it increased to keep pace with changes in the SIFL. Mainly because of fuel cost increases the SIFL rose almost 25 percent between May 1979 and January 1980. During this period fare increases in replacement markets tended to follow increases in the SIFL closely. There was little evidence of any widespread tendency to boost fares dramatically above cost increases.[10]

In the analysis changes in fares between June 1, 1979, and July 15, 1981, were tracked in a sample of 150 commuter markets served by 30 different commuter carriers. The sample included both competitive and monopoly markets, and considerable variation in frequency, stage length, and market type. Commuter fares closely tracked the SIFL adjustment over time, with the dates of commuter fare increases closely matching the effective dates of SIFL increases. In 98 markets (65 percent) fare increases were within 10 percent of the SIFL increase. Another 17 (11 percent) were within 15 percent of the SIFL hike. Those markets where fare increases deviated from the SIFL changes were characterized by changes in the commuter carrier providing service, or by substantial competition from other carriers or from the automobile.

To examine these pricing decisions more closely, all nonstop markets served continuously between June 1, 1979, and July 15, 1981, by a sample of 15 commuters were also analyzed. Nine of the 15 carriers appeared to follow the SIFL increases quite closely while the others followed only the trend of raising fares in response to increasing costs. Again, several of the exceptions, where fare increases were observed to be less than the SIFL increases, were in very short-haul markets where the auto was a particularly viable competitor or in competitive multicarrier markets.

In general, commuters seemingly tied their fare changes to changes in the SIFL and thus to industrywide fare changes, possibly muting consumer resistance. By linking fare changes to SIFL changes, commuters (many of whom lack detailed cost-accounting systems) were also able to keep their fares roughly in line with rapidly changing costs.

The major driving force behind CAB changes to SIFL was the rapidly increasing cost of fuel. Although commuters' cost structures differ from those of jet carriers, commuters were also affected by fuel price increases and, as seen in chapter 4, in a manner not too dissimilar to the jet carriers. Thus, although mirroring SIFL changes may not have been a perfect means of keeping commuter fares in line with changing costs, it had the virtue of being simple, reasonably accurate, and widely followed.

Discount Fares

An important aspect of the early experience with deregulation among the major carriers was widespread use of capacity-controlled discount fares. The commuter industry has not had a parallel experience although a few commuter carriers have offered discounts for military personnel, elderly, clergy, and the like.

Discount fares may, though, become an increasingly important aspect of commuter operations. Because of deregulation commuters can use larger aircraft. Whenever larger planes have been put into service by the commuters, the number and proportion of leisure travelers has typically increased, an observation consistent with the plane size demand elasticity reported in chapter 3. With a greater proportion of price-sensitive travelers flying commuter airlines, the opportunities to stimulate demand via selective discounts may also increase.

Some commuters are also decreasing their historic reliance on feeder markets and moving into point-to-point markets—those markets serving the passenger's origin and final destination. As this happens, commuter discounts should have a larger impact on the total cost of a trip and thus have a greater potential to stimulate traffic.

Several commuter carriers have in fact undertaken interesting experiments in fare discounting. Metro Airlines in Houston introduced off-peak discounts to fill some of the extra seats in its high-frequency operation. Mississippi Valley Airlines initiated 50 percent fare discounts on its Tuesday and Saturday flights, which had previously operated with low load factors. Ransome Airlines of Philadelphia initiated service to Washington, D.C., with a low, one-month inaugural fare to help develop the market. The post-deregulation period has also seen the development of "SuperSaver" commuter fares, as some commuters have adopted pricing discounts pioneered by the major airlines.

The potential importance of discount fares for commuters should not be overstated, however, as business and connecting travel is still most of the industry's bread and butter. Only in a few specialized vacation markets do business travelers not predominate. It is hardly surprising therefore that commuters have not rushed headlong into discounting and have generally avoided fare wars.

Joint Fares

Since about 70 percent of commuter passengers connect to other flights, joint fares comprise a substantial portion of commuter carrier revenues. The effect of joint fares is to lower the cost of a commuter flight for a connecting passenger. Thus the existence and precise nature of joint fares can influence both passenger volumes and profitability.

Commuter carriers were not included in the initial mandatory joint fare program developed in Phase 4 of the *Domestic Passenger Fare Investigation* (*DPFI*) during 1973–74. Under Phase 4 the CAB estimated that the cost of an airline transporting a passenger between cities A and C, with a connection at an intermediate city B, was less than the sum of the local fares between A and B and B and C. This cost saving, the terminal charge, was deducted from the sum of the local fares to establish the joint fare between A and C.[11] The maximum joint fare was to be the sum of the lowest, unrestricted coach fare minus a SIFL terminal charge for each connection. The CAB required that joint fares be established by trunk and local service carriers for all connecting routes generating at least 50 origin and destination passengers each year. First class and discount fares were exempt from the program.

Under the Airline Deregulation Act the commuter carriers could be included in the CAB's joint fare program, if they so wished. Most commuter carriers have chosen to do so. The joint fare program was scheduled under the deregulation act to expire along with all CAB rate-making authority at the end of 1983. Following that, commuters will again have to negotiate joint fares individually with the major carriers, as many did prior to deregulation.

Joint fares have their largest effect on commuters in short-haul markets. To evaluate how substantial these effects might be, several representative markets were selected to survey the range of fare reductions resulting from fares; the results are shown in table 8.5. The markets selected reflect a diversity of commuter markets linked with one long-haul jet route (2,050 miles from Chicago to Los Angeles, one medium-haul jet route (Atlanta–Dallas, 800 miles), and one short-haul jet route (Chicago–Pittsburgh, 450 miles).

The "effective commuter fare," as shown in the far right column of table 8.5, can be derived by subtracting the full jet fare (for the line haul) from the joint fare. In all the markets surveyed this effective commuter fare is substantially lower than the full commuter fare. The size of the reduction is related to the length of the connecting jet flight: "effective" commuter connecting fares averaged 53 percent below the standard commuter fares in the Chicago–Los Angeles market, compared to an average 38 percent decrease for commuter fares in the Atlanta–Dallas market and a 32 percent average reduction in the Chicago–Pittsburgh market. The inclusion of commuter carriers in the joint fare system has thus resulted in effective fare decreases of one-third to one-half for many commuters on connecting flights.

The Regional Airline Association of America (RAAA) has argued that air service to small communities is highly dependent on connecting traffic utilizing joint fares. Without mandatory joint fares, according to the RAAA, commuter carriers will be forced to increase local fares to maintain existing revenues and service levels. The result is that "the combination of higher fares, reduced traffic, and reduced revenues will clearly make many commuter services, which are marginal to begin with, uneconomic, leading to their elimination."[12]

If joint fares have had a significant impact on commuter operations, a shift in growth patterns due to joint fares should be evident.[13] All else equal, the "effective" price reduction in joint fares should lead to an increase in the percentage of commuter passengers that make connections. Data from the CAB indicate, however, that the growth in connecting traffic was *lower* in 1979 (after joint fares) than it was in 1978 (before joint fares). Analysis of individual markets does, though, show substantial variation. Thus joint fares may have had an important impact on some individual commuter carriers.

Another major aspect of the joint fare program, and the source of considerable disagreement between most major airlines and the RAAA, is how joint fare revenues are divided between carriers. Setting joint fares on the basis of SIFL coach fares, but allocating joint fare revenues on a cost formula, has the potential to drive a wedge between the price reduction faced by connecting passengers and the revenues received by the commuter carriers. For example, from Lafayette, Indiana to Phoenix via Chicago the institution of joint fares effectively resulted in a 30 percent fare decrease from $53 to $37 for the passenger on the Lafayette–Chicago leg of the trip. Using the cost prorate formula, however, the carrier received revenues of roughly $68 from $269 joint

Table 8.5 Joint fare comparisons for selected markets, August 1, 1980

Markets	Full commuter fare	Full jet fare	Total full fare	Joint fare	Effective commuter fare (joint fare less full jet fare)
Chicago (CHI) to Los Angeles (LA)					
Akron–CHI–LA	$86	$280	$366	$306	$26
Appleton, WI–CHI–LA	61	280	341	308	28
Battle Creek–CHI–LA	56	280	336	310	30
Bloomington, IN–CHI–LA	67	280	347	322	42
Burlington, IA–CHI–LA	62	280	342	308	28
Champaign–CHI–LA	66	280	346	280–308	0–28
Decatur–CHI–LA	58	280	336	280–308	0–28
Elkhart–CHI–LA	50	280	330	308	28
Flint–CHI–LA	67	280	347	339	59
Ft. Wayne–CHI–LA	53	280	333	310	30
Grand Rapids–CHI–LA	50	280	330	282	2
Kalamazoo–CHI–LA	60	280	340	310–339	30–59
Lafayette, IN–CHI–LA	53	280	333	308	28
Muncie–CHI–LA	53	280	342	317	37
South Bend–CHI–LA	41	280	321	280–308	0–28
Terre Haute–CHI–LA	65	280	345	308	28

Atlanta (ATL) to Dallas (DAL)

Charleston–ATL–DAL	72	139	211	171	32
Charlotte–ATL–DAL	66	139	205	176	37
Columbus, GA–ATL–DAL	45	139	184	156	17
Dothan, AL–ATL–DAL	79	139	218	191	52
Fayetteville, NC–ATL–DAL	97	139	236	200–209	61–70
Greenville–ATL–DAL	53	139	192	177	38
Savannah–ATL–DAL	65	139	204	182	43
Valdosta, GA–ATL–DAL	87	139	226	212	73

Chicago (CHI) to Pittsburgh (PIT)

Appleton–CHI–PIT	61	93	154	139	46
Bloomington, IL–CHI–PIT	67	93	160	129	36
Burlington, IA–CHI–PIT	62	93	155	139	46
Champaign–CHI–PIT	66	93	159	130	37
Danville, IL–CHI–PIT	60	93	153	120	27
Dubuque–CHI–PIT	56	93	149	137	44
La Crosse–CHI–PIT	73	93	166	153	60
Madison–CHI–PIT	47	93	140	124	31

Table 8.5 (continued)

Markets	Full commuter fare	Full jet fare	Total full fare	Joint fare	Effective commuter fare (joint fare less full jet fare)
Springfield, IL–CHI–PIT	55	93	148	137	44
Wausau–CHI–PIT	79	93	172	150	57

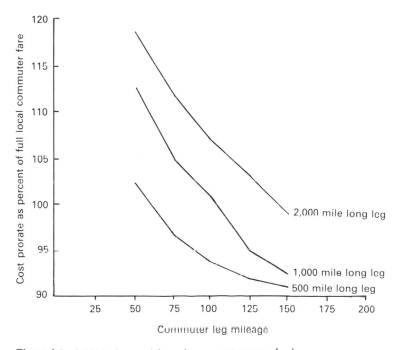

Figure 8.5 Commuter joint fare shares: cost prorate basis

fare—$15 *more* than the $53 full local fare at the time. Thus the commuter carrier benefited in two ways: from lower fares to stimulate passenger volume and from higher revenues than it otherwise would have received.

To analyze the extent of the potential wedge between commuter revenues and effective commuter fares, a sample of commuter markets between 50 and 150 miles and long-haul jet markets of roughly 500, 1,000, and 2,000 miles was examined. The results are presented in figure 8.5 The horizontal axis shows commuter stage length. The vertical axis reflects the average revenue a commuter carrier would receive under the cost prorate formula for each short-haul/long-haul mileage combination, as a percentage of full standard commuter fares. The shorter the commuter leg and the longer the certificated carrier leg, the higher the proportion of the local fare the commuter carrier receives. For a typical commuter flight of about 100 miles, and a jet connection of 1,000 miles, the commuter share is about equal to its local fare. For shorter hauls the commuters receive revenues greater than full local fares, except when the connecting jet leg is short.

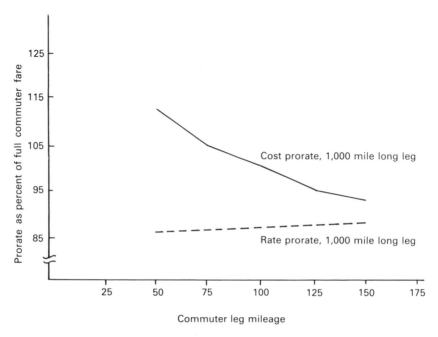

Figure 8.6 Computer joint fare shares: cost prorate vs. rate prorate

The CAB has permitted voluntary agreements between airlines to allocate joint fare revenues on other than a cost prorate basis. A number of major carriers have moved in fact to a rate prorate scheme in which joint fare revenues are divided in the same proportions as the separate fares. For the commuter carriers a rate prorate typically results in lower revenues than the cost-based scheme. For example, the Lafayette–Chicago carrier would receive only $50 under a rate prorate compared to $68 under the cost formula. Figure 8.6 shows commuter joint fare shares under both schemes for a 1,000 mile jet connection. The rate prorate is lower at all points, and it never provides revenue in excess of the full local commuter fare.

A public policy of eliminating mandatory joint fares assumes that the marketplace will be competitive enough to sort out the true value of joint fares. A key unresolved question is thus whether there will be enough commuters and jet carriers in the relevant markets to ensure this competitive result.

Summary

Commuter airlines have grown rapidly since the mid-1970s, with the most striking feature of that growth being the heavy reliance placed on serving new routes, both before and after deregulation. New routes accounted for almost 47 percent of growth in enplanements between 1976 and 1978 and for over 83 percent of growth between 1978 and 1980. Commuter growth since deregulation has been helped by the increased opportunities for commuters to provide replacement service for terminating trunk and local service airlines. About 23 percent of commuter growth between 1978 and 1980 can be attributed to terminations by certificated carriers, and by 1980 about 7.5 percent of total commuter passengers were the result of these terminations.

As commuters have grown, they have also shifted to new and different markets, moving into higher-density markets and particularly those involving small hubs and medium hubs. Despite this shift in emphasis the traditional commuter focus on feeding passengers from nonhubs to large hubs to connect with other flights has not diminished in absolute terms and remains the single most important commuter market. Much of the growth, however, has been in point to point markets involving small and medium hubs, a trend that was evident before deregulation and has no doubt been helped by increased availability of 30-passenger aircraft and the post-deregulation freedom to fly up to 60-seat aircraft. Commuter growth has also been accompanied by a sharp increase in competition, with the number of competitive markets almost tripling between 1977 and 1979.

Commuter fares have generally been bounded from below by the SIFL and from above by 130 percent of the SIFL. In markets under 60 miles, however, the auto has been an important competitor, often pulling air fares significantly below the SIFL. Where commuters have competed head to head with a trunk or local service carrier, they also have usually charged lower fares. Commuter fares were found to be noticeably higher in monopoly markets; on the other hand, markets served by more than one commuter carrier often had fares below the SIFL. Changes in the SIFL also have apparently acted as signals for fare increases; commuter fare changes have tracked the SIFL increases fairly closely both in magnitude and timing. Although discount fares have not been widely used by commuters, some tendency toward increased use of discounts and capacity-controlled fares is discernible, as increased use of larger aircraft has attracted more discretionary travel.

In a larger perspective the commuter airlines have clearly established themselves as an important element in the domestic commercial airline system. The commuters' importance resides not so much in the quantity of their activities—say measured by enplanements or passenger miles— but rather in their ability to meet a specific system requirement of serving small communities at a reasonable cost. Maintenance of small community service was a major worry prior to deregulation, reflecting a traditional American public policy concern with "knitting the federation together." The commuters have not only met this system need but also inject an additional competitive check into airline markets. Specifically, the commuters can contest not only each others' markets but, with ever larger planes and greater financial strength, can more and more contest low-density short-haul markets that might otherwise be largely protected from competition.

Part IV

PUBLIC POLICY ISSUES

Chapter 9

Airport Congestion and New Entrant Access
by Don H. Pickrell

The rapidly growing levels of air traffic and congestion at the nation's largest airports during the mid-1970s raised important questions about the ability of the domestic air transportation system to adapt to deregulation. The largest worry was whether air traffic congestion would increase dramatically as carriers took advantage of the route entry provisions offered by deregulation to increase the number of flights scheduled at already busy major airports. A related question was whether widespread air traffic congestion—combined with insufficient ground or terminal area capacity for the handling of aircraft, passengers, and baggage—would effectively preclude access to some airports by new carriers, thus threatening the success of deregulation as a competitive initiative.

In this chapter airport delay trends beginning several years prior to deregulation are analyzed in an attempt to assess how air carriers' subsequent responses affected air traffic and congestion throughout the U.S. airport system. The focus is on the effect of deregulation on air traffic and delays at major airports, and the issue of access for new entrants at congested airports. The chapter concludes with some observations on the special or unique effects of the air traffic controllers' action of August 1981 and its aftermath.

Air Traffic Congestion and Delays since Deregulation

Deregulation affected passenger volumes primarily by allowing carriers to offer discount fares that apparently increased total passenger volumes, all else equal, by approximately 15 percent.[1] Yet, by increasing passenger loads on scheduled flights, carriers were able to accommodate this increase in passenger travel without scheduling many additional flights at major airports. As table 9.1 indicates, by increasing both the density of seating on available aircraft and the load factor, certificated airlines were able to increase the number of passengers carried per flight by

Table 9.1 Increases in load factors and passengers per flight: certificated air carriers

Year	Average seats per flight[a]	Average load factor (%)[b]	Average passengers per flight[c]
1971	107.1	48.5	51.9
1972	114.7	52.4	60.1
1973	120.8	52.2	63.1
1974	125.3	55.9	70.0
1975	129.2	55.0	71.1
1976	133.5	56.2	75.0
1977	136.3	56.4	76.9
1978	139.2	61.3	85.3
1979	141.2	62.9	88.8
1980	145.0	58.1	84.2
Annual growth rate			
Pre-1977	3.6	1.7	5.3
1977–1979	1.8	5.6	7.5

a. Computed from available seat miles (ASM) divided by plane miles for domestic operations of trunk and local service carriers. Source: CAB Form 41 data.
b. Computed from revenue passenger miles (RPM) divided by available seat miles (ASM) for domestic operations of trunk and local service carriers. Source: CAB Form 41 data.
c. Computed from average seats per flight multiplied by decimal equivalent of load factor.

over 15 percent between 1977, the point marking the CAB's initial relaxation of fare regulation, and 1979.

Table 9.2 shows recent trends in air carrier operations and delays at all commercial airports, all large hubs, and the 10 busiest commercial airports. Clearly both systemwide commercial air traffic and activity at large hubs grew slightly faster immediately after deregulation than in the period preceding it. At the 10 busiest commercial airports, air traffic grew more slowly throughout the entire period, although operations at these very large airports rose slightly during 1980, in contrast to the modest decline at other commercial airports. Table 9.2 also indicates that delays in scheduled air carrier operations are concentrated at a small number of major airports.[2] As few as 10 airports consistently have accounted for over 80 percent of all delays recorded throughout the national airport system, even prior to deregulation, while the other 17 large hub airports account for virtually all remaining delays. These 10 airports are also major air traffic hubs, accommodating about a third of all nationwide commercial air traffic.

Table 9.2   Growth in air traffic operations and delays, 1974–1980

Year	All commercial airports[a]		FAA-designated large hubs[b]		Ten largest commercial airports[c]	
	Operations[d]	Delays[e]	Operations[d]	Delays[e]	Operations[d]	Delays[e]
1974	9,476,535	—	5,063,792	—	3,033,413	—
1975	9,343,958	31,672	5,219,417	31,072	2,868,298	24,846
1976	9,300,526	36,196	5,270,215	35,596	3,036,151	27,682
1977	9,751,791	39,063	5,563,790	38,498	3,200,664	28,750
1978	10,046,699	52,239	5,764,870	51,370	3,313,246	33,941
1979	10,349,332	61,598	6,035,878	60,509	3,381,118	43,553
1980	10,069,277	57,554	5,977,652	57,120	3,406,519	48,085
Percent change						
1974–77	2.9	23.3[f]	9.9	23.8[f]	5.5	15.7[f]
1977–80	3.3	47.4	7.4	48.4	6.4	67.1

a. Includes all airports classified by the FAA as "air commerce airports."
b. Includes those airports at which 1 percent or more of all passengers are enplaned.
c. Ranked by total commercial air carrier operations.
d. Source: FAA, "FAA-Operated Airport Traffic Control Towers by Rank Order of Air Carrier Operations," *Air Traffic Activity Report*, various years, table 7.
e. Delay of 30 minutes or more to arriving and departing aircraft as recorded by the National Air Space Communications System, Federal Aviation Administration.
f. Percent change for 1975 to 1977 only.

Although delays increased fairly rapidly during the last years of regulation, their growth has accelerated markedly since that time, as table 9.2 shows: after rising over 23 percent from 1975 to 1977, total delays rose almost 60 percent during the first two years following deregulation. At the 10 busiest commercial airports, this pattern was exaggerated somewhat: delays grew less rapidly than for the system as a whole prior to 1977 but have risen considerably faster since then. One possible explanation for this acceleration in the growth of delays is that even slight volume increases at major airports already operating near their capacities could produce substantial increases in aircraft queuing and delays.

If this is the case, the four major airports historically subject to FAA quotas (New York's Kennedy and La Guardia, Washington's National, and Chicago's O'Hare), which recorded nearly two-thirds of all delays during the years preceding deregulation, might have been particularly affected. Yet, as table 9.3 indicates, traffic at these airports has consistently declined since the beginning of deregulation, and by 1980 delays there were only about 20 percent above their pre-deregulation level. At the same time, because of the rapid growth elsewhere in the

Table 9.3 Operations and delays at FAA quota airports

Year	Air carrier operations[a]	Percent of all operations	Delays[b]	Percent of all delays
1974	1,358,290	14.3	—	—
1975	1,322,046	14.1	20,154	67.0
1976	1,282,051	13.8	22,799	65.0
1977	1,363,596	14.0	22,103	57.0
1978	1,352,085	13.5	28,330	54.0
1979	1,311,027	12.7	25,989	42.0
1980	1,241,413	12.3	26,390	46.0
Percent change				
1974–77	0.4		9.7[c]	
1977–80	−9.0		19.4	

Note: Includes Chicago-O'Hare, New York-Kennedy, New York-La Guardia, and Washington-National Airports. Landing and takeoff entitlements are limited by the FAA and allocated among carriers by negotiation.
a. Source: FAA, *Air Traffic Activity Report*, various years.
b. Source: Supplied by National Air Space Communications System, Federal Aviation Administration.
c. Percent change for 1975 to 1977 only.

system, delays at these historical problem airports have fallen from two-thirds to well under half of all those recorded.

Thus major airports not subject to administrative controls apparently became new focal points of air traffic and congestion after deregulation. These airports can be roughly classified as either destination points, which handle predominantly passengers originating and terminating trips there, or transfer hubs, which handle large numbers of connecting passengers in addition to those originating or destined there. Destination points are primarily major cities on the nation's perimeter, particularly its east and west coasts, where passengers originating or terminating trips commonly represent two-thirds or more of the total. By comparison, each of the four major regional transfer hubs—Atlanta, Chicago, Dallas–Fort Worth, and Denver—actually handles more connecting passengers than those originating or destined there. In addition each region has at least one secondary transfer hub, which typically handles one-third to one-half connecting passengers; examples of these include Pittsburgh, St. Louis, and Kansas City.[3]

Table 9.4 reports recent trends in operations and delays at the nation's large airports, grouped according to this functional classification. The most pronounced change in operations growth has been at the major

Table 9.4   Distribution of operations and delays at large hubs

| Year | Air carrier operations[a] | | | |
	Major hubs	Secondary hubs	Destinations	Total
1974	1,317,654	794,039	2,952,099	5,063,792
1975	1,480,970	807,819	2,930,628	5,219,417
1976	1,462,571	809,296	2,998,348	5,270,215
1977	1,590,900	850,663	3,122,227	5,563,790
1978	1,663,014	889,035	3,212,827	5,764,870
1979	1,746,286	981,117	3,308,465	6,035,868
1980	1,786,554	958,808	3,232,290	5,977,652
Percent change				
1974–77	20.7	7.1	5.8	9.9
1977–80	12.3	12.7	3.5	7.4

| Year | Aircraft delays[b] | | | |
	Major hubs	Secondary hubs	Destinations	Total
1975	13,812	1,072	16,188	31,072
1976	12,082	1,282	22,232	35,596
1977	14,738	1,679	22,081	38,498
1978	23,594	2,325	25,451	51,370
1979	28,053	3,694	28,762	60,509
1980	26,285	2,431	28,404	57,120
Percent change				
1975–77	6.7	56.6	36.4	23.9
1977–80	78.3	44.8	28.7	48.4

Note: Twenty-seven large-hub airports classified by function according to mix of originating and connecting passengers reported in FAA, *Airport Activity Statistics*, 1979, table 1. Major hubs are those with more than 50 percent of enplanements representing connecting passengers, and include Chicago-O'Hare, Atlanta, Dallas–Ft. Worth, and Denver. Secondary hubs are those with 33 to 50 percent of enplanements representing connecting passengers; they include St. Louis, Pittsburgh, Minneapolis–St. Paul, Memphis, Kansas City, and Las Vegas. Destinations are those with less than 33 percent connecting passengers, and include Los Angeles, Miami, San Francisco, New York-Kennedy, New York-La Guardia, Washington-National, Boston, Houston-Intercontinental, Detroit, Seattle, Honolulu, Cleveland, Tampa, Philadelphia, Newark, Phoenix, and New Orleans.
a. Source: FAA, *Air Traffic Activity Report*, various years.
b. Source: National Air Space Communications System, Federal Aviation Administration.

regional transfer hubs, where traffic has grown only about half as rapidly since 1977 as during preceding years. A similar pattern is evident at destination airports, although their growth rates both before and since deregulation are less than one-third those at the major transfer hubs. The secondary hubs, by contrast, have had considerably more rapid growth in traffic since deregulation began than during the immediately preceding years.

Changes in the distribution of aircraft delays among these airport types have been even more pronounced than those in air traffic levels, as table 9.4 also indicates. The most striking development is the growth of congestion at major transfer hubs; there, delays nearly doubled in the first two years of deregulated operations, followed by a modest decline in 1980. While delays at the secondary hubs varied considerably over the period, their overall growth rates immediately before and after the start of deregulation were closely comparable. At destination airports, delays have continued to grow fairly rapidly since the onset of deregulation, although at a somewhat slower rate than during the immediately preceding years.

It is difficult to reconcile the continued rapid growth of delays since deregulation began with the slowing of operations growth that has ensued. In addition to the overall volume of traffic, another important determinant of the level of congestion and the number of resulting delays is the extent to which arrivals and departures are bunched within a relatively few hours of the day. Queuing of aircraft and delays can occur if the frequency with which aircraft arrive or depart even temporarily exceeds the rate at which they can be accommodated. What seems most likely is that scheduled operations during certain hours at some airports were nearing their respective capacities prior to deregulation, so that even the modest traffic growth since then has produced longer peak-hour takeoff and landing queues, and thus sharp increases in delays recorded.[4]

Because of the competitive pressures introduced by deregulation, airlines have faced strong incentives to coordinate their flight schedules at major hubs, in an effort to minimize passenger layover times. Deregulation may thus have acted indirectly through its effect on route structure to increase peak-hour operating volumes at some transfer hub airports. Table 9.5 reports changes in two measures of the time pattern of air traffic activity at large hub airports: average operations during the busiest single hour of the day and the ratio of busiest hour operations to average hourly operations. The former measure indicates

Table 9.5   Peaking at large-hub airports

Year	Busiest hour operations			
	Major hubs	Secondary hubs	Destinations	Total
1974	385	266	921	1,572
1975	361	269	826	1,456
1976	405	266	893	1,564
1977	440	297	893	1,630
1978	413	296	935	1,644
1979	469	328	958	1,755
1980	491	296	863	1,650
Percent change				
1974–77	14.3	11.7	−3.0	3.7
1977–80	11.5	− 0.3	−3.4	0.4

Year	Ratio of busiest hour operations/average hour operations			
	Major hubs	Secondary hubs	Destinations	Total
1974	2.3	3.0	2.5	2.5
1975	2.1	2.9	2.5	2.4
1976	2.4	2.9	2.6	2.6
1977	2.4	3.0	2.5	2.6
1978	2.2	2.9	2.6	2.5
1979	2.4	2.9	2.5	2.5
1980	2.4	2.7	2.3	2.4

Source: FAA, *Terminal Area Traffic Relationships*, various years.

how total peak utilization of airport capacity has changed; the latter whether an increasing *fraction* of takeoffs and landings is concentrated into a relatively short time period within the day.

By either measure the systemwide degree of daily peaking exhibited by airport operations has not increased markedly since the beginning of deregulation. At the major transfer airports the strengthening of the hub configuration of air carriers' route networks apparently did produce some increase in peak-hour traffic, although total daily traffic has evidently risen at roughly the same rate. At the secondary hub airports peaking would have been expected to increase because of the bunching of flight arrival and departure times produced by scheduling to facilitate flight connections; although peak-hour operations at the five secondary hubs did increase rapidly during the first full year of route freedom, they returned to their earlier levels in 1980. The peaking in traffic associated with the development of hubs probably accounts partly for the pattern of delays at these airports, which also rose sharply from the onset of deregulation through 1979, prior to a substantial decline in 1980. Still, after falling significantly from their 1979 peak, delays at the five secondary hubs were nearly 50 percent above their pre-deregulation level despite the fact that peak-hour operations had returned to their 1977 level, suggesting that factors beyond operations during the single busiest hour also contributed to the growth in delays.

Congestion and Airport Access

These increases in airport traffic congestion—not only in the terminal airspace surrounding major airports but also in the ground handling of aircraft and passengers—may have affected the route development strategies of new and expanding air carriers. From the individual air carrier's perspective traffic congestion in either the terminal airspace or ground facilities for aircraft handling and servicing poses two serious problems: first, delays are costly because they entail nonproductive use of aircraft and flight crew time, and second, delays can impose additional indirect costs by delaying connecting flights, or the subsequent flights to which detained aircraft and crews are assigned. In addition congestion of ground and terminal facilities used in passenger servicing and baggage handling can raise air carriers' operating expenses as well as introduce delays and disruptions of scheduled operations.

Of course airport and airspace congestion and delays impose barriers to competition only insofar as the resulting costs or disruptions are more serious for potential or new users of congested airports than for carriers with established operations there. Because of the first-come, first-served procedure typically employed in both terminal airspace traffic control and ground traffic management, arriving flights that enter the terminal airspace surrounding a busy airport or departing flights taxiing toward the runway area are equally likely to be delayed, regardless of which carrier operates them.[5] Further, with the exception of a relatively few airports where takeoff and landing times are subject to advance reservation, carriers initiating service at congested airports are essentially free to plan arrivals and departures at any hour, with flights scheduled at congested hours no more likely to be delayed than those of established carriers scheduled for the same time.

The expected cost per flight of aircraft delays—actual operating expenses of a typical flight plus an allowance for the cost of the average delay—should be no higher to new or potential entrants than to incumbent carriers. Indeed, added congestion from new entry at an already heavily used airport can be more costly in total to established carriers than to new entrants themselves, since the established carrier is likely to have a larger cumulative number of flights delayed by the increased traffic levels.

A second potential cost disadvantage faced by new carriers attempting to compete with established airlines at heavily used airports can arise if potential entrants face higher costs for access to passenger-boarding gates, baggage-handling services, or related facilities. The primary reason that potential entrants might face higher costs for such facilities is that at some airports, existing ground service capacity is fully leased to incumbent carriers under long-term arrangements. Such (temporary) leasehold "monopolies" can arise because ground service capacity has historically been financed at major airports by proceeds from revenue bonds issued by airport operating authorities, secured partly by revenues from long-term leases on ground facilities agreed to by carriers holding authority to serve those airports prior to the industry's deregulation. Incumbents holding such leases may be reluctant to sublease the use of underutilized facilities to carriers intending to begin competitive service, even at rates reflecting the full opportunity cost they face in reserving facilities for their own operations.

Nevertheless, even if all ground service capacity is fully leased, it seems unlikely that all incumbent carriers would refuse to negotiate subleases for the provision of ground services or facilities with potential entrants. Large carriers with a relatively small presence at particular airports may, for example, have strategic interests in assisting entrants that are likely to provide effective competition for the dominant carriers there. Where entering carriers encounter genuinely anticompetitive actions by established airlines, they will still have both direct appeals to airport operators and conventional legal remedies available to them. Over the longer run, moreover, they can participate directly in financing new additions to airspace and terminal area capacity for use by new or expanding participants. For this variety of reasons, therefore, it seems unlikely that potential entrants will confront widespread protective rental rates or other costly restrictions imposed by established carriers.

Finally, there remains the possibility that new entry into some city-pair markets could be deterred by administrative barriers to competition. Four major U.S. airports (New York's Kennedy and La Guardia Airports, Chicago's O'Hare Airport, and Washington's National Airport) have operated since 1968 under FAA limits on the number of takeoffs

Table 9.6 Quota rules (as of January 1, 1982)

Class of user	Instrument flight rules operations per hour			
	Washington-National	New York-La Guardia	New York-Kennedy	Chicago-O'Hare
Certificated air carrier	37[a]	48	70–80[b]	115
Scheduled air taxi/commuter	11[a]	6	5	10
Other	12	6	5	10
Total	60[c,d]	60[d]	80–90	135[d]
Hours in force	All day	All day	3–8 P.M.	3–8 P.M.

Source: Code of Federal Regulations, Title 14, Part 93, Section K, and subsequent amendments.
a. Effective December 6, 1981.
b. Between 3 and 5 P.M. 70 per hour; between 5 and 9 P.M. 80 per hour.
c. Does not include charter flights or other nonscheduled flights of scheduled or supplemental air carriers.
d. Does not include extra sections of scheduled air carriers.

and landings allowed by aircraft of all types during certain hours of the day. Under the quota system, summarized in table 9.6, air carriers are awarded in advance rights to specific numbers of aircraft operations during each hour for which they are limited, which in effect serve as reservations for takeoffs and landings at those times.[6]

Quotas on aircraft operations at these four airports are implemented by four separate scheduling committees, each made up of representatives of the certificated carriers serving the airport over which it has jurisdiction. Carriers that do not already serve a quota-controlled airport may be represented by observers, who participate actively in each committee's deliberations and can refuse to approve an allocation formulated by the incumbent carriers. Each committee meets twice per year, with carrier's representatives submitting requests in advance for takeoff and landing entitlements, or slots, during each hour that the quota is in effect. These initial requests are subsequently modified, often in several stages, until a final allocation of hourly slots among carriers is approved by unanimous vote of committee members. The trading of slots between carriers, as well as most other forms of explicit bargaining, is specifically prohibited. In the event that a committee cannot unanimously agree on an allocation of the available slots, the FAA retains the authority to impose unilaterally an allocation of its own design.

Under these committee procedures potential entrants have been able to obtain minimal levels of takeoff and landing entitlements, as would be expected under threat of their exercise of veto power over proposed committee slot allocations.[7] Over time the total concession to new carriers should approach incumbent carriers' collective assessment of the allocation that the FAA would impose if the scheduling committee failed to offer a distribution of operating rights agreeable to carriers seeking to begin service to a quota-controlled airport. Thus the slot allocation process is no doubt guided by continuous attempts at strategic assessment of the FAA's intention and capabilities on the part of carriers who now dominate markets involving these four airports.[8]

Table 9.7 summarizes the post-deregulation results of the slot allocation process, including an FAA-imposed allocation at Washington-National Airport during the winter of 1980–81. New entrants have been moderately successful in obtaining slots from the established carriers at the four airports subject to operations quotas, although their success has varied considerably among airports. Virtually all of the slot requests from potential entrants have been submitted by either newly organized certificated carriers or former commuter airlines certificated by the CAB since 1978, rather than by established domestic or foreign carriers seeking to expand operations at airports they served prior to the industry's deregulation.

As the table indicates, more than 80 percent of the slot requests actually granted have been at those airports serving northeast corridor air travel, New York-La Guardia and Washington-National Airports. At the former new applicants have been allocated more than three-quarters of the slots they have requested. Nearly 90 percent of these slots were formerly held by established carriers, and the remainder were created by an expansion of the total number allocated to all carriers. Although the new entrants at National since 1978 have obtained a lower fraction of the slots they have requested (55 percent), they have been allocated nearly as many slots in total as at La Guardia. At Washington-National Airport 90 percent of the slots conceded to new entrants have been transferred from carriers serving the airport prior to deregulation. At each of these two airports, carriers beginning service since the onset of route freedom now hold about 18 percent of the total number of slots allocated to all carriers.

Only at Chicago's O'Hare Airport has the scheduling committee process possibly acted as a significant barrier to new entry. Nevertheless, the table may slightly overstate the extent to which it has done so, because virtually all of the requests for slots by what appear to be new carriers (179 of the total of 185 requests through 1981) have been made

Table 9.7 New carrier slot allocations at FAA quota-controlled airports

	Summer 1978	Winter 1978–79	Summer 1979	Winter 1979–80	Summer 1980	Winter 1980–81	Summer 1981	Net change, 1978–81
New York-La Guardia Airport								
Slots requested by established carriers[a]	754	731	774	714	712	699	700	− 54
Slots allocated to established carriers	735	726	753	716	703	647	616	−119
Slots requested by new and recent entrants[b]	0	0	0	10	40	94	172	172
Slots allocated to new and recent entrants	0	0	0	10	26	88	135	135
Total slots allocated[c]	735	726	753	726	729	735	751	16
Number of new entrants	0	0	0	1	1	3	2	7
Washington-National Airport								
Slots requested by established carriers	626	618	626	636	584	564	601	− 25
Slots allocated to established carriers	618	620	606	594	568	532	525	− 93
Slots requested by new and recent entrants	0	0	28	56	78	142	213	213
Slots allocated to new and recent entrants	0	0	28	42	62	104	107	107
Total slots allocated	618	620	634	636	630	636	632	14
Number of new entrants	0	0	6	1	2	3	1	13
Chicago-O'Hare International Airport								
Slots requested by established carriers	576	581	575	580	571	552	561	− 15
Slots allocated to established carriers	555	557	553	538	537	531	512	− 43
Slost requested by new and recent entrants	0	0	0	31	45	46	63	63
Slots allocated to new and recent entrants	0	0	0	15	14	23	34	34

Total slots allocated	555	557	553	553	551	554	546	—
Number of new entrants	0	0	0	2	0	0	2	9

Source: Tabulated from data supplied by airline scheduling committees.

a. Established carriers are those holding slots during the summer of 1978.

b. New and recent entrants include all carriers obtaining slots since the summer of 1978.

c. Includes only those allocated to scheduled domestic carriers.

by newly certificated commuter air carriers previously operating at O'Hare. These carriers have apparently been required by FAA procedures to obtain slots reserved for certificated air carriers operating large jet aircraft, despite the fact that most newly certificated commuter carriers continue to fly the smaller-sized aircraft (60 or fewer seats) they have historically used.[9] Although established certificated carriers have been understandably reluctant to yield slots for what they view as a simple redefinition of service, the issue has been partially resolved through use by some newly certificated commuter airlines of modest numbers of additional slots obtained on their behalf by major trunk carriers for whom they provide considerable transfer or "feed" traffic.[10] Thus the operation of the quota system has apparently barred competition from new entrants no more, and no less, than general competition among all carriers serving each of the four airports under quota controls.

The PATCO Action and Its Effects on New Carriers

In response to the August 1981 strike by many members of the Professional Air Traffic Controllers Organization (PATCO), the FAA required substantial reductions in flights by certificated air carriers and general aviation pilots at many of the nation's most heavily used airports. These restrictions reduced total aircraft operations during September of 1981 at the 22 airports where they applied to a level about 15 percent below that during September of the previous year. Flight reductions ranged up to 30 percent at Pittsburgh and Chicago-O'Hare Airports, although operations at a few major airports actually increased slightly from their year-earlier levels. The corresponding reduction in available seat departures was only about half as large, because air carriers operated a mix of aircraft having a slightly higher average seating capacity than during the previous year. Because load factors on flights to and from the 22 restricted airports also rose slightly, the number of passengers carried on flights using them fell only about 1 percent from its year-earlier level.[11] By January 1982 total operations at these airports were restored to a level only 4 percent below that of a year earlier, with 10 of the 22 actually experiencing increases in flight frequencies, ranging from less than 1 percent to nearly 14 percent.[12]

The FAA-mandated flight reductions limited the numbers of takeoff and landing entitlements at each of the controlled airports and authorized that agency to allocate them among air carriers. Initially, the FAA required all carriers serving each controlled airport to reduce operations from their September 1981 levels by a percentage equal to the reduction in air traffic control capacity at that airport and prohibited new carriers from beginning service without first being assigned specific takeoff and landing privileges. As would have been expected, there was considerable debate over the proper allocation of increased operations capacity among incumbent airlines and those seeking to begin service to cities having controlled airports, both within the airline industry and the FAA itself.

In May 1982 the FAA approved the exchange, sale, and rental of takeoff and landing "slots" then held by individual air carriers, in effect converting takeoff and landing rights held by incumbent carriers to transferable claims on airport capacity. Amid widespread protests about their propriety, slot sales and rentals were suspended by the FAA after seven weeks, although exchanges continued to be permitted. During this period 194 slots, representing less than 2 percent of all daily capacity at the 22 controlled airports, were sold at prices ranging up to $360,000, while another 120 were exchanged. Overall, about three-quarters of the slot sales apparently resulted in transfers from commuter carriers to major airlines, and about 15 percent of total purchases were made by the newer jet carriers.[1]

The FAA's imposition of operations controls, together with the various measures it adopted to allocate airport capacity among competing users, apparently did produce some changes in the development of several new carriers' route networks. These included pronounced reductions of operations at a few of the controlled airports, interruptions in the previous growth of flight frequencies, and the inauguration or expansion of service to airports not among the 22 subject to operations controls. Table 9.8 summarizes these changes for three of the newer jet-equipped carriers during the first few months following the PATCO action.

In some cases these new carriers were actually able to expand operations at the less intensively utilized airports among the 22 subject to FAA controls, particularly Newark Airport, where both People Express and New York Air increased scheduled flights significantly. Of course these changes probably also reflected carriers' responses to the continued decline in total enplanements over this period, as well as normal cutbacks in scheduled flight frequencies in response to seasonal reductions in travel activity during the fall months. They probably also resulted partly from intentional adjustments of routes and flight frequencies that occurred as carriers gained experience in new markets or redeployed equipment from less successful routes. Hence it is difficult

Table 9.8 Changes in weekly departures by airport category for selected new jet carriers

	Weekly departures		
	7/5/81	11/1/81	Percent change
Midway Airlines			
22 designated large hubs	146	192	32
Reliever airports in designated large-hub cities[a]	185	238	29
Other large hubs[b]	0	14	—
Medium hubs	12	12	0
Total	343	456	33
New York Air			
22 designated large hubs	566	529	−7
Reliever airports in designated large-hub cities	40	54	35
Other large hubs	0	0	—
Medium hubs	19	40	105
Total	625	623	0
People Express			
22 designated large hubs	39	93	138
Reliever airports in designated large-hub cities[c]	195	306	57
Other large hubs	0	0	—
Medium hubs	169	237	40
Total	403	636	58

Source: *Official Airline Guide.*
a. Chicago-Midway Airport.
b. Nondesignated large-hub airports are Seattle–Tacoma, Tampa, Phoenix, New Orleans.
c. New York-Newark Airport.

to assess how much of the reorientation in carrier route networks and service frequencies was actually the product of the FAA's actions, rather than of the adjustment of route structures that new carriers would normally have undertaken as their operations grew and evolved.

Summary

Overall, the changes in air traffic patterns at the nation's major airports following deregulation do not appear to have produced a major surge in air traffic congestion and resulting delays. Although some of the marketing, routing, and scheduling changes made in response to deregulation have probably aggravated demand and capacity imbalances at certain airports, other such changes have probably improved air traffic flows at some congested airports. On balance, deregulation might be responsible for as much as half of the roughly 50 percent increase in total systemwide delays that have occurred during the period of adjustment.

Even if this is an underestimate, the major contribution of deregulation to increased delays would be the accelerated transition toward an intensified hub and spoke configuration of the national route network it prompted. Much of the abrupt growth in delays accompanying this transition would thus represent an acceleration of what would probably have eventually occurred even under the continued regulation of air carriers' routes and fares.

Neither the existence of operation quotas at the four major quota airports nor the mechanisms used to allocate the takeoff and landing rights established by these quotas seem to have effectively prevented new carriers from initiating service. Recognizing their various motivations for avoiding congestion and their use of secondary airports, as well as new carriers' success in obtaining slots at quota airports, it seems unlikely that their route development has been altered critically by any entry-deterring effect of the quotas. Even the controls on carriers imposed by the FAA response to the PATCO strike do not appear to have exerted a disastrous effect on the development of routes by the new jet carriers, partly because of their apparent strategy of avoiding the most congested hubs in favor of secondary airports.

New entrants apparently also benefited from the FAA's reluctance to apply its announced percentage reductions in carrier operations, which ranged up to 60 percent during certain hours at the most congested airports, to carriers operating relatively infrequent flights. Further it appears that beyond the operations cutbacks originally mandated, at least some of the newer carriers were fairly successful in winning approval for flight increases and new station openings at airports other than those 22 airports of most immediate concern to the FAA. Although the new carriers were certainly not immune from the agency's post-strike actions, they appear to have been substantially less affected in their routings and scheduling decisions than were some of the more established carriers.

Chapter 10

Small Community Service and the Role of Federal Subsidy

A principal policy concern prior to airline deregulation was whether easing restrictions on entry and exit would result in reduced service to small communities. Many expected the airlines to redeploy their aircraft away from low-density markets serving small communities to high-density markets, with the result that small communities would have greatly reduced or, in extreme cases, no air service.[1]

In response to these concerns, a provision guaranteeing essential air service to small communities was included in the deregulation act. A so-called Section 419 subsidy was authorized with compensation based on community needs and the use of appropriately sized aircraft. The act also scheduled the eventual end of the previous subsidy program (Section 406 subsidy), which, as seen in chapter 2, had supported small community service prior to deregulation.

The new Section 419 subsidy guaranteed service to a far greater number of communities than had received subsidized air service under the old Section 406 program. Critics of deregulation therefore predicted that the subsidy cost would be much higher than under the old program. Supporters of deregulation argued, however, that since commuter carriers were eligible to provide essential air service under the new program (they had previously been excluded), and that since commuter aircraft were much better suited for small community service, the total subsidy costs would be reduced despite the expanded coverage. In essence, these proponents were arguing that the entrepreneurship unleashed by deregulation would result in a better matching of supply and demand, of operations and equipment with the needs of various communities so that costs would be lowered overall.

This chapter begins with a systemwide analysis of changes in air service to small communities since deregulation. Following this, the implementation of the Section 419 subsidy program is examined, and the subsidy costs of this new program are compared with the costs of the previous Section 406 program. Finally, there is a discussion of potential problems with the new program and how it may distort commuter management incentives.

Table 10.1 Changes in weekly aircraft departures and seat departures

Airport size	Percent change in airport departures	Percent change in seat departures
June 1, 1978, to June 1, 1981		
All airports	9.0	2.6
Large hubs	12.4	5.8
Medium hubs	19.0	6.9
Small hubs	− 1.1	− 8.4
Nonhubs	− 0.1	−12.9
June 1, 1981, to June 1, 1982		
All airports	− 3.5	2.4
Large hubs	− 5.9	1.7
Medium hubs	4.7	9.3
Small hubs	2.8	1.6
Nonhubs	− 8.5	− 7.5

Airline Service to Small Communities

The top portion of table 10.1 summarizes the percent changes in both weekly aircraft departures and weekly seat departures between June 1, 1978, and June 1, 1981; these data thus reflect post-deregulation trends prior to the PATCO strike. The bottom portion of the table summarizes the changes between June 1, 1981, and June 1, 1982, and thus reflects PATCO influences as well.

Comparing the same week for different years controls for seasonal variations in airline service patterns. Total aircraft departures for all sizes of airports rose 9.0 percent during the 1978 to 1981 (or pre-PATCO strike) period. Substantial gains were observed at both large hubs and medium hubs, while small hubs lost slightly, and nonhubs were essentially unchanged. The gains were much larger and more widespread during the first year of deregulation, but subsequent fuel price increases followed by the onset of economic recession severely dampened airline demand, resulting in cutbacks of flights to all size communities.[2] Apparently, though, during this period from mid-1978 to mid-1981 the number of seats per aircraft (aircraft size) was declining (as shown by the seat departure figures being less than those for aircraft departures). Most of the decline was due to the rapid growth of commuter airlines with their much smaller aircraft. Part of the decline was also due to the retirement of some of the older DC-8s and B-707s which were rendered uneconomic by fuel price increases, and the reduced use of wide-body aircraft due to the recession.

The PATCO strike and resulting reduction in air traffic control capacity had a dramatic impact on the distribution of airline service, as shown in the bottom portion of table 10.1. Both large hubs and nonhubs had substantial decreases in aircraft departures while medium hubs and small hubs showed gains. The air traffic control restrictions obviously affected the large hubs most severely. It is evident from the table that nonhubs were also affected by the large-hub reductions. Such a result is not surprising when it is recalled from chapter 8 that large hubs are the principal destinations for flights from nonhubs. Small hubs and medium hubs seem to have been the beneficiaries of the reductions at the large hubs as airlines made more intensive use of airports where excess capacity existed in the air traffic control system.

The trend toward smaller aircraft also seems to have been at least partially reversed following the PATCO strike. Average aircraft size went up between 1981 and 1982 in large hubs, medium hubs, and nonhubs. The increase in nonhubs is quite small and probably reflects commuters taking delivery of larger aircraft and utilizing them more intensively in the face of reduced flights from nonhubs to large hubs. In large hubs the increase in average aircraft size also reflects the increased use of wide-body aircraft as a means of keeping capacity up while reducing flights in response to air traffic control restrictions.

Among nonhubs the very slight average decline in weekly aircraft departures between 1978 and 1981 masks considerable variation in how individual communities fared. Figure 10.1 shows the frequency distribution of percent changes in nonhub aircraft departures per week between June 1, 1978, and June 1, 1981. As can be seen, slightly more communities experienced decreases in service than increases, but the distribution is not markedly skewed to either side.

Prior to deregulation commuters were not regulated with respect to frequency, entry, or exit, and certificated carriers were not regulated with respect to frequency. The main change for small community service brought about by deregulation was the eased ability of certificated carriers to withdraw from communities they no longer wished to serve. Figure 10.1 also shows the distribution of percent changes in departures per week in those nonhubs from which a trunk or local service carrier had exited. Only losses in these "terminated" nonhubs might be properly attributed to deregulation, although even under deregulation some certificated carriers might have been able to exit or at least reduce service

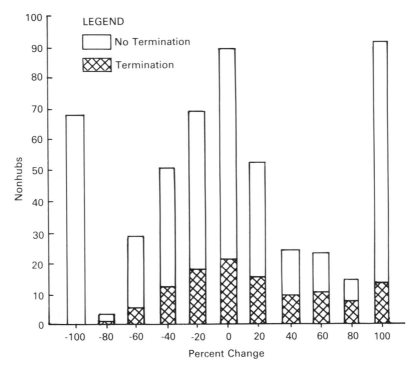

Figure 10.1 Frequency distribution of percent changes in departures per week for nonhubs (June 1, 1978, to June 1, 1981). (Note: Dashed line represents the experience of communities subject to a termination by a trunk or local service airline.)

frequencies.[3] As can be seen in the figure, the "winners" far outnumber the "losers" among these terminated nonhubs: while 38 of these communities had fewer departures, 54 had more and 21 were effectively unchanged. Communities with terminations have thus apparently contributed very little to total service losses among nonhubs, and therefore, by inference, deregulation has little responsibility for any such losses.

The New Section 419 Subsidy

Essential Air Service
The Airline Deregulation Act guaranteed that essential air service (EAS) would be maintained for 10 years to those communities listed on air carriers' certificates as of October 24, 1978 (the date the act was passed). The actual level of service that constituted essential air service for a community was defined by the CAB in terms of five major service factors: equipment, hubs, frequencies, capacity, and stops.

Aircraft eligible to provide essential air service were defined, at a minimum, to be twin-engined, dual-piloted, and with unimpeded cabin entry through airstair doors or similar types of access. Although pressurized aircraft were not to be required normally, the CAB reserved the right to specify pressurized aircraft if circumstances so warranted.

With regard to hubs, the objective established for the EAS program was to insure that small communities were linked to hub airports where opportunities to connect to other flights were available. Service to the closest hub was intended to be the norm, except where there were sufficient traffic, close ties, or other circumstances to justify guaranteed service to a more distant major city or to a second hub.

For frequencies, Congress had specified in the act a minimum frequency of two round trips on weekdays. In practice, under EAS almost all cities were also guaranteed some weekend service with Sunday service preferred over Saturday. A typical service pattern had the same number of seats available over the entire weekend as for a single weekday. No specific departure times were mandated for flights except that they be reasonably convenient.

The EAS capacity requirement was based on accommodating 1978 traffic levels using a target load factor of 50 percent. This load factor represented a compromise between minimizing government subsidy and using low load factors to give travelers a high probability of obtaining a seat on short notice. As a baseline 1978 not only represented the year for which the most recent data were available but was also the best year ever for airline traffic (e.g., rather than a historical average). The maximum number of seats guaranteed a community was 160 per weekday in both directions which, with the 50 percent load factor, represented 40 arriving and 40 departing passengers per weekday; at higher levels of traffic the CAB maintained that a community could support unsubsidized commuter service.

For stops, no rigid guidelines were specified. A two-stop maximum between the community receiving essential air service and its designated hub was usually used, but even this maximum was not inviolate. Several communities voiced interest, for example, in multistop routes that would collect enough traffic to allow the use of larger equipment than with nonstop flights.

Figure 10.2 shows the distribution of EAS-guaranteed seats per point as of November 1981. Almost 65 percent of the 303 points were guaranteed the maximum 160 seats per day. As might be expected, not all of the CAB's initial EAS determinations were accepted without protest.

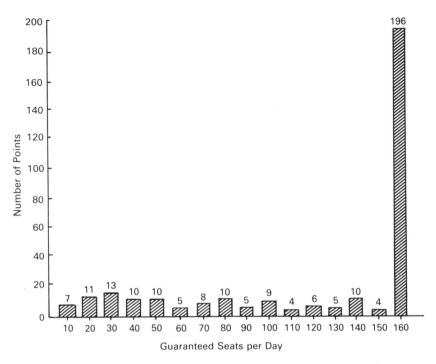

Figure 10.2   Distribution of guaranteed seats per EAS determination (as of November 9, 1981). Source: CAB Bureau of Domestic Aviation.

Appeals were filed in 23 percent of the cases handled in the first year of the program. The appeals came from the communities affected, the local airlines serving them, and state agencies, with multiple appeals filed in almost one-third of the cases.

Table 10.2 classifies the appeals by both the issue on which the appeal was based and by who filed the appeal. Many appeals of course were based on more than one issue. The two most common issues were capacity (the number of guaranteed seats) and the choice and number of hubs. Surprisingly, most of the capacity appeals were from or on behalf of communities that had been granted the 160-seat maximum. These appeals thus represented a fundamental disagreement with the EAS guidelines, rather than with how those guidelines had been applied in specific instances. Very few of these capacity appeals were granted and no exceptions were made to the 160-seat maximum.

For 137 points that had lost certificated air service before deregulation but after July 1, 1968, the CAB had the option, but not the obligation,

Table 10.2 EAS appeals by appellant group and issue (percentage of this issue cited on appeals within each appellant group)

	Community (49)[a]	State (54)	Carriers and others (24)[b]	Total appeals in which this issue is included
Capacity	38%	85%	50%	61%
Hub selection and number	55	48	54	52
Number of intermediate stops	12	19	21	17
Aircraft specifications[c]	25	7	8	14
Guaranteed transition levels	12	2	4	6

Source: CAB orders.
a. Numbers in parentheses are the actual number of appeals for each group.
b. Group consists of 18 air carriers and 6 miscellaneous parties such as local airport commissions.
c. These concern aircraft size, pressurization, and speed.

to grant EAS guarantees. Guidelines were developed based on the traffic potential at each point, isolation as measured by distance to the nearest hub, the reliability of the previous air service, availability of other public transportation, quality of air service at the nearest hub, recent improvements at the local airport, and the potential of the community to support either nonsubsidized air service or subsidized service with reasonable levels of subsidy. By the end of 1981 only seven of these previously decertificated points had been admitted to the EAS program, with an additional nine points remaining under appeal.

If a community's air service fell below its EAS level as a result of a termination, the CAB first attempted to find a new carrier to enter the market to provide replacement service at EAS levels. If a replacement carrier was not found immediately, however, the CAB was empowered by the act to hold the incumbent in the market until a replacement was found. If the incumbent suffered financial losses as a result of being held in, the CAB was required to compensate the carrier for those losses under the Section 419 subsidy program.

Selecting an EAS Carrier
Carriers were selected to provide EAS service on a community by community basis.[4] The process began with the solicitation of proposals

Table 10.3 Competition in 419 subsidy awards (through September 16, 1981)

Number of carriers involved in final selection process	Occurrences	Percentage of total
One carrier	18	47
Two carriers	14	37
Three carriers	4	11
Four carriers	2	5

Source: Compiled from CAB orders.

from carriers. The carrier's fitness to provide essential air service was assessed by federal and state agencies and by the appropriate state attorney general and public utility commission. Concurrent with the fitness determination, the reasonableness of cost and revenue estimates for the proposed service was assessed.

After a proposal had been reviewed by CAB staff, an informal conference was normally held with the carrier to resolve any remaining differences between the CAB and the carrier and to agree upon a subsidy rate.[5] In the early awards the conferences also served as information conduits, with CAB staff providing interpretations of its guidelines. Occasionally, the CAB was also able to provide better cost estimates than the carriers (e.g., when the proposed service was with an aircraft with which the carrier had no experience). The conference also gave carriers an opportunity to explain any costs that appeared excessive or unusual.

Competitive bidding was expected to keep Section 419 subsidy costs low. However, as can be seen in table 10.3, only slightly over half of the awards involved competitive bids. Indeed, from the inception of the Section 419 program, the CAB stressed that it was not simply a low-bid program. Factors such as the quality of service, community support, and the type of equipment were to be considered in reaching a decision. Such claims notwithstanding, the low bidder was virtually always awarded the subsidy (except in the very early months of the program). Table 10.4 lists the five competitive subsidy awards where the low bid was not selected. Four of the five cases occurred during the first six months of the selection process and all five were cases where the incumbent or the more established carrier was favored. Only in the case of selecting Air North over Empire was the cost difference substantial. Air North had served the market for ten years, whereas at that time, Empire would have had to undertake a substantial expansion

Table 10.4 Multicarrier 419 subsidy awards in which low bid not accepted (through September 16, 1981)

Award date	Point(s)	Winning carrier	Bid	Other carrier	Bid
2/20/80	Watertown, Massena, Ogdersburg, N.Y.	Air North	$345,330	Empire	$103,000
5/13/80	Chico, Calif.	Wesair	186,962	Shasta	159,097
5/20/80	Catskill/Sullivan County, N.Y.	Newair	371,858	Air Vectors	326,000
8/1/80	Alamagordo, Silver City, N. Mex.	Air Midwest	445,783	Airways of New Mexico	400,462
3/24/81	Jonesboro, Ark.	Rio	297,515	Scheduled Skyways	232,000
				Jamaire	81,842
				Jamaire/ CAB[a]	295,000

Source: Compiled from CAB order numbers 80-2-100, 80-5-87, 81-6-27, 80-5-135, 80-6-105, 80-8-8, 81-3-129.
a. The CAB considered certain assumptions in Jamaire's bid to be unreasonable and calculated that the bid should have been $295,000 which is what they used for the selection process.

to provide the proposed service. Even so, the difference was enough to provoke a dissenting opinion from one CAB member.[6]

Subsidy awards were generally established for a two-year period, with either a uniform subsidy rate applying for both years or separate rates for each year. If the carrier underestimated the cost or overestimated the revenue, providing subsidized essential air service could result in losses, perhaps even substantial losses. Unlike an unsubsidized situation, where traffic proved to be less than forecasted in an EAS market, the carrier could not simply reduce capacity, and thus costs, to meet the actual demand (unless the community raised no objection to the reduction).

On the other hand, if traffic exceeded forecasts, the carrier could earn the additional revenue while still receiving the same amount of subsidy. Thus it was conceivable that a profitable service could collect a subsidy for up to two years. Such a situation, though not common, was also not unheard of. Indeed, in the absence of recession, the typical experience of a commuter replacing a terminating certificated carrier in a low-density market was that traffic increased substantially in response to higher frequency, with profits improving correspondingly.[7]

Comparison of the Sections 406 and 419 Subsidy Programs

As noted in chapter 2, payments to carriers participating in the Section 406 subsidy program were based on a class-rate formula that paid for the number of days each eligible point was served, the number of departures from each eligible point, and the number of plane miles flown in subsidy-eligible service. An amount was deducted from the subsidy payment for the number of revenue passengers and revenue passenger miles in subsidy eligible service. These class-rate formulas created an incentive to use jet aircraft during peak traffic times of the day between points that were not eligible for subsidy and to reposition the aircraft during off-peak times of the day in multistop, hedgehopping flights among points eligible for subsidy.

In January 1979 the CAB proposed major changes in its methods of determining Section 406 subsidy in an attempt to match more closely the actual costs of small community service with the payments to the carriers providing it. Specifically, the CAB instituted what it called a "service incentive payment" (SIP). The CAB's purpose in establishing the SIP program was to slow the exit of the local service airlines from small community service, thereby providing a smooth and gradual

Table 10.5 Cumulative 406 reductions, 419 expenditures, and 419 savings (October 24, 1978, to July 1, 1981)

406 Reductions	
Adjusted base rate reductions[a]	$30,133,200
Reductions in SIP	11,873,700
419 Expenditures	
Compensation for losses	9,770,100
Trunk and ineligible LSA payments	3,668,400
EAS payments	7,225,700
419 Savings	
Including all 419 payments	21,342,700
Excluding payments to trunks and LSAs	25,011,100

Source: Compiled from CAB orders and CAB, *Claim and Payment Statistical Ledger.*
a. The full ceiling reduction without any payout adjustment was $34,829,300.

transition to the Section 419 subsidy program. The carriers would receive their SIP only if they did not terminate service to subsidy-eligible communities. If a carrier stopped service to a subsidy-eligible point it had still served as of May 24, 1979, it was to lose twice the SIP assigned to that town in addition to the loss of subsidy calculated through the class-rate formula.[8] Under this scheme a carrier could thus lose its entire SIP by withdrawing from half of its subsidy points.

Table 10.5 summarizes the estimated net effect of the change from the Section 406 to the Section 419 subsidy program as the principal means for supporting small community service.[9] As can be seen in the table, the net cumulative effect from the beginning of deregulation through July 1, 1981, has been an estimated savings of over $21 million.

The Section 406 reductions consisted of two components: the adjusted base rate reductions and the reductions in SIP.[10] These components were adjusted for inflation by applying the cost index used by the CAB to adjust the ceilings. Thus the Section 406 savings are an estimate of the cumulative additional subsidy the government would have had to pay if the carriers had continued serving the Section 406 points they terminated.

Although the cumulative impact of the Section 419 program has been a substantial overall savings in subsidy over the Section 406 program, the question arises whether the savings are likely to continue. Figure 10.3 shows the rate of payment for each component of the Section 419 program and the rate of savings from each component of

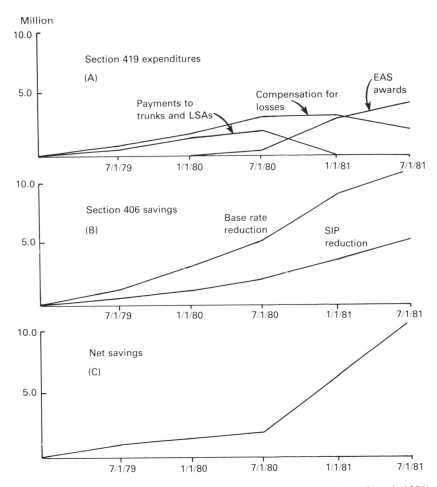

Figure 10.3 Savings in small community subsidy (January 1, 1979, to June 1, 1981).
Source: Compiled from CAB orders and CAB, *Claim and Payment Statistical Ledger.*

Table 10.6 Average subsidy per passenger and total subsidy: comparison of 406 and 419 programs

Enplanement level per day	Subsidy per passenger		Subsidy	
	406	419	406	419
Points enplaning less than 40[a]	$69.89	$47.38	$22,041,100	$8,409,840
Points enplaning 40 to 100	28.36	20.40	29,104,416	4,653,659
Points enplaning more than 100	12.48	—	40,970,149	—
Average all levels	19.92	32.21		

Source: CAB data contained in testimony before the Aviation Subcommittee of the House Committee on Public Works and Transportation, June 25, 1981.
a. For the 419 program, which is based on a six-day week, an annual level of 12,480 passengers per year was considered the equivalent of 40 per day.

the Section 406 program for each six-month period from the onset of deregulation to July 1, 1981 (the same period covered in table 10.5). The rate of savings has increased steadily with substantial increases coming in the last two periods. The increase in the rate of savings comes both from an increase in each of the components of the Section 406 savings (figure 10.3b) and from a reduction in the compensation for losses and payments to trunks and local service airlines (figure 10.3a).

Table 10.6 compares the subsidy per passenger in both programs. As can be seen in the bottom line of the table, subsidy per passenger is over 60 percent higher under Section 419 than under Section 406. However, in the Section 406 program over 44 percent of the subsidy would be paid to provide service to points enplaning over 100 passengers per day which are *not* subsidized at all under the 419 program. In short, the 406 program achieves a lower overall subsidy per passenger by paying relatively small subsidies for many who are not presumed to need a subsidy under the 419 program.

The more relevant comparison is to look at the subsidies per passenger in the specific markets requiring subsidy under EAS guidelines—those enplaning fewer than 40 passengers per day. In these the Section 419 program is clearly more cost-effective even on a per passenger basis. Similarly, even in those borderline subsidy cases enplaning between 40 and 100 passengers per day, the Section 419 program is more cost-effective. It is only in markets far larger than those believed by the CAB to require subsidized service that the Section 406 subsidy per passenger figure is low, and even then it is higher than the implicit zero subsidy of the Section 419 program.

Table 10.7 Composition of 419 expenditures

New obligations incurred by additional scope of 419 program	
Compensation for losses	$3,874,600
Essential air service	1,922,600
Total	5,797,200
Old obligations inherited from 406 program	
Compensation for losses	3,964,100
Essential air service	4,429,700
Other[a]	2,804,800
Total	11,198,600
Payments to trunks and ineligible LSAs	3,668,400

Sources: Compiled from CAB, *Claim and Payment Statistical Ledger*, and CAB orders.
a. Represents flow-through payments to commuters from USAir, an ineligible LSA, as well as transition payments to commuters that are now serving without subsidy.

The Section 419 program also extended guaranteed essential air service to a far greater number of communities than had been covered under the 406 program. Table 10.7 breaks down the payments made through June 1981 into those used to meet obligations transferred from the old subsidy program and those caused by the broader scope of the essential air service guidelines. As can be seen in the table, 28 percent of the total Section 419 payments have been incurred by the added scope of the program.

Summary and Some Concluding Observations

The essential air service program with its accompanying Section 419 subsidy has worked effectively to insure that small communities retain access to the nation's air transportation system under deregulation. While some community leaders have decried the loss of jet service, most passengers have found the operations of well-run commuter airlines acceptable. Moreover the savings in federal funds have been and seem likely to continue to be substantial (at least in relative terms), even though the scope of federal guarantees to small community air service has expanded.

Some potential problems have emerged, however. One problem that quickly became apparent was the lack of competitive bidding in many essential air service awards. Many of the strongest and most financially stable commuters have been unwilling to participate in the subsidy program. Some have participated briefly and withdrawn, while others have shown no interest since the program's inception. The subsidy program seemingly forces managements to make a choice: to specialize in either those skills needed to run a subsidized operation or those skills needed for an unsubsidized one. Thus it is not at all surprising that increasingly commuters have refused to participate in the subsidy program or to specialize in serving subsidized markets.[11]

Other potential problems stem from the definition of EAS levels and their role in the subsidy program. The EAS levels, as noted, were based on traffic in 1978, an excellent year for the industry. Airline traffic, however, has always been highly influenced by general economic conditions. To have neither the subsidy awards nor the EAS levels responsive to changes in economic conditions (as is now the case) puts a large, perhaps undue, burden of the downside risk on the carriers. Moreover the post-deregulation program implicitly argues that the number of seats needed by a community is independent of the current demand for air travel in that community. An obvious question, meriting at least some further consideration, is whether the EAS focus on departing seats is appropriate under varying economic conditions, or whether EAS should be more flexibly defined.

A final area of concern is the seemingly inevitable pressure to expand the scope and nature of the Section 419 program. Communities not currently guaranteed air service can be expected to push vigorously for such guarantees. Other communities guaranteed air service to one hub may lobby for a second hub. Still other communities, in which air service was instituted on an experimental basis, may try to get the experiment made permanent even if traffic does not develop.

In general, concerns that small communities would suffer drastic losses in air service under deregulation have proved largely unfounded. Between 1978 and 1981 nonhubs in the aggregate saw their departures drop less than 1 percent. And even that small loss could be as much the product of the 1981 recession as of deregulation. As expected, the trunk and local service airlines have withdrawn from much of their small community service, but the commuter airlines have filled the void, typically with more frequent and more conveniently scheduled service—and at less subsidy cost to government as well. The entrepreneurship of the commuter airlines, aided and abetted by the flexibility created by deregulation and changes in the subsidy system, has thus largely solved the small community problem that has so long preoccupied U.S. aviation policy.

Chapter 11

Airline Industry Structure and Public Policy

The entrepreneurial carriers—commuters and new entrant jets—are small in size compared to the remainder of the airline industry. Together they enplaned only about 10 percent of all domestic passengers in 1981. Both groups of carriers, however, have been growing much more rapidly than the established airlines. Moreover the impact of these carriers, particularly the new entrant jets, on the structure of the airline industry is potentially far greater than their size might imply.

The growth and development of these entrepreneurial carriers raise three related issues. First, how might these segments of the airline industry eventually be structured? Second, what impact will these carriers ultimately have on the remainder of the airline industry? And finally, what do these structural changes imply for issues of public policy, particularly service to small communities and the inherent competitiveness of the industry? This final chapter draws on the findings of the preceding chapters to address these questions. First, the potential impact of the new entrant jet carriers on the airline industry is examined. Then, the evolving structure of the commuter segment of the industry is considered.

The New Entrant Jets

Cost Advantages

Savings in labor outlays—a major source of lower costs for the new entrants—stem from three features common to most new entrants. The most obvious, and most often discussed, is that these carriers are typically not unionized. Having nonunion labor offers the potential for higher productivity per employee through, among other considerations, the absence of restrictive work rules. A nonunion carrier, for example, is less likely to have to pay flight crews for hours during which they do not fly. Nonunion carriers are also better able to cross-train employees to perform a variety of tasks. For example, pilots not only fly more hours per month than is typical for unionized carriers but may also work as flight instructors, dispatchers, and schedulers. Similarly, flight attendants might also be found working in reservations and at the ticket counters. It has been estimated that this flexibility can reduce the number of people on an airline's payroll by at least 10 percent.[1]

A nonunion carrier also has more flexibility in the use of part-time labor. Operations such as reservations, for example, have daily peaks of activity. To accommodate those peaks with full-time labor would mean having far more reservations agents than are needed at off-peak times.

New entrant carriers may also gain a cost advantage by using lower seniority labor. A new carrier will typically have a younger and less experienced labor force than an established carrier. Thus, to the extent that wages rise with seniority alone rather than greater productivity, a new carrier with the same wage scale and work rules will still have lower unit labor costs than an established carrier.

Finally, a new entrant carrier may gain a labor cost advantage through simply paying lower wage rates. High wages among some airline employees may well be a legacy of 40 years of regulation. In essence CAB regulation enabled carriers to pass along wage settlements directly in higher fares, as long as wage increases were in line with industrywide practices. This effective cost pass through, coupled with a high degree of unionization, apparently resulted in higher than competitive wages for many types of airline workers.

Estimating how much of an advantage a new entrant carrier can gain through lower labor costs and higher productivity is, at best, difficult. As seen in chapter 4, changing crew costs from minimum entry levels to average costs for established carriers raised total costs between 9 and 15 percent, depending on the aircraft and the flight length. Furthermore potential labor cost savings extend beyond the flight crew to ground operations and administrative functions. Overall it would seem that labor cost savings of 10 percent are easily achieved by the new entrants, and 25 to 30 percent reductions are not too difficult.

Another major source of cost savings for new entrant carriers has come from unbundling the package of services offered. A standard ticket on an established carrier usually includes the option of checking baggage to the final destination, even if the trip includes several flights on several different carriers; food and some beverage service at no extra charge; the opportunity to make an interline connection with a single ticket; and the use of a reservations system that includes the flight offerings of other established carriers. Many passengers, however, either do not make use of these services, or would not be willing to pay extra for them.

Rather than follow the established carriers' practice of offering service at a single stipulated price, many new entrant carriers have chosen to unbundle these services and either not offer them or charge extra to those passengers who wish to use them. As seen in chapter 7, most new entrant carriers do not offer interline ticketing or interline baggage handling. Some (e.g., People Express) charge extra for checked baggage. Food and beverage services are usually quite modest on the low-fare carriers and are often available only at extra cost. Some new entrants forsook established centralized reservations systems, preferring instead to handle only their own reservations via the telephone. As a result of unbundling these services, a passenger pays only for the services used, and thus a lower ticket price. People Express estimates that their unbundling, perhaps the most extreme in the industry, has reduced the average ticket price by about $18—a reduction of over one-fourth in many of their short-haul markets.[2]

Streamlined operations are another source of the new entrants' cost advantage. These carriers typically have relatively simple short-haul route networks with an emphasis on turnaround operations. Such route networks allow very high rates of aircraft utilization—in some cases two to three hours per day more than is typical for established carriers. Using secondary airports can further contribute to cost savings. As seen in chapter 9, secondary airports are subject to fewer congestion delays so that carriers are able to turn their aircraft more quickly—again contributing to high aircraft utilization. Secondary airports further contribute to reduced costs by assessing lower gate and terminal fees than those typically found at major airports. Finally, new entrants often use simplified systemwide fare structures with discounts for only off-peak service. By avoiding capacity-controlled discounts and complicated fares, new entrants greatly simplify reservations, ticketing, and perhaps even marketing.

A final major source of cost advantage for many of the new entrants is the lower capital cost of employing used rather than new jet aircraft. The new entrants have also generally bought (or leased) used twin jets which are relatively fuel efficient compared to the older three- and four-engine jets. The old twin jets do, though, incur a fuel consumption penalty compared to the very newest generation of aircraft. At fuel prices in the range of $1 per gallon, however, the fuel consumption penalty is often not sufficient to overcome the capital savings. For example, as seen in chapter 4, despite the DC-9-80's savings on fuel consumption, the cost per available seat mile of the used DC-9-30 was about 20 percent less at a range of 500 miles (assuming a fuel cost of $1.08 per gallon).

Erosion of Cost Advantages

The cost advantages that the new entrant jet carriers have enjoyed over the older established carriers may in no sense prove immune to erosion. Some of the factors that have contributed to the new entrants' cost advantage will likely diminish automatically over time. Others may diminish as established carriers respond to the new entrants by adopting some of their practices. The labor cost advantage, for example, may diminish as the work force of the new entrants gains seniority. Similarly, should the new carriers continue to grow, they may become increasingly attractive targets of organizing efforts by unions.

The cost advantage gained by the use of secondary airports may also diminish. As some of the principal airports in major cities become more congested and subject to higher costs due to more frequent delays, more carriers may establish operations at secondary airports. As a result costs at these airports may go up as demand grows for terminal and gate space, and more congestion delays may also result. A sharp increase in fuel prices would obviously increase costs for all carriers; new entrants, however, might be particularly hurt since their older aircraft are not as fuel efficient as the newest generation of jets.

The new entrants' cost advantage may also be eroded if the established carriers adopt some of the new entrants' cost-saving practices. While some sources of cost advantage would be difficult to emulate—notably some of the labor cost savings—others might not be difficult for an established carrier to adopt. Both United and Braniff (prior to its bankruptcy) introduced low-fare services similar to those of some new entrants. Established carriers can also achieve cost savings by unbundling services and streamlining their operations. Moreover, since the established carriers are a major source of used aircraft, they have the option of retaining and refurbishing their existing jets rather than automatically reequipping with the latest aircraft. Indeed, the established carriers' enthusiasm for the very latest and most fuel-efficient aircraft (e.g., the Boeing B-757 and B-767) abated when interest rates rose and fuel prices declined. Some of the established airlines turned their attention instead to reengining older aircraft; United and Delta, for example, reengined their DC-8s, and American expressed interest in reengining its B-727-200s.

Advantages of the Established Carriers

The established carriers are clearly at a cost disadvantage when competing with the new entrants, and although they can take steps to reduce the magnitude of the disadvantage, they are unlikely to eliminate it totally. The established carriers, however, are not without some advantages of their own.

Foremost among their advantages are their large hub and spoke route networks, made even more extensive by interline agreements. These hub and spoke networks allow established carriers to serve profitably markets that are not dense enough to support either turnaround service or typical new entrant connecting service. Consider a simple example. An established carrier and a new entrant both operate out of the same hub and are both considering establishing service to a new point. The established carrier already serves 15 spokes out of the hub whereas the new entrant serves only 5. In this new market, assuming passengers prefer online to interline connections, the established carrier can expect to compete effectively for passengers bound not only to and from the hub but also to the cities served by any of its 15 spokes. The new entrant, however, can compete only for passengers bound to and from the hub and cities served by any of its five spokes. Thus because of its existing network size the established carrier may be able to serve markets that are not viable for the new entrant.

A second major advantage is the ability to offer capacity-controlled discount fares. Effective exploitation of these fares requires two factors: (1) the "full service" offerings attractive to business and other less price-sensitive travelers, and (2) sophisticated computerized reservations systems. Once an established airline is committed to making a flight, the marginal cost of serving an additional passenger in a seat that would otherwise have gone empty is very low—almost always much lower than the fully allocated cost of carrying a passenger even for a low-cost new entrant carrier. In high-density markets the use of wide-body aircraft may enhance the ability of established carriers to offer a substantial number of seats at discount fares.

The objective of course is to minimize both the use of these discount fares by passengers who would otherwise have paid the higher fare and the displacement of full-fare passengers by discount-fare passengers. Thus carriers have generally tried to segment markets into full-fare business passengers and discount-fare leisure passengers by placing restrictions on the use of discount fares that were unacceptable to most business passengers. Avoiding excessive displacement of full-fare passengers by discount-fare passengers has also been eased by the use of computerized reservations systems. With such systems a carrier can both estimate the likely number of full-fare passengers for a given flight and reserve that number of seats for full-fare passengers only. As a departure draws near, the carrier can adjust the number of seats held for full-fare passengers, depending on the pattern of sales for that specific flight. If advanced full-fare sales are running above expectations, more seats can be held for full fares, whereas if they are running below normal, more seats can be released for discount fares.

Two features of typical new entrant service make it difficult to offer capacity-controlled discount fares. First, to offer such discounts would eliminate the simplified fare structures—both adding to costs and removing a marketing tool. Second, to make effective use of such fares would require a sophisticated computerized reservations system—again adding to costs.

Computerized reservations systems coupled with extensive route networks also enable established carriers to use "frequent flyer" programs as a competitive tool. Carriers offering such programs often keep track of the amount traveled by an individual on their routes. A traveler who has amassed a specified number of flights or miles on the system is entitled to additional travel on the system at reduced or no cost. Such programs can be quite attractive to frequent travelers. To the extent that the travel is for business, and the employer does not try to recapture the bonus travel, the program is an income transfer from the employer to the employee. New entrants find it difficult to compete with such programs. They typically lack both the computerized system to implement the program and the extensive route networks, including routes to vacation spots and abroad, necessary to make it attractive to travelers.

Another advantage of the large established carriers is that their size may enable them to withstand a price war with a smaller new entrant carrier. As seen in chapter 7, established carriers have usually responded to low-fare entry by introducing matching capacity-controlled discount fares. To combat a new entrant, they could simply make a large number of seats available at the discount fare and perhaps loosen the restrictions on the use of that fare, thus matching the new entrant's fare but with a higher level of service. Once the new entrant was "convinced" to leave the market, the established carrier could respond not by raising fares—which might be construed as "predatory pricing"—but by simply reducing the number of seats available at the discount fare and tightening the restrictions. Such a matching of a new entrant's low fare could prevent the new entrant from achieving a break-even load factor but might also generate losses for the established carrier. A large established carrier, however, might withstand the losses for a relatively long period of time.

Established carriers may also derive some advantage to the extent that there are scale economies and lower historical costs embedded in terminal and maintenance facilities. Although nonunion new entrants may be able to erode some of that advantage through the use of cross-training and part-time labor, it is unlikely that they can eliminate all such advantages, particularly where established carriers hold long-term leases at favorable rates.

New Patterns of Low-Cost Service

Most of the new entrants examined in the previous chapters have chosen to take advantage of their low-cost structure by offering low fares. These carriers have followed the basic pattern established prior to deregulation in intrastate service by PSA, and later Southwest and Air California. The only major deviation from this pattern is that some of the new entrants have been able to provide low-fare service in less dense markets with fewer frequencies than some had thought profitable prior to deregulation.

Although the low-fare approach seems to have been successful, there are other ways to take advantage of a low cost structure. An obvious trade-off exists between lower fares and a higher level of amenities. Indeed, Air One, based in St. Louis, has proposed offering first-class service at standard coach fares. Columbia Air, based in Baltimore, has proposed a level of service roughly comparable to a business coach at lower fares than for the comparable service on an established carrier. It remains to be seen whether such approaches will attract sufficient customers to be viable. The point is that the low-fare, no-frills approach is not the only way in which new entrant carriers can exploit their lower costs. With other approaches new entrants may be able to make inroads into market segments currently the sole domain of the established carriers.

Market Potential for New Entrants

To assess the potential for new entrant carriers, each prospective market must be considered on a case by case basis. A market's viability for a new entrant depends on the type of service envisioned; the other markets to be served by that entrant; as well as the population, distance, and demographic characteristics of the cities involved.

As seen in chapter 7, most new entrants started by serving large-hub to large-hub markets of less than 500 miles. The absence of service amenities on such short flights was not a serious drawback to the passenger. In the continental United States there are currently 37 (two-way) large-hub to large-hub markets of less than 500 miles. If the distance is extended to 750 miles, the number of such markets expands to 65. Of these markets 19 of 37 within 500 miles and 26 of 65 within 750 miles were already served by a new entrant or former intrastates as of March 15, 1982. Of course not all such markets are likely candidates for new entrant service. Nevertheless, it seems clear that there is potential for some additional turnaround low-fare service.

New entrants have also successfully served large-hub to medium-hub markets, both as turnaround markets and as part of hub and spoke networks. There are 172 large-hub to medium-hub markets of less than 500 miles and 297 of less than 750 miles. Although some of these might be viable as turnaround markets, they would appear to be more attractive as part of hub and spoke systems.

A rough assessment of the hub and spoke potential can be gained from table 11.1. The table lists for each large hub the number of medium hubs within 500 and 750 miles. Some cities, such as Seattle and Denver, do not appear promising for short-haul service. Other cities, such as Pittsburgh, have fairly congested airports making them difficult places for a new entrant to establish a hub. Even so, there are some interesting possibilities for hub and spoke growth suggested by table 11.1. Moreover it is not inconceivable that a medium-hub airport could serve as the focal point for a new entrant carrier. In short, though the potential for low-fare or other forms of new entrant jet service is not unlimited, there seems to be ample room for additional growth.

Potential Responses of the Established Carriers
Continued growth of low-cost new entrant carriers poses a difficult set of choices for the established carriers. The lower cost structure of the new entrants is a powerful competitive tool to the extent that it persists. To counter that tool, the established carriers seem to have only four basic options. These are beat them, copy them, hire them, or regulate them. These four types of responses need not be used only in their pure form but could be used in combination, depending on the specific circumstances.

Table 11.1 Short- and medium-haul market potential

Large hub	Large hub within 500 miles	Large hub within 750 miles	Medium hub within 500 miles	Medium hub within 750 miles
Atlanta	5	13	12	22
Boston	4	5	6	13
Chicago	4	8	13	22
Dallas–Fort Worth	2	5	6	12
Denver	0	4	4	8
Detroit	6	9	15	20
Houston	2	4	5	9
Las Vegas	3	4	8	10
Los Angeles	3	3	6	9
Miami	2	4	2	5
Minneapolis–St. Paul	2	5	4	14
New York	5	7	10	17
New Orleans	4	7	5	15
Orlando	3	5	3	10
Philadelphia	5	7	13	18
Phoenix	2	4	6	9
Pittsburgh	7	9	17	19
St. Louis	4	9	13	22
San Francisco	2	4	5	9
Seattle	0	1	2	6
Tampa	4	4	2	9
Washington	5	9	15	19
Totals	74	130	172	297

The "beat them" alternative relies on exploiting the advantages of the established carriers. In such a strategy the established carriers would further differentiate their services from those of the new entrants. With the important exception of the use of capacity-controlled discounts, the strategy calls not for confronting the new entrants head to head with low fares but rather making very sure that the new entrants cannot effectively take full-service, full-fare traffic from the established carriers. The drawback to this approach is that it may result in the established carriers having a much smaller share of total airline traffic, as well as less traffic in absolute terms. Moreover, to the extent that it cedes important travel segments to the new entrants, it facilitates new entrant network growth. And, if and as new entrant networks grow, the established carriers may see their network-related advantages diminish and their traffic further eroded.

The "copy them" alternative entails the established carrier emulating the new entrants in an effort to lower costs so as to compete head to head. For an established carrier this may not require that the new entrants' lower-cost structures be fully duplicated. Narrowing the cost gap and thus reducing the fare differential might be sufficient to prevent the established carrier from losing much traffic to the new entrant.

Several barriers face established carriers trying to replicate the low-cost structures of the new entrants. Labor relations are the most obvious impediment. With the notable exception of Delta the established carriers are highly unionized. The work rule and wage concessions necessary to approach the cost structures of the new entrants might be difficult for a union to accept. However, should the industry be clearly in trouble, some union concessions are not beyond the realm of possibility. Indeed, some concessions have been made. Pilots at United and Western, for example, have agreed to fly B-737s with two rather than three crew members in the cockpit. Employees at several established airlines have accepted salary cuts or pay deferrals or payment in company stock in lieu of layoffs. The extent to which these concessions would remain in an improving economy is, however, unclear. And even with substantial concessions new entrants would retain the short-term advantage of a greater proportion of workers at or near entry-level wage rates.

The unions are far from the only impediment to lowering the established carriers' costs, and indeed may not even be the major one. Management itself may be equally difficult to reorient to a different type of operation. Most established carriers operate with sizable management staffs, in some cases a plethora of vice-presidents. To match new entrant cost structures, these staffs would have to be trimmed considerably, and managers themselves would have to undergo cross-training in different tasks (not too dissimilar from that of labor). Once management levels were trimmed, those managers who remained would also have to focus on far different planning, operational, and marketing goals than had been the case prior to deregulation and the rise of the new entrants.

The "hire them" alternative is based on acquiring some of the cost advantages of the new carriers rather than trying to combat or replicate them. Such a strategy might work, for example, in a market served by an established carrier in which the carrier was breaking even or just barely making money. The established carrier, realizing that a lower cost structure combined with the market stimulation from lower fares might make the market profitable, could offer the market to a low-cost carrier. The established carrier could continue to provide those specialized services at which it was particularly effective—computerized reservations, terminal facilities, and aircraft scheduling and maintenance, for example. In addition it might offer to lease its used aircraft to the low-cost carrier. It is easy to imagine arrangements along these lines, where both the established carrier and the new entrant would benefit.

Such arrangements are not without precedent. The Allegheny Commuter System franchises have worked in a similar manner. Allegheny Airlines (now USAir) realized that with its cost structure it could not economically operate the commuter aircraft appropriate for many of the points on its certificates. Instead, it contracted with independent commuter operators to provide feeder air service to USAir points. In exchange for a modest fee and some added operating requirements, USAir provided the commuters with both name identification and a variety of services difficult for the commuters to provide by themselves. Both USAir and the individual commuters appear to have benefited from these arrangements. Another approach was that taken by Texas International in setting up New York Air as a low-cost new entrant. Texas International—a unionized local service airline—was organized as part of a holding company, Texas Air Corporation. The holding company was able to set up New York Air as a nonunion, low-cost carrier with aircraft leased from the parent. Other established carriers are organized as part of holding companies. Similarly, the trunks have already grown accustomed to transferring used aircraft along to foreign airlines, so that passing them to domestic carriers who would not compete directly might not be too large a step.

A similar approach has also been used in the American auto industry in response to the ability of foreign manufacturers to build small autos at lower cost than U.S. automakers. Although the U.S. automakers embarked on small car development programs, they also purchased cars from Japanese manufacturers and marketed them under their own names. For example, Mitsubishi has supplied cars to Chrysler, and Isuzu has supplied trucks to General Motors. The American Motors/ Renault agreement represents still another form of such cooperation. Auto manufacturers have also turned to "out-sourcing"—purchasing component parts from lower-cost nonunion suppliers rather than using their own union plants—as a response to high costs.

The hire them approach could face, however, substantial barriers to implementation. First of all, the unions are unlikely to embrace such arrangements eagerly. Indeed, the Texas International employees tried, unsuccessfully, to block the formation of New York Air in court. In exchange for other concessions United has agreed that United's union pilots will fly all aircraft operated by the holding company, UAL, Inc. Although there seem to be no insurmountable legal obstacles to moves aimed at minimizing use of union labor, carriers trying to make such arrangements might face work stoppages or slowdowns in their ongoing unionized operations. There could also be problems in transferring routes involving slot-controlled airports to low-cost carriers. Despite these and other potential barriers variations of the hire them approach could prove viable for some established carriers.

The "regulate them" approach would try to use the government to stop or reduce the threat posed by the new entrants. Although, at first glance, such a tactic might seem futile in the face of deregulation, it is not nearly so far-fetched as it might seem, particularly if applied with subtlety. One possible approach stems from the reduction in air traffic control capacity following the PATCO strike. Landing slots at many airports have become much more of a scarce resource than when the system operated at pre-strike capacity. Such restrictions could serve to favor incumbents at the expense of potential entrants. Although, as seen in chapter 9, no widespread problem emerged during the period shortly after the PATCO strike, should these restrictions continue and air traffic resumes its growth, the ability of new entrants to expand could be severely curtailed. Moreover established carriers could intensify the restrictions by pushing for further curtailments in the name of airline safety. In the process they might also increase the usefulness of their own surplus of wide-body aircraft.

The established carriers might also be able to restrain the freedom of the new entrants by raising the issue of the air transportation system's integrity. The argument could be put forward that the new entrants, with their lack of interline agreements and use of secondary airports, are fragmenting the air system and that such fragmentation imposes social costs. The potential problem with such an argument is that it might lead to mandatory interline agreements. While such agreements might increase the new entrants' costs, they might also make it easier to integrate flight segments on new entrants into multiflight trips and end up stimulating growth for some of the new entrants.

Another approach might be to argue that the low fares of some of the new entrants are promoting destructive competition, with resulting instability in the industry. It could be argued that some of these fares cannot possibly be cost based and that fares only be permitted that bear some relationship to the SIFL. Indeed, World Airways, something of a new entrant itself, has made just such a request, and other established carriers have also made claims that some of the new entrants' fares are noncompensatory. Again, however, the established carriers must be careful in pushing this line of argument. Mandating cost-based fares could remove their ability to respond to lower-cost new entrants with capacity-controlled discount fares and thus ultimately work to the established carriers' disadvantage.

Commuters

The principal role of commuter carriers continues to be providing feeder service from small communities to hub airports where passengers connect to other flights. While some commuters have begun moving toward providing more point to point turnaround service, the future structure of the commuter industry will hinge largely on feed relationships among commuter and medium- to long-haul jet carriers. These relationships are likely to be much more amicable and cooperative than those among new entrant jets and established carriers, since the feeder service provided by commuters is of value to the jet carriers rather than a competitive threat.

The Value of Feed
Assessing the value of commuter feed traffic to a jet carrier is more complex than merely counting the number of commuter passengers who connect to the jet carrier's flights and adding up the contribution

of revenue over cost for these passengers. Such an approach would only be valid if none of these passengers would have flown on any of that jet carrier's routes had the commuter service been unavailable or if the pattern of commuter service had been different. The true value of commuter feed is based on the excess of revenues over costs for those passengers who would not otherwise have flown on the jet carrier.

There are four ways in which differing patterns of commuter service can affect the traffic carried by the jet carrier: (1) altering the market share at a hub, (2) altering the passenger's routing to the final destination, (3) changing the passenger's final destination, and (4) stimulating new trips by air.

The market share effect is probably the largest of the four. Consider, for example, a hub airport dominated by two jet carriers where both of these carriers compete in many of the same markets out of that hub. Which of the two carriers a passenger connecting in that hub will use for the jet portion of the trip may well depend on the specifics of the commuter link to the hub. If the commuter's flights are timed to meet with the connecting flights of one of the carriers, that carrier would probably get a much larger share of the traffic from the communities served by that commuter than would the other jet carrier. In such a situation the value of having the commuter scheduled to meet a carrier's flights is the excess of revenues over costs from the added connecting passengers over the alternative of the commuter scheduling to suit the other carrier's operations (or perhaps scheduling independently of either).

One example of such a situation where the commuter link might matter is Chicago's O'Hare, where both United and American have large-hub and spoke systems. For example, both United and American serve Boston out of Chicago. For a traveler wishing to go from Bloomington, Indiana, to Boston via Chicago, the timing of the commuter flight might easily influence the choice of jet carrier. If the Bloomington traveler wanted to go to New York, however, the timing of the flight would be of less importance since both United and American have very frequent flights. For travel to New York other factors such as the relative locations of the commuter and jet carrier gates, the reservation system used by the commuter, or the amount of joint advertising might be deciding factors.

Routing will also influence which hub a passenger will use to connect to a flight to a final destination. Again, using Bloomington as an example, a passenger has the choice of connecting through Chicago or through

Indianapolis. If a Boston-bound traveler connects through Indianapolis, the jet carrier is most likely to be USAir, which has the most flights from Indianapolis to Boston, or perhaps Delta. Neither United nor American fly directly from Indianapolis to Boston. Similarly, between Indianapolis and New York, USAir is the dominant carrier, with a substantial presence by Trans World and a single flight offered by American (as of July 1, 1982). Since different hubs are dominated by different carriers, the choice of hub will generally have a strong influence on the choice of the jet carrier. In this example one would expect USAir to benefit from frequent commuter flights to Indianapolis, whereas United and American would benefit from frequent commuter flights to Chicago.

The destination effect represents an extension of the routing effect and might be expected to apply to some vacation travel. Vacation destinations are to some extent substitutable for one another. Where travel via either of two hubs is possible, and where some destinations are better served from one hub than the other, the commuter links to the two hubs may influence the choice of vacation destination. The effect is not likely to be large, but it could be significant where different low-fare carriers are present at the different hubs.

The trip stimulation effect simply reflects the added convenience and any lower cost of travel provided by convenient commuter links. There are two aspects of trip stimulation that should not be confused. The first is the diversion of trips to the hub from auto (or some other mode) to commuter carrier. These air trips can be considered stimulated trips from the commuter's perspective but not from the jet carrier at the hub, as the jet carrier gets the traffic in either case. The second is that more trips are made due to added convenience. In this instance there is more traffic for both the commuter and the jet carrier.

There are also situations where commuter feed would be of little value to the jet carrier. If a small community had only one convenient hub, there would be little potential for a routing or a destination effect. If a single carrier was dominant at that hub, the market share effect would be small. If the hub was quite close so that private auto was an easy link to the hub, the stimulation effect would be small. In other words, in such situations the jet carrier dominant at the hub is likely to get very little additional traffic from a commuter link to the small community and thus has little incentive to assist or subsidize the commuter serving that link.

Elements for Commuter/Jet Carrier Cooperation

Generally, there are potential gains to the jet carrier from cooperating with the commuter. Such cooperation can take many forms in varying degrees. One obvious form of cooperation is through the commuter having interline agreements with jet carriers. Under such interline agreements baggage can be automatically transferred, common tickets can be issued, and so forth. There is little competitive edge in such agreements, since the most common practice is for commuters to have interline agreements with all jet carriers with which their passengers could possibly connect.

A form of cooperation that can impart a competitive edge is for the commuter to use the jet carrier's reservations system. Most reservations systems have a bias built into them. While a carrier's system will list connections involving other carriers, connections involving their own flights will typically be listed first. In a situation where a commuter serves a hub where several carriers have operations, the bias imparted by a reservations system can have an appreciable impact.

Commuters and jet carriers can also cooperate in scheduling. A jet carrier can get a substantial advantage if the commuter flights are specifically scheduled into its connecting banks of flights rather than independent of the banks or into another carrier's banks. Although a commuter may pay a small penalty in aircraft utilization by constraining its flights to hit specific times, that penalty may be outweighed by the added commuter traffic from providing better connections. Scheduling to meet connecting flights typically involves close cooperation between commuter and jet carriers. For example, the commuter must get advance notice of schedule changes so that the connections can continue to be listed in the *OAG*.

Commuters may also undertake joint advertising with a jet carrier to promote the connections available to commuter passengers. Joint advertising often accompanies attempts to schedule connecting flights and typically involves publishing joint schedules. Commuters may also establish special joint fares with jet carriers for promotional and market stimulation purposes.

A closer level of cooperation may also involve coordinating plans for market entry by the commuter with the planned exit from the market by the jet carrier. Such planning may enable the jet carrier to leave a low-density market without losing the feed from that market. A jet carrier can also often provide assistance in determining the market potential in cities the commuter is contemplating entering.

Jets and commuters may also cooperate in ground operations. For example, a jet carrier may lease gate space to a commuter, thus making connections from the commuter to the carrier's flights easier. A jet carrier may also provide counter space in the terminal. Similar arrangements with accompanying efficiencies may be made for luggage handling, fuel, and aircraft ground handling.

The Range of Commuter and Jet Carrier Relationships

Relationships between commuters and jet carriers can range from a contractual franchise to complete independence involving head to head competition. There are many gradations between these two extremes, but most relationships can be classified into one of four types: (1) a franchise with name identification with the jet carrier; (2) close cooperation exclusively with one carrier; (3) local cooperation where a commuter may cooperate with one carrier at one airport but with a different carrier at another airport; and (4) independence where, though there may be some cooperation with jet carriers, there are no specific tion.

The Allegheny Commuter System is the oldest and largest of the contractual franchise arrangements. The system began in November 1967 when Henson Aviation began operation as an Allegheny commuter replacing Allegheny (now USAir) in service between Hagerstown, Maryland and Baltimore. The program continued to grow and by 1980 involved 12 different commuter carriers. Allegheny formed the commuter system, prior to deregulation, as a means of withdrawing from small communities without losing the feed traffic these small communities provided. Transferring small communities to commuters was necessary for Allegheny to move off of subsidy and to move into larger aircraft and longer routes.

Allegheny sought successful established commuters as their franchisees. The agreements between Allegheny and the commuters were all similar, although there was some room for tailoring them to the specific circumstances of the commuter and the community. The planes were painted in Allegheny colors and with the Allegheny commuter logo. The commuter had the use of Allegheny's reservations system and communications network in exchange for a fee per passenger. Allegheny provided ticketing and check-in services at major airports, as well as the use of terminal facilities at these points. In some instances Allegheny guaranteed a break-even financial operation during the first two years and guaranteed loans for the purchase of aircraft. Ground services were provided at major airports for a fee, but the fee was typically less than it would have cost the commuter to provide equivalent services independently.

In exchange the commuter had to operate minimum specified schedules and routes and had to maintain sufficient backup aircraft to achieve a 95 percent flight completion rate each year of operation. The commuter had to operate the ground facilities at the small community airports in accordance with Allegheny's standards. Aircraft had to be operated with an ATP-rated pilot and a copilot. While under contract the commuter could not move into other Allegheny markets without approval, nor could the commuter merge or give up majority ownership. If the commuter served other routes, it could not use Allegheny's services and facilities, or serve those routes with aircraft marked with Allegheny's logo.

Allegheny obviously exercised rather tight control over the commuters in its system. While some may have found the restrictions confining, the Allegheny name identification was quite valuable—particularly during the period prior to deregulation. As the commuter industry grew, and some commuters began to achieve name recognition, the route restrictions were felt by some commuters to be no longer worth the benefits gained from the relationship with Allegheny. As a result several commuters withdrew from the system, for example, Britt, Aeromech, and Ransome. In addition under deregulation Allegheny was able to remove most small communities from its certificate. With these obligations removed, Allegheny was no longer required to subsidize commuter service anywhere and therefore severed its relationship with certain previously subsidized commuters (e.g., Air North).

Franchise relationships need not be as tightly defined as in the Allegheny Commuter System. Indeed, close cooperation between a commuter and a jet carrier is also possible without the commuter taking on the name or identification of the jet carrier. Ransome, for example, after withdrawing from the Allegheny Commuter System, established a similar but less restrictive relationship with Delta in which Ransome operates under its own name. Mississippi Valley Airlines, operating feeder service to Chicago, has very close ties with United yet retains its own name and has had more managerial discretion than under a formal franchise agreement.

A commuter may also cooperate with a jet carrier at one airport only, while cooperating with another carrier at a different airport. Britt, for example, has a cooperative agreement with Ozark at St. Louis, yet it does joint advertising with American for connections through Chicago, and it feeds USAir flights at Indianapolis. Similarly, Air Wisconsin has its gate near American in Chicago and has joint advertising with them, but it operates quite independently in other markets.

Finally, some commuters may not engage in joint advertising or any other formal cooperation with jet carriers. For those commuters focusing on point-to-point service, feeder-related cooperation is not particularly important.

Point-to-Point Commuter Service
The bulk of commuter traffic connects to flights of jet carriers, but point-to-point commuter service has been growing (as reported in chapter 8). Indeed, some commuters are explicitly seeking out markets with point-to-point traffic. Such market opportunities are likely to grow in the future. Recall that commuter costs are often lower than jet costs at short distances and low passenger volumes (figure 4.7). Indeed, commuters can provide less costly service for virtually any market with fewer than 100 enplanements per day. In very short-haul markets, such as 150 miles, commuters have a cost advantage up to about 130 enplanements per day.

The commuter cost advantage could easily grow. The analysis in chapter 4 was based on fuel prices of $1.08 per gallon. Should fuel prices rise—a possibility not without historical precedent—the commuter advantage would be enhanced. Moreover, as the new generation of commuter aircraft come on the market in the mid-1980s, both the comfort and speed with which commuters can transport passengers will increase.

The most promising point-to-point commuter opportunities may well be with low-density overflight strategies. As the range, comfort, and speed of commuter aircraft increases, commuters should find themselves better able to compete with hub and spoke jet carriers by circumventing the hub. A passenger may well prefer to fly nonstop on a commuter to connecting through a hub on a jet. Certainly the commuter aircraft, although somewhat slower, may sometimes have a significant travel time advantage over a jet connection at a hub that involves both a more circuitous routing and an intermediate stop.

Evolving Commuter Industry Structure
Commuter carriers seem increasingly likely to specialize in only one type of operation, that is, being (1) a feeder carrier, (2) a point-to-point

carrier, or (3) a small market fringe carrier. The management skills, and to a lesser extent the equipment, needed to be successful at each type of operation are different.

Feeder carriers will of course concentrate in markets where most passengers connect to another flight provided by a jet carrier. For them the key to success will be the relationships they establish with jet carriers. The advantages of having close cooperation with a jet carrier are potentially so great that a shakeout among feeder carriers might be expected as those unable or unwilling to establish close working relations with jet carriers lose out to those that do. While an increase in name identified relationships such as those of the Allegheny commuters might also occur, the relationships need not be nearly so tight as in the Allegheny case to be effective. It is unlikely that a successful commuter that is well established in a region need take on the name of a jet carrier to compete effectively, especially if it has the other benefits of close cooperation.

Feeder carriers will be operating relatively short flights, with most being less than 150 miles. As a result pressurized aircraft will not be critical for success except in mountainous areas. On such short flights in-flight amenities will also be relatively unimportant. Thus 19-seat aircraft without a flight attendant will be viable, although many markets will be served by 30-seat aircraft. The key to success, from an operations standpoint, will be frequency and scheduling to meet connections. One would not expect to see 50-seat aircraft become dominant except, possibly, in feeder service to airports where landing slots were limited (so that compromises with frequency had to be made) or where very high traffic levels existed.

Since most passengers on feeder carriers will connect to other flights, the commuter fare will not be too critical as it will represent only a portion of the total trip cost. Although joint fares are likely to be a part of any relationships with jet carriers, feeder commuters will probably not make extensive use of discount fares. The discount fares that are used are likely to be focused at point-to-point passengers. Some predominantly feeder commuters, however, may carry an appreciable amount of point-to-point traffic since most large hubs are located in large cities that are destinations for many travelers. Another role for discount fares for feeders could be on off-peak flights that do not link up well with connecting flights.

The point-to-point carriers will operate under substantially different circumstances than the feeder carriers. The major difference will be that close relations with a jet carrier are not important, as few passengers will connect to a jet carrier. These carriers will generally fly longer flights, often among small and medium hubs. As a result pressurization, in-flight comfort, and amenities will be more important. Although some 19-seat aircraft will be used, their use may be limited on long flights by a low level of comfort and the absence of a flight attendant. Rather, these carriers should benefit substantially from the new generation of 30- to 40-seat commuter aircraft to be put in service during the mid- and late-1980s. Indeed, the lack of suitable aircraft may have slowed commuter moves into hub overflight strategies. Even so, as seen in chapter 8, commuters have entered into such point-to-point service among small and medium hubs relatively rapidly.

Because commuter carriers providing point-to-point service often provide all of the air travel for the trip, actual fares paid by travelers are likely to be more important, as distinguished from revenues received under joint fare arrangements. As a result far greater use of discount fares would be expected among these carriers than among those providing mainly feed traffic. The relative roles of frequency, scheduling, and fares are unclear, however. (The demand analysis in chapter 3, for example, lacked the data to analyze this type of service.) Point to Point carriers will also benefit substantially from the demise of Section 406 subsidies, since they will be well positioned to serve many of the markets supported by that program.

The small market fringe will serve very low-density markets—those too small for service by the 19- and 30-seat aircraft of feeder and point-to-point carriers. The key to these fringe operations will be the very low costs of single-pilot operations in nine-passenger aircraft. These operators will be small in scale since the number of opportunities in a geographic area are likely to be limited. Many of these carriers will come from the ranks of fixed-base operators, and they will probably be tied to the fixed base for maintenance. Barriers to entry for this type of operation will be low, and thus high turnover will likely persist.

Summary

The rebirth of the airline entrepreneurs has been an integral part of the airline deregulation experience. Specifically, commuters and new entrant low-fare jet carriers have played central roles in three of the principal developments in the airline industry following deregulation: (1) rationalizing service to small communities, (2) broadening the range of fare and service offerings, and (3) improving productivity and lowering cost structures.

Prior to deregulation much small community service had been provided by local service airlines using jets and large turboprops while receiving government subsidy. Since these aircraft were poorly suited for low-density short-haul service, the service was often provided using multistop hedgehopping flights during off-peak travel hours. Even this poor service was usually unprofitable and required large (and growing) amounts of subsidy. Commuter carriers, with smaller turboprop aircraft better suited to these markets, have been able to provide service at far lower cost. Moreover, since the use of smaller aircraft allows higher service frequencies and more convenient schedules, commuters have often stimulated traffic.

Commuters made inroads into small community service even prior to deregulation, as evidenced by their sustained high rate of growth throughout the 1970s. With deregulation the door has been opened more fully for commuters to pursue their advantages in providing short-haul low-density service. Service terminations by trunk and local service airlines have contributed as much as 25 percent to commuters' post-deregulation growth. Making commuters eligible to provide subsidized small community service saved taxpayers over $20 million in small community subsidies by June 30, 1981, and can eventually be expected to result in annual subsidy savings of at least $50 million.

To be sure, the service provided by commuters is not exactly the same as that provided by the jet carriers. For one thing, it is almost invariably not done in a large jet aircraft, a change that is deemed offensive by some. Commuter airlines, as a whole, are also somewhat less safe than jet carriers, but the difference is far less than usually perceived. Also the larger commuter carriers, who carry over half of all commuter passengers, have a safety record virtually the same as the jet carriers.

Overall, commuters have apparently helped solve one of the major public policy problems anticipated with deregulation: namely, they have ensured a continuation, even an extension, of essential air service to small communities while maintaining an acceptable safety standard. Furthermore they have done this at less total cost to the economy and government than would otherwise have been the case.

The new entrant jet carriers, by contrast, have been much more instrumental than the commuters in broadening the range of fare and service offerings available to travelers. Before the deregulation act was passed, many proponents of deregulation had expected across-the-board fare cuts similar to those found in intrastate markets of Texas and California. In the initial period following deregulation, however, the established carriers responded to pricing freedoms with an often bewildering array of discount fares. These discount fares had two characteristics in common: they were capacity controlled (i.e., they were available for only a limited number of seats on each flight), and they were market segmenting, as a discount-fare traveler had to meet certain restrictions designed to prevent the use of such fares by business travelers.

The new entrants, with their simplified fare structures, have helped spread unrestricted low fares. They have done this both by their own pricing policies and by competing away the restrictions placed on the discount fares in the markets the new entrants contested with established carriers.[3] It remains to be seen whether the established carriers will extend unrestricted low fares to markets not served by a new entrant. The prognosis, though, would seem favorable. The new entrants have proved that they can enter and exit markets relatively inexpensively and quickly, almost exactly as hypothesized to provide the contestability needed to create a reasonably competitive market outcome.

The new entrant jet carriers have also been a force in improving airline productivity and lowering costs. The increased competition fostered by deregulation would have increased pressure on the airlines to lower their costs to some extent even in the absence of new entrant jets. The new entrants, however, have greatly intensified that pressure by demonstrating just how low costs can be driven by streamlining service offerings and being free of the work rule restrictions of unionized labor. In intensifying the pressure for low costs, the new entrants have apparently weakened labor's ability to capture productivity gains from technological improvements, at least to the extent done under regulation. The new entrants have also forced the established airline managements to evaluate their aircraft acquisition decisions, as well as their pricing and route decisions, with much more care than in the past.

The entrepreneurial airlines, then, have been pivotal in bringing about some of the most significant changes wrought under deregulation. The new entrepreneurs have already profoundly altered the structure of the domestic airline industry. Through their own continuing initiatives, and the responses elicited from the established carriers, that record of constructive change is likely to be maintained. The benefits should be substantial, not only for those who are successful entrepreneurs but for the flying public and ultimately the entire aviation industry as well.

Notes

Chapter 1

1. J. A. Schumpeter, *The Theory of Economic Development* (Cambridge, Mass.: Harvard University Press, 1934).

2. Entrepreneurial responses have also been elicited from a few of the older established trunks. Almost all of them in fact have matched at least some of the low fares instituted by their new competitors. But few of the established carriers have fundamentally restructured their operations to make them cost competitive with the new entrepreneurs. Two exceptions to this rule have been Braniff and United Air Lines. Braniff did so in an effort to salvage itself just before entering bankruptcy. United did so on a limited scale to rid itself of what it considered to be a particularly pernicious "make-work" union rule (3 men in the cockpit of the two-engined Boeing 737). Although both these experiments are of considerable interest, they seemed too *sui generis* and limited to warrant analysis in this study. Several carriers lowered costs through wage and work rule concessions from their unions. Yet even these moves represent more of an income transfer from one group to others than entrepreneurial innovation.

3. The only exceptions were commuter airlines operating with very small aircraft on short-haul low-density routes.

4. As described in the next chapter, the CAB did, however, allow some other (nontrunk) types of new entrants into the industry under special circumstances and restrictions.

5. It could be argued of course that a sufficiently broad definition of ease (or cost) of entry would include an allowance for the contingency of exit, in which case the "old" industrial organization focus on entry would incorporate much or most of what is added by the concept of contestability. Furthermore, if entry is equally difficult in two circumstances, but exit is easy in only one, it needn't always be true that the easy-exit case embodies greater competitive pressures. Indeed, the contrary could well be true. Thus a broadly defined measure of entry barriers (explicitly allowing for exit contingencies) may well encompass all the information relevant to assessing market power. For a review of the recent literature on contestability, see Elizabeth Bailey and Ann Friedlaender, "Market Structure and Multiproduct Industries," *Journal of Economic Literature* 20 (September 1982):1024–1048.

6. The safety of the new entrant jet carrier has been questioned by some following the January 1982 crash of an Air Florida B-737 on takeoff from Washington's National Airport. However, the experience with new entrant operations is too limited to permit drawing any conclusions based on empirical observations. Thus new entrant safety is not addressed in chapter 5.

7. For a discussion of the initial adaptations, see John R. Meyer and Clinton V. Oster, Jr. (eds.), *Airline Deregulation: The Early Experience* (Boston: Auburn House, 1981).

Chapter 2

1. 6 CAB 1, p. 10.

2. Donald R. Whitnah, *Safer Skyways: Federal Control of Aviation 1926–1966* (Ames, Io.: Iowa State University Press, 1966), p. 263.

3. 6 CAB 1, p. 2.

4. George C. Eads, *The Local Service Airline Experiment* (Washington, D.C.: Brookings Institution, 1972), p. 76.

5. 6 CAB 1, p. 13.

6. John R. M. Wilson, *Turbulence Aloft: The Civil Aeronautics Administration Amid Wars and Rumors of Wars, 1938–1953* (Washington, D.C.: GPO, 1979).

7. The CAB envisioned that feeder service might be provided by the existing trunks in 24-passenger DC-3s "whose greatest utility and competitive advantage were in the longer distance transportation markets."

8. 6 CAB 1, pp. 29–30.

9. Ibid.

10. Eads, *Local Service Airline*, p. 77.

11. A skip-stop flight would involve dropping some of the intermediate cities along a route while stopping at selected points. A nonstop would eliminate all intermediate points and fly directly to the terminal destination.

12. Eads, *Local Service Airline*, p. 86.

13. 8 CAB 360, p. 360.

14. Eads, *Local Service Airline*, p. 88.

15. 6 CAB 1, pp. 4–5.

16. 6 CAB 1, pp. 689–690.

17. Civil Aeronautics Act of 1938, Pub. L. 75-706, 52 Stat. 973.

18. 6 CAB 980 (1946).

19. 6 CAB 1, p. 690.

20. 8 CAB 191 (1947).

21. Eads, *Local Service Airline*, pp. 93–94.

22. Wilson, *Turbulence Aloft*, p. 158.

23. Eads, *Local Service Airline*, p. 97.

24. John R. Meyer and Clinton V. Oster, Jr. (eds.), *Airline Deregulation: The Early Experience* (Boston: Auburn House, 1981), p. 22.

25. National Transportation Safety Board, *Air Taxi Safety Study* (Washington, D.C.: GPO, 1972), p. 2.

26. Wilson, *Turbulence Aloft*, p. 160.

27. 6 CAB 1049 (1946).

28. Ibid.

29. Wilson, *Turbulence Aloft*, pp. 161–162.

30. Civil Aeronautics Act of 1938, Pub. L. 75–706, 52 Stat. 1705 (1938), 49 USC 411(a).

31. 12 Fed. Reg. 3076.

32. 14 CFR 298.1(f) (1981).

33. 37 Fed. Reg. 19609.

34. U.S. Senate, Committee on the Judiciary, "CAB Practices and Procedures," report of the Subcommittee on Administrative Practice and Procedure (Washington, D.C.: GPO, 1975), p. 41.

35. For a more detailed discussion see Simat, Helliesen and Eichner, Inc., "The Intrastate Air Regulation Experience in Texas and California," in Paul W. MacAvoy and John W.

Snow (eds.), *Regulation of Passenger Fares and Competition among the Airlines* (Washington, D.C.: American Enterprise Institute for Public Policy Research, 1977).

Chapter 3

1. Robert D. Rowe and Ronald A. Dutton, "Determinants of the Demand for Commuter Air Service in Wyoming," paper presented at the 60th annual meeting of the Transportation Research Board, Washington, D.C., January 1981, pp. 13–15. These authors estimated the elasticities of demand with respect to flight frequency and aircraft size to be approximately 0.7 and 0.8, using a cross-sectional sample of enplanements of 11 Wyoming communities, over a 10 year period.

2. Steven E. Eriksen, "Demand Models for U.S. Domestic Air Passenger Markets," report FTL-R78-2, Flight Transportation Laboratory, Massachusetts Institute of Technology, June 1978, pp. 236–239; Philip K. Verleger, "A Point-to-Point Model of the Demand for Air Transportation," Ph.D. dissertation, Massachusetts Institute of Technology, 1971, pp. 188–190; and Terry P. Blumer, "A Short Haul Passenger Demand Model for Air Transportation," M.S. thesis, Massachusetts Institute of Technology, 1976, pp. 60–65.

3. One of the few studies to explore such issues is that by Eriksen, "Demand Models," pp. 241ff.

4. The FAA's definitions are based on the percent of total U.S. enplanements at each point. Large hubs each enplane more than 1.0 percent, medium hubs between 0.25 and 0.99 percent, small hubs between 0.05 and 0.24 percent, and nonhubs less than 0.05 percent.

5. Travel volumes were estimated from CAB Form 298 data.

6. Equations for the frequency of air service, which depends partly on the level of passenger traffic, and passenger volume, which in turn depends partly on the frequency of service, are estimated simultaneously using the techique of two-stage least squares.

7. Formally, the arc elasticity along a demand function is defined at the percentage change in the quantity of a commodity that is purchased—in this case airline trips—in response to a 1 percent change in their price. Thus a fare elasticity of −1 suggests that a 1 percent rise in the number of airline trips will accompany a 1 percent reduction in their average fare.

8. Precise figures are not available; commuter airline managements, however, commonly estimate that 70 to 80 percent of their passengers are traveling primarily for business-related purposes, although the actual figure no doubt varies among specific routes.

9. The Regional Airline Association (formerly named the Commuter Airline Association of America) estimated that in 1980 about 70 percent of commuter airline passengers transferred to onward flights from their commuter flights; again, exact estimates are unavailable.

10. Since each commuter route feeding a medium or large hub accounts for only a small fraction of enplanements there, the problem of simultaneous interdependence between the model's dependent variable, passenger traffic, and one of its explanatory variables, hub enplanements, is probably not serious.

11. John R. Meyer and Clinton V. Oster, Jr. (eds.), *Airline Deregulation: The Early Experience* (Boston: Auburn House, 1981), table 7.3.

12. Meyer and Oster, *The Early Experience*, table 7-13.

13. Meyer and Oster, *The Early Experience*, chapter 4.

14. In 1980 the average number of seats per certificated carrier flight in the 100 most heavily traveled markets between 200 and 1,000 miles in length was 124; from 501 and

1,000 miles the figure was 143 seats. See David R. Graham and Daniel P. Kaplan, "Developments in the Deregulated Airline Industry," staff report, U.S. Civil Aeronautics Board, Office of Economic Analysis, June 1981, table 3.

15. U.S. Civil Aeronautics Board, *Report on Airline Service, Fares, Traffic, Load Factors, and Market Shares: Service Status on August 1, 1981*, issue number 17, October 1981, tables 7 and 22.

16. For tentative evidence supporting this hypothesis, see Peter R. Stopher and Joseph N. Prashker, "Intercity Passenger Forecasting from the National Travel Survey Data of 1972," final report to the National Railroad Passenger Corporation, the Transportation Center, Northwestern University, September 1976; and Alan Grayson, "A Disaggregate Model of Mode Choice in Intercity Travel," paper presented to the 60th annual meeting of the Transportation Research Board, Washington, D.C., January 1981.

17. Eriksen, "Demand Models," table 6.2, p. 246.

18. Ibid., pp. 243–247.

19. See Meyer and Oster, *The Early Experience*, chapter 4, for a discussion.

20. For a detailed presentation of this view, see William E. Fruhan, Jr., *The Fight for Competitive Advantage: A Study of the United States Domestic Trunk Air Carriers*, (Boston, Mass.: Division of Research, Graduate School of Business Administration, Harvard University, 1972), pp. 126–132.

Chapter 4

1. Block time and block fuel refer to the total time and fuel consumed between an aircraft starting its engines and leaving the departure gate and shutting down its engines at the arrival gate. Both taxiing and flying are included.

2. For this analysis all captains' salaries were assumed to be $20 per block hour, whereas all first officers received $10 per block hour.

3. The Shorts is somewhat of an exception from the 100-mile segment on. The Shorts' performance is due to having been designed for a different mission—shorter, lower-altitude flights—than that of the other turboprops.

4. During the development of the airline industry under regulation, certificated airline pilots achieved significant bargaining power with the airlines. This power was translated into high salary levels, which were partially based on the relative productivity of the aircraft they flew. Commuters have adopted a similar salary structure, although the level of salary is of course lower. The salary structure used in the analysis reflects that relationship—paying the pilots of more productive planes (measured by both capacity and speed) higher salaries than those flying less productive equipment.

5. John R. Meyer and Clinton V. Oster, Jr. (eds.), *Airline Deregulation: The Early Experience* (Boston: Auburn House, 1981), chapter 8.

6. David R. Graham and Daniel P. Kaplan, "Competition and the Airlines: An Evaluation of Deregulation," staff report, U.S. Civil Aeronautics Board, Office of Economic Analysis, December 1982, chapter 4.

7. Douglas Aircraft Company, *Estimating Aircraft Maintenance Costs*, October 1980, p. 1.

8. Ibid., p. 10.

9. Simat, Helliesen and Eichner, Inc., *Methodology for Estimating Operating Costs of Commuter Air Carriers*, January 1975, appendix A.

10. *Commuter Air*, June 1981, p. 13.

Chapter 5.

1. Lester Reingold, "Travelers' Advisory: The Commuters Are Coming," *Washington Monthly* (December 1979).

2. Robert Kaus, "The Dark Side of Deregulation," *Washington Monthly* (May 1979).

3. Federal Aviation Administration, *First Commuter Air Carrier Safety Symposium* (Washington, D.C.: FAA, 1980), pp. 26–28.

4. Ibid., p. 3.

5. The best measure would be fatalities per passenger departure rather than per enplanement. Unfortunately passenger-departure data are not available. For nonstop flights the measures are identical, but for multistop flights a passenger may make several departures yet be counted as a single enplanement. Thus the tables that follow may slightly overstate the risk for nonstop flights while slightly understating the risk for multistop flights. This bias, however, is not believed to affect the validity of comparisons within the commuter industry.

6. For this and all remaining tables in this chapter, the groups of carriers being compared had statistically significant differences in their overall rates of fatality, producing accidents per 100,000 aircraft departures. Using an *F*-test, all differences were significant at the 95 percent level or higher. Passenger fatality rates reported in the tables could not be tested directly because it could not be assumed that each fatality was an independent event.

7. National Transportation Safety Board, *Air Taxi Safety Study* (Washington, D.C.: NTSB, 1972).

8. National Transportation Safety Board, *Special Study: Commuter Airline Safety 1970–1979* (Washington, D.C.: NTSB, 1980).

9. U.S. House, Subcommittee on Oversight and Review, *Commuter Air Safety*, February 26–29, 1980; U.S. House, Subcommittee on Government Activities and Transportation, *Airline Deregulation and Aviation Safety*, September 8–9, 1977.

10. One exception was an investigation conducted by Frank Munley entitled *Commuter Airline Safety: An Analysis of Accident Records and the Role of Federal Regulation* (Washington, D.C.: Aviation Consumer Action Project, 1976) that based its conclusions on the results of a statistical analysis of the data on the commuter airline industry. Using accident data for the period 1969 to 1974 for over 100 commuter airlines, Munley tested the hypothesis that "less stringent safety regulation has resulted in a lower level of safety for commuter airline passengers" (p. 2). Munley calculated accident and injury rates for both commuter and trunk carriers, based on the number of accidents per million departures and concluded that the probability of a passenger being killed on a commuter carrier was approximately three times that of being killed on a trunk carrier (p. 10). He also analyzed commuter accidents in terms of their probable causes and the phases of flight in which they occurred and found the accidents to be the result of inadequate maintenance, inadequate preflight preparation, and pilot error. Munley maintained that each accident reflects the differences between the regulations applicable to certificated carriers (FAR Part 121) and those regulations applicable to commuters (FAR Part 135), and he concluded that an upgrading of standards would result in a higher level of commuter safety (p. 15).

11. NTSB, *Special Study*, p. 25.

12. Munley, *An Analysis of Accident Records*, p. 79; NTSB, *Special Study*, p. 25.

13. U.S. House, Subcommittee on Oversight, *Commuter Airport Safety*, February 13, 1980, p. 2.

14. NTSB, *Special Study*, p. 36.

15. NTSB, *Air Taxi Safety Study*, p. 13; NTSB, *Special Study*, p. 18; and U.S. House, *Commuter Air Safety*, p. 75.

16. NTSB, *Air Taxi Safety Study*, p. 8.

17. Ibid., p. 7.

18. NTSB, *Special Study*, p. 29.

19. For a further discussion of this phenomenon, see Andrew McKey, "Commuter Airlines: Predicting a Rational Industry Structure," senior thesis, Harvard College, 1981.

20. Rene Riecke, "Commmuter Airlines: Impact of Carrier Size and Rate of Growth on Safety," honors thesis, Indiana University, 1981, pp. v–58.

Chapter 6

1. Regional Airline Association, *1981 Annual Report of the Regional/Commuter Airline Industry*, Washington, D.C., February 1982.

2. There are limited public data on the financial performance of the commuter industry, because so few carriers are publicly held and only those that are certificated are required to file financial reports with the CAB.

3. The Internal Revenue Service guidelines under which a lease qualifies as a "true" lease for tax purposes were substantially liberalized under the so-called Safe Harbor Leasing Provisions of the Economic Recovery Tax Act of 1981 (ERTA). Under new Safe Harbor lease provisions it was much easier to meet the standards and qualify for an advance ruling, thus insuring that a proposed transaction would be treated as a lease for tax purposes. Other changes included the lowering of the 20 percent at-risk requirement for the lessor to 10 percent and the elimination of the requirement that a lessee's purchase option be at fair market value at the time of purchase. Finally, the prior requirement that the lessor of the plane must make a profit directly from the lease and not merely from the tax benefit transfer was abandoned.

As part of the 1981 tax act new Accelerated Cost Recovery System (ACRS) provisions were also enacted, under which the depreciable life of aircraft was reduced to five years from the previous seven to nine; in some cases this almost doubled the yearly depreciation deductions for the lessor. The combined effect of the new Safe Harbor lease provisions and ACRS resulted in greater tax benefits to lessors at lower risks, which translated into more attractive lease rates for the lessees.

4. Regional Airline Association, *1981 Annual Report*, p. 128.

5. Ibid.

Chapter 7

1. For a more complete discussion of the effects of the fuel price increases on short-haul markets see John R. Meyer and Clinton V. Oster, Jr. (eds.), *Airline Deregulation: The Early Experience* (Boston: Auburn House, 1981), chapter 8.

2. It was not possible to tell with certainty from the *OAG* the extent to which PSA was using off-peak fares or the magnitude of any off-peak fare cuts.

3. A similar caveat would apply to New York Air which also operates in both La Guardia and National.

4. David R. Graham and Daniel P. Kaplan, "Competition and the Airlines: An Evaluation of Deregulation," staff report, U.S. Civil Aeronautics Board, Office of Economic Analysis, December 1982, p. 104.

5. Midway tried service to Cleveland's secondary Lakefront Airport for a while but withdrew in favor of service to the larger Hopkins Airport.

6. For a good survey of the issues involved as well as some interesting suggestions on this topic, see Janusz A. Ordover and Robert D. Willig, "An Economic Definition of Predation: Pricing and Product Innovation," *Yale Law Journal* 91 (1981):8–53.

7. Philip Areeda and Donald F. Turner, "Predatory Pricing and the Sherman Anti-Trust Act," *Harvard Law Review* 88 (1975):697–714.

8. Frederick M. Scherer, "Predatory Pricing and the Sherman Act," *Harvard Law Review* 89 (1976):868–890; Richard A. Posner, *Antitrust Law*; and Paul L. Joskow and Alvin K. Klevorick, "A Framework for Analyzing Predatory Pricing Policy," *Yale Law Journal* 89 (1979).

9. David R. Graham, Daniel P. Kaplan, and David S. Sibley, "Efficiency and Competition in the Airline Industry," *Bell Journal of Economics* (Spring 1983):134.

Chapter 8

1. The largest 40 commuters were selected based on enplanements in 1980; two of the 40 commuters were excluded from the analysis because of incomplete data. Commuters were broadly defined in this analysis to include carriers that had become certificated, such as Air Midwest, Air Wisconsin, and Air New England, but continued to operate predominantly propeller aircraft with 60 or fewer seats.

2. The first line of the table indicates, for example, that of city-pair markets served by these commuters in 1976, 26.4 percent were markets involving a nonhub as both origin and destination (nonhub–nonhub).

3. Although the date on which the notice of intent to terminate was filed with the CAB would, at first glance, seem the appropriate cutoff for inducement, several commuters had sufficiently close relations with trunk or local service carriers that they apparently knew in advance of the intent to terminate.

4. This figure is consistent with a study of the top 20 carriers and the Allegheny Commuter System which attributed a maximum of 29 percent of the station growth and 31 percent of the route growth to terminations. See Jennifer Wetmore, "A Disaggregate Examination of the Commuter Airline Industry," honors thesis, Indiana University, 1981.

5. These seven carriers were Air Midwest, Air North, Air Oregon, Apollo, Cascade, Cochise, and Scheduled Skyways. Prior to deregulation Air North had been part of the Allegheny Commuter System.

6. Specifically, only those operating under a Part 298 exemption are included. Those carriers with commuter-type operations that became certificated prior to the third quarter of 1980 were not included. Also markets in which commuters compete with certificated carriers were not included.

7. The slight apparent decline between 1979 and 1980 in the number of multiple carrier commuter markets is the product of two factors. The first is the growing understatement due to the exclusion of certificated commuters. The second is that as traffic growth slowed in most markets, with actual declines in traffic in many markets as recession deepened, some commuters involved in competitive markets may have withdrawn. It would not be surprising to see renewed growth in competitive markets with an improving economy.

8. Airlines operating in Alaska, Hawaii, and the Caribbean were excluded because of the unique roles of air transportation in these areas.

9. Joint fares, however, play a large role in commuter fares and are examined later in this chapter, using a different methodology.

10. Exceptions to the trend of replacement fare increases in line with SIFL increases were found, though, in some California, Oregon, and Washington markets where commuter fares rose considerably more than costs during the 1979–80 period. The terminating carriers, United and Hughes Airwest, had not generally increased fares in these markets in line with the SIFL during the six months prior to termination. It is therefore doubtful that the extremely low fares charged by the terminating carriers were sustainable over the long run since, in light of the service terminations, these fares were probably not at profitable levels. Fares may have been kept low to keep consumer resentment to service termination at a minimum.

11. In some cases the applicable joint fare is computed differently; however, for commuter airlines this method is most common.

12. "Answer of Commuter Airline Association of America to Petition of American Airlines, Inc. for Rulemaking," CAB docket 38585, section 17, 1980, p. 14.

13. The conclusions presented in this section are drawn from a memorandum to CAB board member Gloria Schafer from the Policy Analysis Division of the CAB entitled "The Mandatory Joint Fare Program and Commuter Airlines," February 21, 1980.

Chapter 9

1. See John R. Meyer and Clinton V. Oster, Jr. (eds.), *Airline Deregulation: The Early Experience* (Boston: Auburn House, 1981), chapter 4.

2. The FAA has developed three systems to record the number of delays exceeding specific thresholds: the National Airspace System Communication (NASCOM) program, which has manually recorded delays of 30 minutes or more at large commercial airports since 1968; the Performance Measurement System (PMS), which since 1975 has recorded delays of 15 minutes or longer at 15 of the busiest airports; and the Automated Delay Measurement System (ADMS), which has recorded the frequency distribution of delays by 15 minute increments at a few of the busiest airports since 1977. This chapter relies on the delay data reported by NASCOM, because of ready availability for large hubs over a time period covering several years prior to deregulation as well as the period since it began.

3. Federal Aviation Administration, *Airport Activity Statistics Report*, 1979, table 1.

4. For example, peak-hour operations on typical days at Chicago-O'Hare Airport increased from 144 in 1977 to 150 in 1978, which can raise average delays by 5 to 15 minutes per aircraft, according to a relationship reported in Federal Aviation Administration, *O'Hare Delay Task Force Study*, Vol. 1: Executive Summary, exhibit 15.

5. Air traffic control procedures generally accord precedence to arriving flights over departing ones. Within this constraint, however, they tend to treat individual carrier's flights in order of appearance.

6. Air carriers value the takeoff and landing rights represented by these "slots" partly because they are able to charge higher fares for flights to and from the airports at which they are required. The best estimate appears to be that fares for such services are at least 5 percent and perhaps as much as 15 percent higher than those charged on routes of equivalent distance, passenger volumes, and levels of competition. See David R. Graham, Daniel P. Kaplan, and David S. Sibley, "Efficiency and Competition in the Airline Industry," unpublished paper, U.S. Civil Aeronautics Board, September 1981, pp. 23–25; and Michael Rissman, "Entry and Pricing at FAA Quota-Controlled Airports," senior thesis, Harvard College, March 1982.

7. During the process of slot allocations at Washington-National Airport for the winter period of 1980–81, a scheduling committee initially refused to allocate operation rights

to Texas Air Corporation (then Texas International Airlines) for use by its newly formed New York Air subsidiary. That carrier's refusal to certify any distribution excluding it led the FAA to impose a slot allocation providing it with 18 of the 24 daily takeoff and landing rights it initially requested.

8. For a detailed description, see David M. Grether, R. Mark Isaac, and Charles R. Plott, "Alternative Methods of Allocating Airport Slots: Performance and Evaluation," Polinomics Research Laboratories, report to U.S. Civil Aeronautics Board, August 1979, section IV.

9. This interpretation, obtained in a telephone interview with Air Transport Association personnel who cooperate with the scheduling committees, is apparently in the process of being revised to recognize the fact that smaller aircraft can often utilize noncompetitive facilities.

10. Interview with Dean Sparkman, Vice-President, Mississippi Valley Airlines, November 10, 1981.

11. U.S. Civil Aeronautics Board, "The Impact of the PATCO Job Action: August through October," memorandum from Office of Economic Analysis to members of the board, February 5, 1982, table 1.

12. Michael Feazel, "Airline operations Down Only 4% from Last Year," *Aviation Week and Space Technology*, January 18, 1982, pp. 31–32.

13. Agis Salpukas, "The Cash Market in Airport Slots," *New York Times*, July 10, 1982, p. 21; and "Plan Mulled on Slot Priorities," *Aviation Week and Space Technology*, June 21, 1982, p. 83.

Chapter 10

1. See, for example, Robert Kaus, "The Dark Side of Deregulation," *Washington Monthly* (May 1979); and the Kysor Industrial Corporation, advertisement in *The Wall Street Journal*, March 7, 1980.

2. For an examination of the early gains in service and the impacts of fuel price, see John R. Meyer and Clinton V. Oster, Jr. (eds.), *Airline Deregulation: The Early Experience* (Boston: Auburn House, 1981), chapters 7 and 8.

3. David R. Graham and Daniel P. Kaplan, "Competition and the Airlines: An Evaluation of Deregulation," staff report, U.S. Civil Aeronautics Board, Office of Economic Analysis, December 1982, pp. 135–137.

4. In some cases two or more communities were considered as a package because of their proximity to one another or common linkages to the same hub. For example, the first Section 419 subsidy case implemented was for five upstate New York points considered in two groups: Plattsburgh and Saranac Lake/Lake Placid with service to Albany as a hub; and Massena, Ogdensburg, and Watertown with service to Syracuse.

5. Some carriers proposed unsubsidized service. The CAB understandably gave these proposals priority over those requesting government subsidy, and these no-subsidy proposals were not always given careful analysis. In some early cases, however, after initiating service, a no-subsidy carrier filed to terminate and was awarded hold-in compensation. These situations forced the CAB to solicit service proposals for some points a second time, and as a result the CAB began to review no-subsidy proposals with greater attention.

6. Subsequent to the award, demand in these upstate New York markets fell significantly below projections, and Air North indicated that the subsidy amount was inadequate.

7. Meyer and Oster, *The Early Experience*, chapter 7.

8. Towns that had been suspended prior to May 24, 1979, would result in a loss of the SIP assigned to that town but not twice the amount.

9. The Section 419 costs are simply the sum of the total payments for each of the categories for the period. A host of assumptions and approximations underlie the other figures in the table. The most difficult component to estimate was the savings in Section 406 payments from service terminations. Two problems complicate the estimate. First, payments under Section 406 are not tied to service to specific communities—the need adjustment masks that relationship (see note 11 for further details). Second, the time period since deregulation has been one of rapidly increasing costs. To correct for this, cost increases due to fuel price increases, and the like, were accounted for as much as possible in the comparison.

10. The base rate reductions were calculated using the change in subsidy ceilings published in the CAB amendments to Class Rate IX. The subsidy ceiling was based on the service patterns in subsidy service in 1978. If a carrier terminated service to a subsidy-eligible community, the CAB would reduce the ceiling based on the 1978 level of departures and plane miles involving that community. However, the 1978 ceiling also incorporated any service above the subsidy maximum of two flights per day. The carrier could collect 100 percent of the ceiling only if the carrier continued to provide the 1978 level of service. If, however, service prior to termination had been less than the 1978 level, then the carrier had not been collecting the ceiling level for that point and the savings would be less than the reduction in the ceiling. To approximate the actual savings, the carrier's ratio of payment to ceiling for the period when the termination occurred was applied to the reduction in the ceiling due to the termination. If the full ceiling reductions had been used instead, the estimated savings would have been about $4.7 million greater.

11. For example two western commuter airlines—Pioneer operating out of Denver, Colorado, and Big Sky operating out of Billings, Montana—together served over one-quarter of all points subsidized under Section 419 in 1981. Considering the sizes and distances between cities in the west, it is not surprising that a high proportion of subsidized points are in this region. What is surprising and somewhat disturbing from a public policy perspective is the degree to which these two carriers depend on subsidized service. In 1981 over two-thirds of Big Sky's flights involved a subsidized community, as did virtually all of Pioneer's.

Chapter 11

1. Statement of Donald Burr, Chairman of People Express Airlines, cited in "A Champ of Cheap Airlines," *Fortune*, March 22, 1982, p. 28.

2. Ibid.

3. Another force for easing restrictions has been discount-fare competition among the established carriers.

Index